D1357717

Us and Them?

Us and Them?

The Dangerous Politics of Immigration Control

Bridget Anderson

OXFORD

UNIVERSITY PRESS

OXFORD

UNIVERSITY PRESS

Great Clarendon Street, Oxford, OX2 6DP,
United Kingdom

Oxford University Press is a department of the University of Oxford.
It furthers the University's objective of excellence in research, scholarship,
and education by publishing worldwide. Oxford is a registered trade mark of
Oxford University Press in the UK and in certain other countries

© Bridget Anderson 2013

The moral rights of the author have been asserted

First Edition published in 2013

Impression: 4

All rights reserved. No part of this publication may be reproduced, stored in
a retrieval system, or transmitted, in any form or by any means, without the
prior permission in writing of Oxford University Press, or as expressly permitted
by law, by licence or under terms agreed with the appropriate reprographics
rights organization. Enquiries concerning reproduction outside the scope of the
above should be sent to the Rights Department, Oxford University Press, at the
address above

You must not circulate this work in any other form
and you must impose this same condition on any acquirer

British Library Cataloguing in Publication Data

Data available

ISBN 978–0–19–969159–3

Printed in Great Britain by
Clays Ltd, St Ives plc

UNIVERSITY
OF SHEFFIELD
LIBRARY

Acknowledgements

This book is the culmination of several years of thinking about the nature of immigration controls. It draws on research projects, conference and seminar discussions, lectures, endless listening to Radio 4 and the World Service, casual reading of newspaper and magazine articles and long conversations at home, at work, and the spaces in between. I don't know the names of all the people I ought to thank, and some of them I will have forgotten. This reflects my absent mindedness not your contribution—sorry!

Firstly, I would like to thank Laura Brace and Ali Rogers for their insightful comments on a first draft. This book is much, much better for their input. I could not have asked for more encouraging and constructive criticism. Thank you too to Phillip Cole for believing in this project from the outset. Academia's loss is science-fiction's gain. Not just this book, but my work more generally would be much the poorer without Julia O'Connell Davidson's razor mind, her kindness and care, and her being one of the funniest people ever.

I have benefited from the intellectual generosity of Nandita Sharma, Caroline Oliver, and David Feldman, who took the time to read chapters and engage with me on them, saving me from some nasty errors and opening new lines of enquiry. They belong to a 'community' of scholars, shorthand for engaged and critical thinkers who are as prone to talking about immigration and citizenship in the pub as they are in the office: Nick Clark and Matthew Gibney, COMPAS colleagues, past and present, including Nando Sigona, Isabelle Shutes, Sondra Hausner, Xiang Biao, Hiranthi Jayaweera, Vanessa Hughes, Mette Berg, Sarah Spencer, and Rutvica Andrijasevic. This has made for an intellectually stimulating environment, and I have been extremely fortunate in my position as a researcher at the ESRC funded Centre on Migration, Policy and Society (COMPAS) in the School of Anthropology at the University of Oxford. I should have written this book a while ago, and it was COMPAS director Michael Keith who really made me do it. I have found my years of arguing with Martin Ruhs really productive and I hope he has too. Our conversations are reflected in the book though he might not recognize them. Thanks to John Davies, for permission to use a version of his great title as my title for Chapter 3. 'Temporary Labour Migration to the UK: Does it all have to end in "tiers"?' was the title of a workshop he organized in 2010 as part of his work with the Bangladeshi Trade Support Programme.

I appreciate it is invidious to separate academic and support staff. I have learned as much from the insights of our administrative team, past and present, including Vicky Kingsman and Jenny Newman, as I have from dozens of conferences, and they have tolerated sometimes even encouraged and engaged with my diatribes and expositions (and added some of their own). But I want to acknowledge the fantastic work that they do to support the logistics and dissemination of research. They make it look so easy. But it takes effort. Thank you too to Michele Drasdo who printed out hundreds of newspaper articles and reports, and photocopied endless papers and opened the door when I forgot my key without ever betraying any irritation. Bhoomika Joshi helped me with formatting, and Melanie Griffiths was a star, patiently updating my endnote, formatting, checking my references, and staying in the office with me until the end. Thanks to the IT anthropology team for sorting out a printer cable that meant I could work from home, and to Kathryn Tyne, a senior library assistant at the Bodleian Law Library, who found and faxed over a copy of the 1388 Statute and took the time to find me an article about the Merciless Parliament. Without this kind of support, books would never get written. A special thanks to Emma Newcombe, the COMPAS communications manager, genius artist, organizer, sounding-board, and friend. My work would be very different without her.

The work of Justice for Domestic Workers, their mutual care and struggle for justice is an inspiration. Together with groups like the Migrants Rights Network, Kalayaan, Legal Action for Women, the All Africa Women's Group, and Detention Action they are a reminder about what is important in life. There are many people who already recognize the centrality of migrants' struggles to citizens' lives and who have dedicated themselves to this: Sue Conlan, Margaret Healy, Aodh O'Halpin, Don Flynn, Bill MacKeith, Liz Peretz, Lucy Rix, Niki Adams, Sofi Taylor, Brida Brennan, Chris Brian, and the No-Borders crew and many, many more. I know that they, like me, draw inspiration from the struggles of the many low waged migrants and asylum seekers who build lives and relationships in situations of desperate difficulty.

Ideas and thinking don't just stop at the office door, and I have to thank many non-academics who have come up with ideas and facilitated the writing of this book. Dosie and all the Alices (you know who you are), Joanna Sephton, Clare Mahoney, Mary Paciello, Margaret Henry and the Snell family, Chris and Gabbi, my aunt, Sister Jane of Mary, circuit trainers Matt and Sid, and circuit buddies—especially Kevin Byrne who really nagged me to finish Chapter 4. A big thanks to Mum and Dad for their love, encouragement, and support, and for being people of the deepest integrity. But of course, especially for the red wine, delicious dinners, and Newport bread when I was getting the first draft of the book done. And thanks to my great brothers Anthony, Michael, and Steve, and the staff of the fabulous Seu Xerea restaurant in Valencia for being so generous and looking after me when I need it. Nona, Liam, Roisin, and Patrick know far more about immigration and citizenship than they ever wanted to and tolerated absences, obsession, and hasty cooking. They've also taught me how to behave. And finally thanks so much to lovely, loved, and loving Rob Lemkin aka Roberto. I'm so lucky to be your friend and I love and admire you more than I can ever say.

Contents

List of Abbreviations

A/EU8   Countries which joined the EU in 2004 (Hungary, Poland, Slovakia, Slovenia, Czech Republic, Estonia, Latvia, and Lithuania)

A/EU2   Bulgaria and Romania, which joined the EU in 2007

ABNI   Advisory Board on Naturalization and Integration

ASBO   Anti-social behavioural order

BME   Black and minority ethnic

CICC   Citizens of Independent Commonwealth Countries

CUKC   Citizens of the United Kingdom and Colonies

EEA   European Economic Area

EU   European Union

EU15   EU member state countries prior to the accession of ten candidate countries on 1 May 2004. These are Austria, Belgium, Denmark, Finland, France, Germany, Greece, Ireland, Italy, Luxembourg, Netherlands, Portugal, Spain, Sweden, and UK

EVWS   European Voluntary Worker Scheme

FNP   Foreign national prisoner

GDP   Gross domestic product

GP   General practitioner

HSE   Health and Safety Executive

ICE   Immigration and Customs Enforcement

IO   Immigration officer

LFS   Labour Force Survey

LIT   Local Immigration Team

LTIM   Long-term international migrant

MAC   Migration Advisory Committee

NGO   Non-governmental organization

NRM   National Referral Mechanism

OECD   Organisation for Economic Co-operation and Development

ONS   Office of National Statistics

PBS	Points Based System
UASC	Unaccompanied asylum seeking child
UCATT	Union of Construction, Allied Trades, and Technicians
UK	United Kingdom
UKBA	United Kingdom Border Agency
UKHTC	UK Human Trafficking Centre
UN	United Nations
US	United States of America
UVD	Unnotified voluntary departure
VoT	Victim of trafficking
WRS	Workers Registration Scheme

Introduction

Citizenship and the Community of Value: Exclusion, Failure, Tolerance

Once upon a time, a poor woodcutter, of no great skill, decided go in search of work. He left behind his family and his home in the forest, with promises that he would one day return with wealth and comfort. 'Here, food is scarce and life is hard', he told his wife, 'but I have heard tell of other places where there are chances for a man like me to make my fortune'. After much hardship and long days of travel, he reached the edge of the forest where he found the borders of a wealthy kingdom. There he found his way barred by guards. 'Who are you and why do you seek to enter?' they asked. 'Please let me in', he replied, 'I am a poor man, but I work hard. I promise through my labour I will make your kingdom even greater and richer than it already is'. The guards agreed to let him in saying that they would give him five years and a day to prove his worth. So the poor man entered and worked hard, digging, scrubbing, and labouring for the Kings' subjects. And the longer he stayed the more his affection for the kingdom and its people grew. After five years and one day, the guards acknowledged he had proved his worth and welcomed him as a true subject of the kingdom. 'But may I ask for one thing more?' said the man. 'I have a wife and children at home. They are poor and have nothing. If you value all I have done, would you permit them to come to your kingdom and make their life with me?' And the guards, being wise and fair, and recognizing his endeavours agreed. His family, overjoyed when he sent for them, came at once, and they all lived happily ever after.

This is the migration fairy story. There are important variations. Sometimes the woodcutter is escaping an evil tyrant, sometimes he is a silversmith of great skill, sometimes he is single, sometimes a woman. Ideally, the story follows the trajectory of survival to civilization with everybody benefitting, but there is not always a happy ending. The woodcutter can become lost in the forest or rejected at the border. He may not obey the guards, sneaking in or refusing to return, and sometimes he is not a woodcutter at all but a thief.

Moreover, a single woodcutter is one matter, but hordes of them might threaten the order or nature of the kingdom. However, the fundamentals are that the kingdom is a far more desirable place to live than the shack in the woods, and migration demonstrates this over and over again.

This book sets out to disrupt this story and the categories that underpin it: kingdom and forest, subject and foreigner. To do so, it foregrounds borders, not primarily those that are policed by the guards, which is how immigration controls are commonly imagined, but the borders between citizen and migrant, between us and them. International borders are commonly presented as filters, sorting out the desirable from the undesirable, the genuine from the bogus, the legal from the illegal, and permitting only the deserving to enter state territory. However, as has been observed ever more frequently in recent years, borders are not simply territorial, but they reach into the heart of political space. Together with their associated practices, and in particular, laws and practices of citizenship, they may be more usefully analysed as *producing* rather than reflecting status, as creating specific types of social, political, and economic relations. These relations are not solely the concern of migrants. The politics of immigration reveal the volatility of categories that are imagined as stable, including citizenship itself. Judgements about who is needed for the economy, who counts as skilled, what is and isn't work, what is a good marriage, who is suitable for citizenship, and what sort of state-backed enforcement is acceptable against 'illegals', affect citizens as well as migrants. The exclusion of migrants helps define the privileges and the limitations of citizenship, and close attention to the border (physical and metaphorical) reveals much about how we make sense of ourselves. This book will argue that rather than simple competitors for the privileges of membership, citizens and migrants define each other, and that they do so through sets of relations that shift and are not in straightforward binary opposition.

The Community of Value: Exclusion and Failure

Central to my argument is that modern states portray themselves not as arbitrary collections of people hung together by a common legal status but as a *community of value*, composed of people who share common ideals and (exemplary) patterns of behaviour expressed through ethnicity, religion, culture, or language—that is, its members have shared values. They partake in certain forms of social relations, in 'communities': 'bound by common experiences ... forged by friendship and conversation ... knitted together by all the rituals of the neighbourhood, from the school run to the chat down the pub'.[1]

---

[1] Cameron (2011).

The community of value is one of the ways states claim legitimacy, and in this way it often overlaps with ideas of the nation. The British people uphold the rule of law, reward hardworking families, respect human rights, etc. The notion of 'community' facilitates a seamless switch between scales, between the imagined national community and the imagined local community. This slippage of scale facilitates depictions of Britain as the land of 'long shadows on county cricket grounds, warm beer, invincible green suburbs, dog lovers and pools fillers and...old maids bicycling to holy communion' (Major 1993). Its localism not only captures a popular communitarianism but implies the importance of daily practice and suggests different parameters of inclusion to those indicated by the explicitly patriotic language of 'national identity'. In theory, 'we' could all belong to the community of value by appreciating the virtues of bicycling to Holy Communion or chatting down the pub, and by chatting and bicycling ourselves, although arguably this appeals to the more distinctively 'English' fantasy rather than the 'nations' of Ireland, Scotland, or Wales. It is certainly a far cry from the rain, high street chain stores, traffic jams, and daytime TV that might perhaps be more realistically conjured as common elements of many people's experiences of the United Kingdom.

The community of value is populated by 'good citizens', law-abiding and hard-working members of stable and respectable families. The policy maker and politician are often self-consciously 'good citizens', and so too, if less self-consciously, are the academic researcher and the anti-deportation campaigner. All may take different positions on different issues. There is not a single liberal tradition giving rise to a unified set of tick boxes about the specifics of the Good Citizen and his or her response to immigration, and the Good Citizen can argue for very different policies, but all draw on the individual as the key unit of analysis. The Good Citizen is the liberal sovereign self: rational, self-owning, and independent, with a moral compass that enables him to consider the interests of others. In this sense he is the product of a liberal history and culture, but it is a history and culture that does not acknowledge its own particularity. For the good citizen, culture is extrinsic rather than constitutive, a way of life, not power and rule (Brown 2006: 168). The Good Citizen is firmly anchored in liberal ideas about the individual, autonomy, freedom, belonging, and property. As Brace has demonstrated in her exploration of the politics of property, conservatives, socialists, and liberal individualists go on to offer differing visions of the good society and how the autonomous and separated self can connect with others (Brace 2004).

As well as manifesting values, the community of value *is* valued. In this sense, it needs protection, and increasingly it seems it needs protection from outsiders. At the national level, outsiders are equated with foreigners. The 'non-citizen (or the Migrant) may be defined legally as a person with a particular citizenship status, but the 'non-citizen', together with its associated terms (foreigner, migrant, immigrant, etc.) is also normative. Part of being an outsider is not sharing the same values—which easily becomes not having the 'right' values. Terms like 'asylum seeker' are not simply descriptive of legal status, that is, formal membership, but they are value laden and negative.[2] Immigration and citizenship are not simply about legal status, but fundamentally about status in the sense of worth and honour—that is, membership of the community of value. The debates around immigration are about the contours of the community of value as much as they are about trade-offs and economic impacts. Bonnie Honig's (2001) exploration of the figure of the foreigner founder has shown how the foreigner, (the non-citizen) defines the nation and its citizenry from the outside. Foregrounding the community of value rather than the nation per se serves to emphasize that not all formal citizens are good citizens. The community of value is defined from the outside by the non-citizen, but also from the inside, by the 'Failed Citizen'.

'Failed citizens' as a term describes those individuals and groups who are imagined as incapable of, or fail to live up to, liberal ideals. It includes a wide range of people, folk devils like the Benefit Scrounger with too many children, the paedophile, the rioter, the Criminal, and others (Cohen 1972). The Failed Citizen is both a disappointment and threat to the local community and/or the nation. They have a problem of culture, fecklessness, and ill-discipline leading to them making the wrong choices and also to welfare dependence. The Failed Citizen, like the non-citizen, can be legally fixed, although again like the non-citizen, this by no means exhausts the category. The Failed Citizen may be defined as a person who has a criminal conviction—that is, through the sub-category of 'the Criminal'. Criminals may be formal citizens but they are strongly imagined as internal Others, who have proved themselves unworthy of membership of the community of value. A citizen criminal cannot be ejected from the state (although of course in the past they could be transported) but they can be excluded from membership in multiple other ways, including, in some states, through capital punishment. Even a minor conviction can result in a permanent loss of rights and these 'invisible punishments' can have grave consequences. In the US, for example, a felony conviction by anyone in a household may be grounds for the household's eviction from public housing, and in many states convicted drug felons lose the right to vote, to Medicaid, to food aid, public housing, and to any form of government education grant, *for life* (Brewer and Heitzeg 2008). For these people, the promise of formal citizenship

---

[2] To give just one example, the *Daily Mail* headline of 11 January 2011: 'Asylum seeker who claimed to have been gang-raped and witnessed family's murder in Somalia exposed as £250K benefit fraudster' (Seamark and Cohen 2011) situates the asylum seeker firmly outside the community of value. Later in the article it becomes apparent that 'she cannot be deported because she is a British citizen'—that is, she is not an asylum seeker in the legal sense of the term. The phrase was not used to describe her formal status, but her moral status.

is largely reduced to the bare toleration of their presence on state territory. Put like this, and purged of its moral claims, the distinction between some categories of non and failed citizens begins to look more hazy. The community of value is defined from outside by exclusion, and from inside by failure, but the excluded also fail, and the failed are also excluded.

Acknowledgement of the minimal legal rights of the Failed Citizen may be through gritted teeth, as is evident from the reluctance with which some states take in their returning ex-prisoners. In the UK, there is often press antipathy to British nationals who are returned to the UK after serving sentences for criminal convictions abroad: 'A career criminal . . . was yesterday returned to Britain as a free man. The taxpayer now faces spending tens of thousands providing housing and benefits to CT even though he has spent most of his life in Australia' (Doyle and Slack 2011). The tone of this and many similar articles suggest that it is not right that citizens with criminal records cannot be excluded from British territory. As Goldberg (1993) has put it, the Good Citizen has rights because he has values, and has values because he has rights. The Failed Citizen does not have rights because he does not have values, and he does not have values because he does not have rights. The Failed Citizen typically lacks both values AND value, as the virtue of the community of value may be priceless but is also about economic worth, independence, self-sufficiency, and hard work. Lack of values and value is the hallmark of the undeserving poor, and this book will argue that the non-citizen and the Failed Citizen are both categories of the undeserving poor: one global, the other national.

The Tolerated Citizen and the Politics of Citizenship

The borders of the community of value are permeable. The following chapters will demonstrate how easy it is for the non-citizen, whatever their immigration or citizenship status, to be imagined as the 'illegal' and thereby associated with the Criminal. In the same way the category of the 'deserving' benefit dependent is at continual risk of sliding into the benefit scrounger. For example, in April 2011, Prime Minister David Cameron stated that:

> We are finding a large number of people who are on incapacity benefits because of drug problems, alcohol problems or problems with weight and diet and I think a lot of people who pay their taxes and work hard will think, 'That's not what I pay my taxes for. I pay taxes for people who were incapacitated through no fault of their own'. (*Daily Mail* 2011).

The welfare claimant, not having the self-mastery to control her consumption, effortlessly becomes the Benefit Scrounger, and once again, it is easy to move from there to criminality.

Different groups and individuals can slip in and out of the community of value: sometimes accepted, sometimes marginal, sometimes examples of Britain's fine institutions, generosity, and tolerance, and other times a threat to British identity and themselves intolerant. That is, as well as Good, non-, and Failed Citizens, there are also (not-quite-)good-enough citizens. These are 'tolerated citizens'. The fragility of hold of the Tolerated Citizen, the contingently accepted, permeates the politics of citizenship. Those at risk of failure or of not belonging seek to dissociate themselves, one from another. Migrants and their supporters are usually eager to differentiate themselves from failed citizens with whom they are often associated. Assertions that refugees are not criminals, or that migrants do not claim benefits, are attempts to counter these associations by affirming the community of value. Migrants and refugees are fit to belong because they have the right kinds of values, unlike criminals and benefit scroungers. Similarly, citizens at risk of failure may seek to dissociate themselves from non-citizens in order to bolster their claim to rights. For example, in 2010, the papers splashed the headline 'British grandmother returns home after twenty three years in Spain and is branded an asylum seeker' (Levy 2010a). The woman in question was a white British national who had been living and working in Spain but had fallen on hard times. She had returned to the UK to find that she was ineligible for housing benefits having lived for a long time abroad. Unlike CT deported from Australia, her right to enter the UK ('return home') is not questioned, and neither is her right to claim housing benefit. The explicit comparison with asylum seekers is a repeat of a recurrent trope that the government treats asylum seekers better than its 'own', resulting in injustice and resentment (Millington 2010). Feeling like a 'refugee in my own country' was not an invitation to reflect on the commonality of exclusion, on either side—the woman claimed an asylum seekers' association 'just laughed at me', and for her part, it served to assert a prior claim over the rights of asylum seekers.

Contingent acceptance turns tolerated citizens, who must often struggle for acceptance into the community of value, into the guardians of good citizenship. Because these categories and boundaries are constructed, even though they are often imagined as real, they easily collapse into one another, legally and metaphorically. Those who are not firmly established in the community of value, must endlessly prove themselves, marking the borders, particularly of course by decrying each other to prove that they have the right values. For example, the Migrant (hardworking, legal, and a taxpayer) must distance herself from the Illegal Immigrant, and her impressive 'work ethic' (disciplined by deportability and the figure of the illegal) is a reproach to the lazy and lacklustre benefit dependent (Anderson and Ruhs 2010). On the other hand, the Illegal Immigrant is a foil to British folk who are not getting jobs because they are being undercut by people prepared to flout the rules. This is the white working class as 'beleaguered native', let down by a government that failed to provide British jobs for British workers (Rogaly and Taylor 2010). Both claimants and scroungers may manifest their resentment in racism—which of course is never endorsed, though it is explained through reference to illegality, and is implicitly set in contrast to the 'multiculturally sophisticated middle classes', including those designing and writing the policy documents (Rogaly and Taylor 2011). But in the end, both hardworking immigrant and deserving claimant are only tolerated members of the community of value, and neither are good citizens. The Illegal Immigrant, the Benefit Scrounger, and the Criminal are not just parallels but they are intricately related both to each other, and to their shadows, the Migrant and the Claimant.

In contrast to the Good Citizen, neither the non-citizen nor the Failed Citizen is properly modern. The Failed Citizen is not the flexible neoliberal subject, with a portfolio career, making the most of every opportunity, improving skills, and selling his labour to the highest bidder. Moreover, tellingly, the depiction is often one of 'uncivilized' gender relations of oppressive masculinity and excessive femininity (Webster 2008). Similarly the non-citizen is often depicted as subject to slave-labour and feudal obligations. Non-citizens too comprise a site of oppressive gender relations. Poverty, deservingness, and citizenship are highly gendered. The Good Citizen, the non-citizen, and the Failed Citizen are male. Women's citizenship has always been mediated, essential yet indirect, and this is also true of citizenship's Others. In the same way that the 'wife' is necessary but subordinated to the Good Citizen, so the Others of the Good Citizen are male, but space is made for the female as a victim of trafficking and as the Benefit Scrounger. In the latter case, women can be depicted as instrumental single mothers, having children not out of love and proper maternal feeling but in order to claim benefits and housing. This is similar to the portrayal of migrant mothers as having what are called in the USA and in Ireland 'anchor babies', in order to claim settlement and citizenship. The relation of women to membership of the community of value is not only about race and class, but also about the right kind of motherhood.

There is a strong tendency to naturalize the categories of migrant, benefit dependent, and criminal which are racialized as well as gendered. People typically continue to be designated as migrants or asylum seekers even when they have attained formal citizenship. The (racialized) foreign born are often only contingently accepted into the community of value, and their children and grandchildren are second- and third-generation migrants. For migrant, claimant, and criminal, exclusion and failure can have strong 'genetic' versions, or weak 'cultural' versions with claims of generations of family dysfunction, bad motherhood, and poor attitudes to employment. The book explores how the politics of immigration must engage with this messy business, and complicate narratives that set up a homogenized 'migrant' in conflict with a homogenized 'white working class'.

Outline

In recent years there has been a remarkable consensus on immigration policy in the UK but also elsewhere. Right and left all want the 'brightest and the best', all want 'sensible policy'. The question is reduced to how many? This overlooks the ways in which the Migrant and the Citizen are normative as well as legal constructs. This is a fundamental challenge to immigration policy, which often seeks to appeal to a vein of populist politics where the Migrant is a folk devil, but at the same time draws the sting of politics through appeal to technocratic experts who advise on 'sensible' policy. The problem is that because of their normative content, like crime, immigration statistics have always been too high. From the reign of Elizabeth I, who famously expelled 'blackamoors' because there were too many in the kingdom, to the complaints of 1621 that aliens 'causeth the enhancing of the price of vittels and houserents' (Dummett and Nicol 1990: 43), to the mid-eighteenth century fears that an influx of Jews would result in St Paul's becoming a synagogue, to contemporary claims about jobs, welfare, and births, there have always been too many foreigners. Making visible the role of the Good Citizen and the community of value and using the same lens to analyse the non-citizen and the Failed Citizen opens up a far more interesting and productive agenda that helps us think about when and why migration matters, and centralizes the community of value.

Us and Them? theorizes immigration debates in order to re-politicize them and reveal what is at stake, not only for migrants, but also for citizens. It is multidisciplinary, drawing on insights from sociology, history, politics, law, economics, geography, and normative political theory. The study of migration needs to cut across traditional boundaries of knowledge making (Brettell and Hollifield 2000). As an articulation of social transformations that has received increasing public and political attention, migration transcends disciplinary boundaries. Yet there are risks attendant on multidisciplinarity: different disciplines have different epistemologies, methodologies, and research agendas, and there is always the risk that to erase these differences may erase the strengths of their insights even as it pushes at their limitations. What is common is the centrality of subject making in the study of the Migrant and the Citizen, and this is manifest across disciplines: when does the use of the category 'migrant' obscure more than it reveals, and what does it tell us about the status of 'the Citizen'?

There is an opportunistic element to this book in that it makes use of examples, particularly of press and media coverage, that have been picked up by chance rather than uncovered by database searches. The community of value is hard to avoid once you start noticing it. Engagement with the detail of law, policy, media coverage, and public debate, and the relation between them means that the book necessarily has a national specificity, and the focus is very much on the UK. It often uses examples from TV and radio coverage, and the national and local press to illustrate how migration is framed and discussed. However, the examination of the relationship between migration, citizenship, work, and belonging in theory and practice, has a more general application, as does the central argument: that immigration is not just about 'them' but is fundamentally about 'us'.

Us and Them? begins with two historical chapters tracing the origins of the figure of the Migrant. Global immigration is often presented as a distinctly contemporary phenomenon with more people on the move than ever before, but human beings always have moved. Chapter 1 will locate contemporary immigration within the long historical concern of rulers with the mobility of the ruled, the relation between geographical and labour mobility, and settlement and claims on the community. It examines the attempts to control the mobility of the poor in England from the fourteenth century onwards and how this was related to labour and an anxiety about social order. For centuries, it was the vagrant rather than the immigrant who was seen as a threat to social cohesion, the breeding ground for an anti-society of rogues and witches. The chapter explores the contemporary relevance of insights derived from this history of mobility in which control of movement which would now be characterized as 'internal' eventually became displaced on to national borders.

Chapter 2 examines the hardening of borders from the 'outside', the differentiation between subjects, foreigners, and aliens, and the emergence of the Migrant via the alien and the subject, set in contrast to the British citizen. It makes the argument for a more nuanced account of race, racism, and immigration controls that explores the relation between race, the community of value, and 'the poor'. The return to a historical 'Year Zero' which erases the history of colonialism and its legacies, in particular the imposition of particular forms of statehood, government, and nationalisms, and the lasting impact of global inequalities, combines with an affected 'racelessness' to construct the immigrant as the poor and the desperate.

The following three chapters map and interrogate UK immigration controls, citizenship policies, and public debate. Public debate tends to homogenize the figure of 'the Migrant' but the law creates a multiplicity of differentiations, and this tension, between homogeneity and heterogeneity, further complicates the question, who counts as a migrant? Chapter 3 gives an overview of contemporary migration controls in the UK. It argues that these are structured in a way that imagines the political, the social, and the economic as fundamentally separate spheres. Each imagines certain types of ideals, so in the same way as asylum policy promotes the doing of a certain kind of liberal politics (an ideal that has become increasingly difficult to sustain in a post-Cold War world), policy on migrant workers promotes certain ideas about skills and employment relations, and policy on family and dependants promote a certain type of family and family life.

Labour markets are a key site for the construction of us and them, and foreigners taking jobs has been a trope of concerns about aliens and immigrants for generations. This is contemporaneously framed as also being about the lazy 'white underclass' overprotected by state benefits who allow themselves to be displaced by migrant labour. Chapter 4 examines the interplay between institutions, systems, policies, and politics, and argues that immigration controls are not necessarily labour protectionist but rather can create a group of workers who are more attractive to employers and who are particularly vulnerable to precarious labour. The temporalities of immigration controls and migratory processes work with and against each other to shape the relations of migrants to labour markets in very particular ways.

Economic migrants are unashamedly cast in terms of the value that they bring, but the emphasis moves from value to values when migrants apply for citizenship. Chapter 5 examines naturalization and the processes of citizenship acquisition. It is through naturalization that the Migrant who has entered as a political activist, economic actor, or family member becomes integrated, both as a full person, and into the national community. Naturalization procedures are the gateway to formal state membership, but they also strongly assert the nation as a community of value. An examination of the changing laws governing citizenship acquisition are set within the context of British debates on citizenship from the 1990s onwards which have seen mobility, settlement, and naturalization moving from a minor complication to a central focus of concern.

Chapters 6 and 7 explore the dilemmas posed by illegality, immigration enforcement, and deportation. There is general frustration in many liberal states, including the UK, at governments' perceived inability to control migration and particularly to deport 'illegal immigrants'. Chapter 6 describes the instability of the category of illegal, and relates it to questions of deportability. It examines the shift in emphasis of UK immigration enforcement policy from the border to in-country raids and removals, and explores how immigration enforcement leaves its marks not just on individual non-citizens, but on communities and citizens more generally. Increasingly citizens are required to police and be policed by immigration control mechanisms, and to instantiate borders in their daily lives. Some challenge this through participation in anti-deportation campaigns, which can appeal to the same claims to good citizenship that are promoted in naturalization procedures, raising the question of who has the right to determine entry into the community of value.

The spectacular display of state power on individual bodies that is at the core of deportation can be deeply troubling to liberals who value personal bodily integrity and individual freedom. Chapter 7 considers the attempt to reconcile immigration enforcement with human rights through the language and policy of trafficking. Responses to trafficking present the UK as a site of free labour and a space of equality that is free from slavery, but they also reveal anxieties about the nature of the market, its relation to society, and more particularly, its compatibility with the idea of the nation. While labour migration policy depoliticizes through 'fact', trafficking depoliticizes through 'value', placing the plight of the victim of trafficking beyond politics. Trafficking as modern-day slavery emphasizes the experiential and individualized, in contrast to the language of labour migration set out in Chapter 4. The focus on the personal relations of dominance establishes the state as protector and passes over its role in producing the category of migrant with its attendant vulnerabilities in the first place.

Chapter 8 takes the case of domestic labour as exemplifying the ways in which all the issues outlined above come together in the lives of migrants and their employers. It examines two types of visa for domestic labour, the au pair visa and the visa for domestic workers accompanying their employers, and considers them as illustrations of profound tensions within liberalism about the nature of labour, the family, women, and the nation. It considers how immigration status reveals domestic labour as both work and not work in the UK, and how visas not only trap migrants in ambivalent social relations, but also affect the sector more generally. It also considers the relationship between immigration controls, life stage, and political subjectivities.

Us and Them? outlines the challenges posed by liberal democracies to migrants, but it is focused more particularly on the challenges that migration and migrants pose to liberal democracies. It argues that these challenges run far deeper than risks to cohesion, benefit fraud, or unemployment, and go to the heart of liberal principles of equality, rights, autonomy, freedom, and membership. Our analysis is infused by assumptions about sovereignty, property, and social relations, but it is these very assumptions that are called into question by migration and state responses to it. How do ideas about self-ownership, property, freedom, and a commitment to equality, fit with the restrictions on employment placed on migrant labour? How are ideals of citizenship as a unitary and sovereign status compatible with the language of 'foreign born' citizens? The deep contradictions within liberalism that emerge when confronted by migration, which mean that, in practice, liberalism often stops at the border (Cole 2000), are not only matters for migrants but go to the heart of citizens' politics.

1

The Chrysalis for Every Species of Criminal? Vagrancy, Settlement, and Mobility

The history of the world is unavoidably a history of mobility. Thinking historically is a useful counter to political and academic claims of the exceptionalism of contemporary migration. As Lucassen puts it, 'the claims that current developments are new or without precedent . . . are mostly not supported by extensive knowledge of migrations in the past' (Lucassen and Lucassen 2009: 2). Beginning with early humans from Africa, and their spread throughout the globe, the mobility of people is often not conceived of as 'migration', but read as conquest, trade, war, kinship networks, itinerancy, and so on. Those who move are pioneers and pilgrims, settlers and troubadours, slaves and conquistadores (Hoerder 2002). All mobilities are by no means equivalent, but are differentially constructed and experienced, forced, encouraged, and prevented. Thinking historically encourages us to link migration to other social and economic processes—to the extent that we often stop thinking of it as 'migration' at all. The *longue durée* suggests that human mobility in itself is far more 'normal' than we are given to expect. It reminds us that mobility is not a feature only of contemporary globalization, nor indeed only of capitalism, that ideas of 'nation' and of 'state' are relatively recent constructions, and that the contours of the relation between people and land are contingent. Land has not always been straightforwardly 'territory' and certainly not bounded territory. The unruly person who moves, the vagrant, has for centuries been regarded, as Christopher Tiedeman (1886) put it, as, 'the chrysalis for every species of criminal'. Thinking historically predisposes us to an analysis that allows that mobility does not just happen within ordered social and political structures, but rather it undermines, reshapes, and reinforces power relations and institutions. This brings centre stage questions such as: when is mobility imagined as a problem? Who so designates it? Who controls (their own) mobility?

There have been some considerable developments in the study of migration history in recent years. Research by scholars such as Hoerder (2002), McKeown (2004), Manning (2005), and Jan and Leo Lucassen (2009), has offered a significant contribution to the field of global history, beginning to go beyond the European and Atlantic perspective that has tended to dominate histories of migration. In the UK, scholars have studied early deportation and attempts to regulate the incomings of foreigners (Stevens 1998; Stevens 2004; Schuster 2005; Wilsher 2012), the history of black people in the UK, from Roman times to the present day (Fryer 1984; Killingray 1994; Gilroy and Hall 2007), and the relation between migration and Empire (Gilroy 2004). This chapter needs to be placed within this context. It considers the attempts to control the mobility of the poor within the geographical space that is now called 'England', and what attention to vagrancy and alms giving/poor relief beginning from the late Middle Ages tells us about migration in the contemporary era. The chapter will begin by considering the first vagrancy and labour statutes of the four-teenth century, and consider how the mobility of the poor was linked to labour control, disorder, and a concern with alms giving. It will then examine the Tudor period, the height of the vagrancy legislation, when vagrancy became associated with criminality, but also resistance to enclosure and the loss of the commons. It will discuss alms, the move from hospitality to charity to poor relief and its association with settlement and belonging. At the edges of all this lurks the figure of the 'valiant beggar' or the 'sturdy rogue', idle and work-shy, the undeserving poor. In this way the vagrant is the one of the ancestors both of contemporary 'failed citizens' and 'migrants'.

1.1 Mobility, Labour, Disorder, and Alms

A desire to control the movement of the poor on the part of rulers pre-dates the British state. The first English law on vagrancy was the 1349 Ordinance of Labourers, revised in 1351 to the Statute of Labourers. This was prompted by acute agricultural labour shortages and the rising cost of labour. During feudal times, geographical mobility was clearly linked to labour mobility: to be mobile was to be able to sell your labour to a different master and there had been a growth of commutation (that is, labour services were being replaced by money payments). In 1349 there was anxiety about labour for the harvest because of the precipitous population decline resulting most immediately from the plague outbreak that had begun a year earlier and was to kill between a third and a half of the population. Rural labour shortages were exacerbated by an increase in the number of chartered towns that had purchased freedom from feudal obligations. 'Town air breathes free', so the saying went, and these chartered towns attracted a floating population of former serfs fleeing increasingly harsh conditions imposed by landowners (Chambliss 1964; Morton 1965).

The 1349 ordinance makes clear the relation between physical and labour mobility and processes of proletarianization, as it was an 'attempt to...substitute for serfdom' (Foote 1956, cited in Chambliss 1964: 240), controlling mobility of labourers in order that 'they may be compelled to labour for their necessary living' (Ordinance of Labourers 1349). It had three main labour provisions: regulation of wages, the enforcement of labour contracts, and the introduction of compulsory service. The first of these, the curbing of 'excessive wages', required masters to pay pre-plague wages, even if they had previously agreed to pay more.[1] The second stipulation attempted to curb labour mobility by requiring that servants should not leave before their agreed term was up on 'pain of imprisonment', making the labour contract, as Bennett puts it 'public, long-term and unbreakable' (Bennett 2010: 13). She argues that the first two of these provisions developed previous statutes, and that what was innovative was in fact the third provision which significantly extended compulsory service. This required that able-bodied men and women who did not have work or land to make a living on 'shall be bounded to serve him which shall him require' or imprisoned until they agreed to do so. Bennett emphasizes the importance of this being compulsory *service*, rather than compulsory labour. The imposition of a service relation indicated 'that the compulsory employment of idle people was not to be casual or short-term, but was to entail dependence and durability' (Bennett 2010: 10), particularly in the light of the limitations on leaving imposed by the second stipulation. This duty to work for whoever required their service could be imposed upon anyone under sixty-years old without 'craft', 'proper land', or visible means of support, whether they were a serf or a free tenant.

The imposition of compulsory labour on free tenants was a new departure from previous forms of compulsory labour. It extended the power of landowners over all tenants, and this included smaller farmers, a group proliferating as large landowners divested themselves of holdings that the labour shortage meant they could not use. The ordinance enabled an 'idle tenant' to be compelled elsewhere, and thus runaway serfs could be replaced by compelled servants. Masters were not permitted to compete for labour by offering higher wages, but they were allowed to demand service from labourers that would previously not have been available to them because they were another person's tenants. Bennett claims that there is evidence to suggest that

---

[1] It also regulated the price of 'victuals', and food sellers were enjoined 'to sell the same victual for a reasonable price, having respect to the price that such victual be sold at in the places adjoining, so that the same sellers have moderate gains and not excessive, reasonably to be required according to the distance of the place from whence the said victuals be carried'.

the relations of compulsory service were hated more than serfdom and that this power of compulsion was to have particular consequences for women. Women are specifically mentioned in the compulsory service clause and they frequently figure in legal court cases detailing enforcement and resistance. 'There is a marvellous illogic to the notion that the landless poor were mostly men, given that men inherited more land than women ever did, were more often gainers than losers in the land market, found employment more readily than women and, of course, earned higher wages' (Bennett 2010: 43).

Woodward (1980), Steinfeld (1991), and Bennett (2010) among others have argued for the importance of vagrancy legislation in controlling wage rates and the employment relations between master and servant, and master and labourer. Bennett (2010) has described how in the late fourteenth century, vagrancy laws were used to compel people to sell their labour locally. Local people could be classed as 'vagrants' if they refused to work:

> Employers, constables, jurors and justices broadened the compulsory service clause to constrain labour of all sorts, even skilled labour and day-labour. The spectre of refused compulsory service was invoked against many sorts of recalcitrant workers; those who took wages deemed excessive, or proved uncooperative at harvest time or spurned the obligatory oath to obey the labour laws, or refused to work generally. (Bennett 2010: 18)

Steinfeld (1991) argues that the threat of vagrancy worked alongside compulsory labour clauses to force labourers into service—that is, into particular form of relation. He cites a 1444 statute which pronounced that those who did not have sufficient land to justify their annual employment should serve by the year 'upon the pain to be justified as a vagabond' (cited in Steinfeld 1991: 3).

The Ordinance of Labourers also criminalized the giving of alms to 'valiant beggars' who 'as long as they live of begging, do refuse to labour, giving themselves to idleness and vice, and sometimes to theft and other abominations' (Ordinance of Labourers 1349). Those giving alms to such people were to be subject to 'pain of imprisonment'. The valiant beggar marks the first appearance of a figure of idleness and indiscipline which is to haunt the statute books to this day. Notably the figure appears at a time when alms giving was a requirement of Christian charity, as manifest in the Sermon on the Mount. This idea of the poor as a threat to social order marked a change from medieval religious notions of apostolic poverty as a holy state. To forbid alms giving to a group of people meant challenging deeply socially embedded norms about poverty, charity, and Christianity, and the Ordinance asked bishops, vicars, and other religious 'to exhort and invite their parishioners by salutary admonitions, to labour' (Ordinance of Labourers 1349).

Attempts to control the geographical and hence the labour mobility of the poor were heightened in 1388 with the Statutes of Cambridge. These confirmed the 1349 clauses, instituting specific wage rates for servants ('because that servants and labourers will not, nor by a long season, would serve and labour without outrageous and excessive hire and much more than that been given to such servants and labourer in any time past' (Statute of Cambridge 1388)). They instigated new mechanisms for the control of labour, by requiring that no servant or labourer was to leave their hundred,[2] even if their term of service was over 'unless he bring a letter patent containing the cause of his going and the time of his return, if he ought to return, under the King's seal which for this intent shall be assigned and delivered to the keeping of some good man of the hundred' (Statute of Cambridge 1388). People found 'wandering without such letter' were to be put in the stocks until they returned and found work (Statute of Cambridge 1388). This punishment was also applied to 'every person that goeth begging' but importantly there was a distinction made between those who were 'able to serve or labour', and 'impotent beggars' (Statute of Cambridge 1388).

The 'good men of the hundred' charged with authorizing or forbidding, through the King's seal, the mobility of the poor, were the local expression of central, kingly, authority. In this way, control over mobility was bound up with the expansion of this central authority. Torpey (2000) has argued that it is not possible to have modern states without control of movement across international borders. Modern states are both territorial and membership organizations, and it is, he argues, a defining feature of modern states that they have the 'monopoly of the legitimate means of movement' (Torpey 2000: 1). He therefore claims that control over movement as manifest in the emergence of immigration controls and passports is 'an essential aspect of the "state-ness" of states' (Torpey 2000: 3). Attention to the history of vagrancy suggests that the monopoly of the legitimate means of movement was first imposed on what is now regarded as *internal* movement.

1.2 Mobility, Crime, and Sovereignty

The Tudor era saw a significant increase in numbers of vagrants (Stone 1966; Beier 1978; Beier 1985). This was in the context of multiple interrelated factors: demographic growth, the end of feudalism, the dissolution of the monasteries, and an increase in what we would now call un(der)employment. People were 'unsettled', physically mobile, endlessly changing jobs, and in occupations which were often dangerous, dishonourable, and criminalized (Beier 1985; Fumerton 2006). These factors contributed to increasing mobility,

---

[2] A 'hundred' is an administrative unit within a shire for military and judicial purposes. Its size was sufficient to provide for one hundred families.

but more particularly a move towards the towns, especially after 1550. Between 1550 and 1650 towns such as Norwich, Bristol, and York doubled or trebled in size, but the largest growth was London whose population increased sixfold (Stone 1966). Given the high urban death rates, this increase in population suggests a massive migration from the countryside, and, when migrants failed to find accommodation or work, they often fell in to vagabondage. Beier describes how the proportion of vagrants that originated from within ten miles of London Bridge noted in Bridewell Court Books increases from 25 per cent in the first half of the sixteenth century to nearly 50 per cent by 1634 (Beier 1978: 207). He argues that, 'whether they were born there or not, the experience of living in a rapidly urbanizing area brought about vagrancy . . . vagrants did not come to London as vagrants but became vagrants in London' (Beier 1978: 208). In short, London was 'unable to assimilate all its immigrants' (Beier 1978: 208).

It was Tudor times that saw the fullest development of vagrancy legislation, and a shift in emphasis from wage control to labour discipline and the countering of social disorder. The prescription to work was, by Elizabethan times, very much about social order. As the legislation on labour developed and become consolidated in 1563 with the Statute of Artificers, vagrancy continued to be a way of disciplining the poor. The 1563 Statute, for example, authorized the ways in which masters could recover runaways and made those mobile poor without testimonials from their masters, punishable as vagabonds (Steinfeld 1991). The vagabonds and beggars were not simply people without jobs who were able to sell their labour in a competitive labour market, but they were people without positions. Compulsory service was therefore the solution, not just to the rising price of labour but to social unrest. The vagrant had become, to use Beier's (1985) term, 'masterless', without position, and threatened social hierarchies and order. Importantly, being 'masterless' did not mean that they were masters of themselves or of their own destiny—ideas of self-ownership and 'property in the person' which were to become so important from the seventeenth century until today, were not developed by the late Middle Ages. In a society in which 'ideas of labour and belonging were inextricably entangled in each other' (Brace 2004: 14), their mobility was a sign that they, quite literally, were not keeping to their place. Their 'masterlessness' indicated the relation between geographical and labour mobility, and between mobility and anxieties about status and social disorder.

Vagrancy seems by this time to be a particularly male crime, with single females accounting for under a quarter of vagrancy proceedings, although pregnancy among unmarried women and abandonment among the married, were particularly common reasons for female vagrancy (Beier 1985). This might be partly because it was more difficult for women to take to the road because of the growth in sexual assault and because of their caring responsibilities. However, most of the data pertains to court cases and it may be that some of the gender difference is a result of poor women being more likely to be tried as witches or as prostitutes than as vagrants (Federici 2004)—this does not mean that they were not on the move.

This shift in vagrancy statutes, from a concern with the mobility and cost of labour, to a concern with crime and social disorder, was not only a result of the development of a separate strand of labour legislation. It was also to do with the demise of feudalism (in 1575 the last serfs in England were manumitted by Elizabeth I) and the increasing loss of common lands. It was access to the commons as well as mobility that had previously given bargaining power to the poor. The rights of the commons enabled poor free men (though not serfs) to access natural resources. They had been enshrined in the Charter of the Forest of 1217, also known as the 'Charter of the Common Man', because it was the first time free men (that is, not the nobility or the clergy) had been granted rights. It was the complement to the Magna Carta, enshrining the rights of common people to royal lands—not just forested, but including pasture and moor.[3] In effect it gave economic rights in the same way that the Magna Carta gave what we would now call civil and political rights (Linebaugh 2008). The Charter of the Forest had enabled many poor people to graze, gather fuel, hunt and fish, and squat—that is, to eke out a subsistence living. This access to subsistence meant that, unlike servants who were generally contracted by the year, labourers and artificers could hire themselves out by the day. These sorts of arrangement could be preferred to relations of service which tied servants to masters for prolonged periods as they were more profitable and offered more autonomy (Steinfeld 1991).

Access to the commons was increasingly under threat from the claims and actions of the wealthy who overgrazed and denied access to the commons. There was a rise in enclosure during Tudor times, partly because of an increase in demand for wool. Landowners switched to sheep, meaning land was enclosed, commons were over-grazed, and demand for labour fell. The options of the poor were becoming more limited as newer, more commercial farming methods required investment, and land became a source of profit. In his 1516 work, *Utopia*, Sir Thomas More was sanguine about the relation between vagrancy and crime, suggesting that the practice of enclosure was responsible for some of the social problems affecting England at the time, specifically theft:

> But I do not think that this necessity of stealing arises only from hence; there is another cause of it, more peculiar to England. 'What is that?' said the Cardinal:

---

[3] In 1184, Henry II had decreed that any land he designated 'Royal Forest' could not be used by ordinary people for foraging, grazing, building, etc. The Charter of the Forest removed these restrictions for all lands designated forest in the intervening period.

'The increase of pasture,' said I, 'by which your sheep, which are naturally mild, and easily kept in order, may be said now to devour men and people, not only villages, but towns; for wherever it is found that the sheep of any soil yield a softer and richer wool than ordinary, there the nobility and gentry, and even those holy men, the abbots not contented with the old rents which their farms yielded, nor thinking it enough that they, living at their ease, do no good to the public, resolve to do it hurt instead of good. They stop the course of agriculture, destroying houses and towns, reserving only the churches, and enclose grounds that they may lodge their sheep in them'. (More 1992 [1516]: 16)

Changing conditions and rebellions meant poverty was becoming dangerous (Beier 1985; Linebaugh 2008). In 1531 there was a further distinction introduced between the able-bodied idle and criminal offenders,[4] with harsher penalties imposed on the latter than the former. Nevertheless, the distinction between the idle and the criminal was not a clear one. Vagrancy, as Braddick (2000) emphasizes, was above all a crime of status. It was being a vagrant itself that was a challenge to the social order as well as crimes committed as a vagrant. In 1536, a vagrant who was found to be a repeat offender could be sentenced to death 'as a felon and an enemy of the commonwealth' (Act for the Punishment of Sturdy Vagabonds and Beggars 1536).

> The threat they posed to society was not just physical but normative and this informed a number of exaggerated stereotypes. They became routinely associated with disease and sedition as well as a whole series of crimes...The forces of patriarchalism are reflected then, not just in the imaginings of sexual license attached to vagrant women but to wholly anti-social values that masterless men must represent. (Braddick 2000)

Vagrants had broken not just with masters, but often with family life, vagrant women were prostitutes, vagrant men were unruly and a sexual threat. 'These offences also involved a new concept of collective crime: of a good society versus a wicked one; of Christians against covens of witches; of rightful rulers against treasonous plotters; of law abiding citizens against anti-societies of rogues' (Beier 1985: 12).

Vagrant, idle, and criminal were moral categories, with idleness 'the mother and root of all vices' (Statute of Labourers 1351). Seventeenth-century radicals such as Gerard Winstanley put a different spin on this and viewed idleness not as a problem of the poor, but of the rich, who thereby, shamefully, lived off the labour of others. Winstanley led a group of radicals called the Diggers who urged the re-coupling of land and labour and an end to the private ownership of land. Encouraged by the reclaiming of the commons in the upheavals of the

---

[4] The able-bodied idle were to be whipped 'til his body be bloody', but for those who use 'divers and subtil crafty and unlawful games and plays', the punishment was to be whipped for two days in a row (Act for the Punishment of Sturdy Vagabonds and Beggars 1536).

Civil War, they went further than the call for maintaining the traditional rights of the poor to the commons, denying the property rights of lords in the commons, and demanding collective cultivation of waste land. They argued that true freedom was access to the land not ownership. Private property created tyranny, exploitation, and a lack of freedom, and they asserted the earth as a 'common treasury for all': 'By his laws, made and upheld by his power, he hedges the weak out of the earth, and either starves them or else forces them through poverty to take from others, and then hangs them for so doing' (cited in Brace 2004: 18–19).

Scarcely fifty years later, Locke in contrast argued that this lack of freedom and exploitation was not a concomitant of private property. His argument rested on the idea of property in the person: 'Every Man has a Property in his own person. This no Body has any Right to but himself. The Labour of his Body, and the work of his Hands, we may say, are properly his' (Locke and Macpherson 1980: 19). For Locke, freedom was about self-ownership, and those who were 'industrious and rational' (but not the 'quarrelsome and contentious') would labour on common land and would thereby improve it. Hill characterized the turbulent times of the Civil War as characterized by two potential revolutions, one which reinstated private property and extended democracy within capitalist relations, and one which called for the 'world turned upside down' (Hill 1972). It was the liberalism of Locke, founded on the idea of the liberal sovereign self, rather than the radicalism of Winstanley, that won out. It is this thinking, as much as the Treaty of Westphalia, that installed the ideology that continues to inform ideas about labour, property, mobility, and belonging today.

1.3 Documentation and Control

As social and political changes occurred, authority, bureaucracy, and violence coalesced in response to the movement of the poor. Documentary controls of subjects were required to enable the exercise of such power: 'Despite widespread fraud, the passport was the only effective method of controlling the movements of the vagrant poor' (Beier 1985). The initial testimonials of employment of 1388 had become complex documents by Tudor times. They were issued for a particular period of time, and they had to be signed by a magistrate or justice of the peace in every settlement passed through. The need to distinguish between those with permission to be mobile and disorderly persons meant that the importance of testimonials for the able bodied and of 'licenses to beg' for the impotent poor continued for several centuries, and the mobile poor were all expected to have papers by the time of Henry VIII.

These impositions were subverted. The problem of fake testimonials was anticipated by the early legislation, and the 1388 Ordinance of Labourers had already instituted a punishment of forty days imprisonment for labourers holding documents 'found forged or false' (Statute of Cambridge 1388). By 1570, false papers could be bought almost anywhere at the cost of between two and four pennies and some vagrants would hold more than one set. Counterfeiters by this date could be highly skilled. Not only had they to be able to write, but, if they were to produce a good document, they had to know the names of the relevant officials and be able to vary handwriting in fake endorsements.

In 1569–72 and 1631–9, 'great national searches' were instituted to root out vagrancy—'local officials and keepers of lodgings for travellers examine lodgers' names, dwelling places, destinations, and reasons for travel and bring away suspicious persons before a Justice of the Peace' (Beier 1985: 155). The first of these national searches saw 13,000 people rounded up and punished. Like today, there was a problem with the administering of the penalties for mobility: there were not enough gaols to imprison vagrants, and members of the judiciary were too few to try them. The punishments were summary and severe: scourging, branding, being held in the stocks, expulsion even death. Vagrants were also required to 'move on'. This was initially from village to village, but it was also possible to move people much further away. In 1597, the Act for the Repression of Vagrancy abolished the death penalty for vagrancy and introduced penal transportation in its place. A 1603 Order of the Privy Council mentions Newfoundland, the West and East Indies, France, Germany, Spain, and the Low Countries as suitable destinations.[5] Thus 'civilized England shall be disburdened of its worst people' (cited in Beier 1985: 150). Both aliens and subjects could be transported if they committed a criminal offence, and the 1718 Act made the return of people who had been transported punishable by death.

The distinction between subjects and aliens (later citizens and migrants) was not a feature of early controls over mobility, and the power of the sovereign to immobilize and to expel was first exercised principally over the sovereign's subjects. Restrictions over who could enter or leave the realm were not determined by whether or not people were subjects, and the entry of aliens was not restricted. The first substantial regulation of alien entrants was not until 1793 when the Aliens Act was passed, a response to concern with numbers fleeing the French Revolution (Haycraft 1897; Bleichmar 1999). While this Act allowed that aliens could be refused landing in Britain, the main thrust of the Act was the enumerating of aliens and their control within the territory,

---

[5] See <http://luna.folger.edu/luna/servlet/detail/FOLGERCM1~6~6~790664~150423:Procla mations–1603-09-17—By-the>.

rather than the prevention of their entry in the first place. Names, numbers, and occupations were to be written on a 'passport' that would be issued by a magistrate or a justice of the peace. The passport also detailed where the alien was allowed to travel to, and it was renewable. Thus passports were issued, not to subjects as in the twentieth century, but to non-subjects.

1.4 Settlement and Alms

For all the monstrousness of begging and idleness, there continued to be a problem of indiscriminate giving to those who were able to work. In 1536, the Act for the Punishment of Sturdy Vagabonds and Beggars forbade indiscriminate personal giving and provided that parishes collect and disburse alms to the disabled poor. Alms collectors were compensated and were also required 'to compel all and every sturdy vagabond and valiant beggar to be set and kept to continual labour' (Act for the Punishment of Sturdy Vagabonds and Beggars 1536). This was at the time of the dissolution of the monasteries which is likely to have had an impact on both the numbers of poor, as numbers were swollen by monks thrown on to the road, and on the giving of alms, an important function of monasteries for many centuries.

In 1563, the first act requiring the levy of compulsory poor rate was passed. This was formalized in the 1601 Elizabethan Poor Law which created a complex system administered by parishes, and paid for by levies on local ratepayers. The 'settled' poor were eligible for outdoor relief in their home or indoor relief in the alms houses (or later in workhouses). But who counts as 'settled poor' in a society that is ever more mobile? The vagrancy statutes had long required that those who were not resident in a hundred or parish were to be punished and expelled or forced to labour, but this received new urgency as ratepayers attempted to limit their responsibility to those who were settled in the parish. There were reports of people gravitating towards more generous parishes simply to claim poor relief financed by ratepayers. As poor relief moved from the responsibility of monasteries or social solidarity to the responsibility of local parishes, a new emphasis was placed on the problem of the claiming of relief by those who did not belong. From the 1640s, phrases such as 'likely to prove a charge to the parish' begin to appear more frequently in records of removal and Feldman observes, 'The phrase was always used to the same purpose; namely, to justify the removal of people who though poor were not vagrants' (Feldman 2003: 10).

The 1662 Poor Relief Act sanctioned the removal of incomers 'likely to be chargeable to the Parish' (Act for the Better Releife of the Poore of this Kingdom 1662), and ordered that poor relief or work could only to be given to those who were 'settled' in a parish or who were in their parish of birth. Like the vagrancy statutes, it promoted the immobility of the poor other than for the purposes of temporary labour. Those who were mobile were not qualified for relief in their parish of temporary residence; if they were to beg, they became 'sturdy beggars', and should they return to a parish from which they had been removed, they could be pursued as vagrants. Like the vagrancy statutes, the Act enabled the forced removal of the 'unsettled' poor to their last parish of settlement or their parish of birth. In the case of Scotland and Ireland, which did not have the parish system, paupers were simply removed to Scotland or to Ireland. While previously parishes and corporations had required landlords and employers who profited from migrants to also carry some of the risks by demanding bonds and securities, these risks were now carried by migrants alone: 'In this way the 1662 law ... to a degree defused a host of local conflicts that arose between landlords and large farmers and manufacturers, on one side, and the larger body of rate payers, on the other, over the burden placed by the migrant poor on the poor law and other collective resources' (Feldman 2012: 18).

The problem was perceived to be not with the transient, or, to use Simmel's phrase, 'the wanderer who comes today and goes tomorrow' (1976). As long as labourers had a certificate of permission and 'hath left Wife and Children or some of them there' (Act for the Better Releife of the Poore of this Kingdom 1662), they could move for temporary work. Rather, the problem was 'the person who comes today and stays tomorrow' (Simmel 1976: 402), and strong efforts were made to limit settlement. To be considered settled one had to have lived in a parish for forty days 'without objection', and seasonal labourers who did not return when their work was finished could not count their time towards settlement. Various other administrative obstacles were placed in the way of forty-day settlement so that over the years, in practice, this became increasingly difficult to obtain. From 1685, newcomers were required to give written notice of their arrival and their location, and the forty days would begin only from receipt of this notice. Settlement could be attained with evidence of paying £10 a year for a tenement or by marriage, or by indenture and service. Amendments in 1697 required servants to remain for a year, with only the last forty days of their annual service fulfilling settlement. According to Feldman this was 'a device to reconcile ratepayers to the needs of employers at the expense of the servants' entitlements' (Feldman 2012: 22)—it was an attempt to balance the demand for labour by masters/employers with the costs to ratepayers by limiting the rights of labourers and encouraging employers to dismiss servants just before they completed their year of service.

Whereas previously there had been claims that the threat to the commons emanated from the rich, it was now the mobility of the poor that was regarded as the problem for the settled population, and the costs were presented as not only carried by the ratepayers, but by poorer people who made use of common rights. The preamble to the 1662 Poor Relief Act claims that: 'poore people are not restrained from going from one Parish to another and therefore doe endeavor to settle themselves in those Parishes where there is the best Stocke, the largest Commons or Wastes to build Cottages and the most Woods for them to burn and destroy' (Act for the Better Releife of the Poore of this Kingdom 1662). In 1690, Locke argued that while God gave the world to men, they were not all fellow commoners, and land, 'though it be common, in respect of some men, it is not so to all mankind; but is the joint property of this country, or this parish' (Locke and Macpherson 1980: 21). Some parishes went so far as to use the 1662 Act to limit access to the commons (Landau 1990; cited in Feldman 2003: 86).

The control of mobility of beggars and labourers was achieved far more successfully after the development of the Elizabethan Poor Law and most particularly, the 1662 Act, than it ever had been through vagrancy law. Beier (1985) regards this Act as ushering in a new means of legalizing mobility and limiting vagrancy both by ensuring that there was relief available in the last parish of settlement and by restricting long distance migration. In contrast, Feldman regards the 1662 law as extremely harsh. 'The greatest effect of the law of Settlement was to force the non-settled poor to survive without support from the poor law' (Feldman 2003: 90).

The 1662 Act fixed the poor in a particular place but importantly, being so fixed did not mean an automatic entitlement to poor relief which was still at the discretion of the overseers. It made provision for corporation workhouses in London, Westminster, and Middlesex, which provided materials for outworkers, and shelter for orphans. In 1696 a Quaker workhouse was established in Bristol and within a few years other cities followed suit. From 1710 the Society for the Promotion of Christian Knowledge promoted the idea of parish workhouses, and in 1723 Knatchbull's Act enabled workhouses to be established by parishes, and gave expression to the 'workhouse test': in order to discourage irresponsible claims, a person who applied for relief had to enter a workhouse and undertake a set amount of work. Workhouses could be contracted out to third parties who 'farmed' the poor. They were paid a weekly rate by the parish for each inmate, and could also keep any income generated by the workhouse labour. Women were particularly affected by these changes, as they were more likely to be admitted to workhouses (MacKay 1997:60), but also the power of removal was exercised particularly strongly against unmarried pregnant women, as the child born into the parish would thereafter be the financial responsibility of the local ratepayers.[6]

---

[6] The Removal Act of 1795 prevented non-settled people from being moved on only on suspicion that they might apply for relief, but an exception was made for these women.

Removals and settlement requirements served to make the mobility of labour more difficult. The numbers of removals between parishes seems to have been quite significant even through to the early part of the nineteenth century: between 25 March 1827 and 25 March 1828, 43,677 individuals were removed from parishes in England and Wales (Feldman 2003: 90). Yet the functional value of migration to the cities of a rapidly industrializing society is clear. In 1834, the Poor Law fundamentally overhauled the Elizabethan arrangements, partly to encourage the able-bodied rural poor to migrate to manufacturing districts. It established national oversight of parish practices, discouraged out-door relief, and required every person in need of support to receive it in a workhouse. This centralization meant that the boundaries between parishes became less important. Concerns began to be expressed at 'parochial selfishness' and attention paid to the harshness of enforced removals. In 1846, the Poor Removal Act made it illegal to remove a person who had been in a parish for five years, even if they did not have settlement, and this was gradually extended over the next two decades. It also applied to the Irish in England, despite public hostility to the Irish and fears of immigration.[7] There was a rebalancing of the response to the mobility of the poor. Being mobile and moving from one's parish was increasingly about being 'free' improving oneself through selling one's labour rather than being 'masterless'.

1.5 Moral Reform and Pauperism

Yet this still left the problem of the 'valiant beggar' who wandered without a view to self-improvement, but who could also become 'settled' into a life of easy dependency. The perennial problem of distinguishing between the valiant beggar and the genuinely needy and managing the idle poor continued. The 1834 Poor Law adapted the Knatchbull workhouse test and had as one of its guiding principles 'less eligibility'. The able-bodied person in receipt of poor relief 'on the whole shall not be made really or apparently as eligible as the independent labourer of the lowest class' (Poor Law Amendment Act 1834)—that is, the conditions for the pauper were to be more difficult than for the working poor, a principle said to originate in the work of the utilitarian, Jeremy Bentham and taken on enthusiastically by Malthus:

> If the condition of persons maintained without property by the labour of others were rendered more eligible than that of persons maintained by their own labour

---

[7] Feldman points out that 'improvements in the welfare entitlements of the Irish arose in the nineteenth century when there was a complete absence of state controls on their entry to the country' (Feldman 2003: 104). This is interesting because it suggests that access to welfare does not have to entail restrictions on entry, which challenges some of the assumptions in contemporary debates about migration and welfare benefits (Feldman 2003).

> then . . . individuals destitute of property would be continually withdrawing them-
> selves from the class of person maintained by their own labour to the class of
> persons maintained by the eligibility of others. (Bentham 1796: 25–6)

This principle informed the development of Victorian welfare and penal policy, and it is also possible to see how the doctrine of less eligibility continues to inform debates today. 'It can't be right to have people on housing benefit living on streets which hard-working families cannot afford to live on', pronounced Housing Minister Grant Shapps on 12 April 2012. Now and in the nineteenth century, the poor needed to be educated away from crime and the deliberate choice of poverty over work, and moral reform was an important response to the problems of both crime and poverty. The distinction between the 'impotent' and the 'valiant' beggar, between the deserving and undeserving poor, the person who can't work and the person who chooses not to, is relevant from vagrancy controls to poor relief to the welfare state.

The problem of some poor people's refusal to submit to the discipline of labour, was and continues to be presented as a problem of values. As Mitchell Dean says, writing of the system of regulation emerging in the early nineteenth century:

> Pauperism is as much about 'morals,' forms of every-day life, families, breadwin-
> ners, households, and self-responsibility, as economics, the state, poor laws, and
> poor policies. It is about the formation of particular categories of social agent, and
> of specific class and familial relations in so far as they are promoted by govern-
> mental practices. (Dean 1991: 3; cited in MacKay 1997: 61)

The disorderly poor were and are seen as lacking both value and values (in contrast to the reformers and the bourgeoisie). They were often identified as immoral, out of control, and sexually incontinent in the same way that black people were thought to be (Davidoff 1979; McClintock 1995). They were thought improvident, irregular, and above all, uncivilized, and, like the natives of the colonies, in dire need of missionary work (Jones 1974).

The separation of land and labour, of 'community' and relations of belonging has been regarded as a problem for order for several centuries in England. It has been managed by different bodies of law on vagrancy, labour, and alms/poor relief, and continues to be manifest in contemporary policies, including in responses to mobility. An historical approach that does not assume nation state boundaries allows us to perceive continuities, not only between the valiant beggar and the welfare scrounger, but also between the unsettled vagrant coming to parishes where they did not belong and the Migrant. In the days before the hardening of the borders of the nation state, when 'foreign' meant outside the parish or town boundary, it was not the Migrant or the Muslim that threatened social cohesion, but the vagabond. As one examines the ways in which, first rulers, and then the state, coerced and coerce the poor into mobility and immobility, one moves away from the pathologizing of the 'Migrant'. The fear that the 'poor stranger is crept among us' (cited in Hindle 1998: 91), and encroaching on the commons, that they are idle, dependent, and undermining the insecure position of the worker, the call to protect morality, values, and culture, have earlier parallels. In earlier centuries, it was the vagabond who was 'without craft' ('low skilled'), who did not 'know their place', and who moved in an unregulated way outside the place where they rightly belonged.

Benefit scroungers and migrants are often imagined as competing with each other for resources, and both exemplify the contested relation between mobility and labour that was expressed first in the Statute of Labourers' understanding of vagrancy, and later in the legislation governing poor relief. The requirement for the population to be fixed in order to claim poor relief and to be mobile for the purposes of selling their labour continues to have relevance today. National boundaries mean that welfare benefits can be a right (albeit increasingly circumscribed) of citizens. But they also establish the territory of the nation within which the benefit claimant is bound to look for work. Labour mobility across state borders must be controlled, but inside the state, labour must be on the move, as will be discussed in Chapter 4. In contrast to non-citizens, citizens are supposed to be mobile to find work, to 'get on your bike', to find the work that has been reserved for them. In contemporary discourse, and in contrast to immigrants, those who have access to the welfare state are often depicted as not mobile enough, stuck in their housing estates, and not bothering to make the journey to the next town to look for work. For them, work is a *duty*, but for non-citizens work, like welfare benefits, is a *right* to which they cannot automatically claim entitlement. A historical perspective enables us to understand why it is that the poor 'at home' can be depicted as not mobile enough, at the same time as the poor 'abroad' are too mobile, and how work can be a right for some and a duty for others.

While both the (illegal) migrant and the dependent/scrounger have their origins in the vagrant, both have different emphases and relations to work. The problem of migration is perceived as being, not that the (illegal) migrant seeks to labour and to earn a wage, but that they do so in the wrong place. The problem of welfare dependency/scrounging in contrast is that, like the valiant beggar, they do not seek to labour at all, and in this they are assisted by the over-eager migrant. The Migrant, as will be discussed in Chapter 4, is often portrayed as undermining the livelihoods of those who already have very little, taking jobs that rightly belong to the Citizen, as well as facilitating benefit scrounging by giving unscrupulous employers access to cheap labour. Migrancy, like vagrancy, is above all a crime of *status*, of refusing to accept one's position. Nowadays however, this is not cast as one's position as a serf, as belonging to a master, but one's position as 'belonging' to a state.

The Lockean individual is tied in the first instance, not to a plot of land, nor to a master, but to a nation state. As Henry Ireton put it in the Putney Debates: 'This, I perceive, is pressed as that which is so essential and due: the right of the people of this kingdom, and as they are the people of this kingdom, distinct and divided from other people, and that we must for this right lay aside all other considerations' (Firth 1901: vol. 1). Thus the relation between self-ownership, freedom, and belonging are far from fixed. While today there is an assumed naturalness to belonging to a state that is imagined, through ideals of the nation, as originating somewhere in the mists of time, these are recent social and political formations, not natural arrangements disrupted by industrialization and globalization.

1.6 Conclusion

Non-citizens are urged to differentiate themselves from failed citizens. Migrants are often presented as hardworking, good family members, law-abiding people. They are explicitly NOT criminals, NOT benefit dependents, NOT sex workers, NOT single mothers. This argument may work to support the claims of some 'migrants', and it may even work for many of them. Indeed too often this is what migration 'debates' are reduced to: are 'some', 'many', or 'most' migrants 'Good Citizens'? But what then of those migrants who ARE single mothers, or benefit dependents, or who have criminal convictions, or work in the sex sector? And similarly, what of those citizens who find themselves labelled in the same way? Ultimately this serves only to reinforce the logic of exclusion and failure.

Historicizing the Migrant challenges the taken-for-grantedness of nation, citizenship, and state. A historical perspective reveals the relation between the expansion of state authority and control, first over the mobility of subjects within the realm, more particularly of poor people, and later over the mobility of non-citizens outside the state. Thus although mobility in the contemporary world is often regarded as a challenge to states, the control of mobility was a factor that facilitated the emergence of certain types of (nation) states. But a historical perspective also highlights the taken-for-grantedness of contract, property, and self-ownership which in turn ground other assumptions underpinning migration debates about gender, work, decision making, and skill. It indicates the importance of ideas of property, sovereignty, and the self that were highly contested, particularly in the seventeenth century, but that are now readily assumed in our analyses. Situating our analyses of migration within this historical context reveals that it cannot be extricated from struggles over labour and labour control and anxiety about the uncontrolled masses.

2

Subjects, Aliens, Citizens, Migrants

The previous chapter outlined how vagrancy was a crime of status, and the vagrant the embodiment of the undesirability of mobility. It also described the ways in which poor relief 'settled' vagrancy. This chapter will examine how 'the Migrant' came to exist as a category of person whose mobility was to be controlled. In a global context this cannot be analysed in isolation from the history of colonialism and the development of modern nation states (Chatterjee 1993). In terms of the making of migrants, the question 'Who is "the Migrant"?' or 'Who counts as a migrant?' requires an examination of the vexed question of the relation between immigration controls, racism, and ideas of autochthony and belonging.

The chapter begins by considering the history of the distinction between subjects and aliens, and examines how the codification of British subjects by nationality was used to control the mobility of racialized subjects between different 'dominions'. While the movement of subjects was not free between different areas of the British Empire, all subjects were free to enter the UK and the chapter describes this movement and how it was managed in the post-war years. In particular, it charts the shift between subjecthood and citizenship and how the alien became the immigrant. It is in this context that I examine the arguments about the relation between racism and immigration in public debate in the UK. I argue that we need a more nuanced account of racism and immigration that considers nationalism and the ways in which the nation is framed as a community of value in which migrants, and multiple others, are at best contingently included, and from which they are often overtly excluded.

2.1 Subjects and Aliens

Allegiance was the forerunner of nationality law. All those who owed allegiance to the sovereign were the subjects of the English Crown and the key distinction was between subjects and aliens rather than citizens and migrants.

In the Middle Ages, children born outside the realm were generally not subjects even if their parents were (although exceptions were made for the children of the sovereign and the children of serving ambassadors), but this had little bearing on the lives of ordinary people. Before the 1200s there is no evidence of any legal distinction between a class of aliens and a class of subjects, and the emergent distinction between the two was marked, not by the regulation of entry and stay, but by the regulation of property ownership and inheritance (Dummett and Nicol 1990). By the end of the thirteenth century, birthplace was of primary importance in determining subjecthood, but the question of who exactly was an alien was more ambiguous.

As the territorial claims of the English sovereign expanded, so the reach of subjecthood widened. In 1541 Henry VIII proclaimed himself 'King of Ireland', but even before that people born in Ireland had been considered natural-born subjects of the monarch of England (Dummett and Nicol 1990: 45). In 1603 when the son of Mary Queen of Scots, James VI of Scotland, acceded to the English throne on the death of his aunt, Queen Elizabeth I, he became James I of England. The famous Calvin's Case in 1608 asserted that a child born in Scotland when ruled by the English Crown (*post natus*) was thereby a subject of the Crown. However, it was not the case that subsequently all those born in dependent territories were British subjects. Unconquered 'native Americans', for example, could be 'protected' but were not necessarily subjects (Dummett and Nicol 1990; Welke 2010). Early settlements in the Caribbean and the 'New World' developed with a considerable degree of variety, and in various gradations of relations with the English government. Some types of non-subjects could apply for subjecthood in order to be able to assert land ownership rights in certain territories. Local colonial leaders had the authority to naturalize and those naturalized by them were then subjects of the sovereign, but this left open the question of what this local naturalization meant for subjecthood in other territories. In effect, write Dummett and Nicol, 'there was a system of separate nationalities within the British empire though there was only one name for them all: the British subject' (Dummett and Nicol 1990: 77). Therein lay the root of multiple differentiations and categories within what was supposed to be a unitary and unmediated category of allegiance (Cohen 1994).

2.2 Racial Subjects

Settlements in the Caribbean and North America were claimed and established in the seventeenth century, and the reach of England grew. Irish resistance to the Protestant 'settlers' that were given land in Ulster by James I, and subsequent support for the Royalists in the English Civil War was countered by Cromwell in 1649. The New Model Army, led by Henry Ireton (who participated in the Putney Debates) conducted an infamously brutal and successful campaign, and in 1652 the English Parliament required almost every Irish landlord to forfeit their land. Less than sixty years later, Scotland came under English rule and in 1707 the Act of Union was passed, the Scottish Parliament voted itself out of existence and England (with Wales) and Scotland became one United Kingdom of Great Britain. Among the pressures acting on Scotland was access to English colonial trade following the disastrous and highly costly failure of Scotland to establish a colony in Central America (the 'Darien Scheme'). A further factor was the very first Aliens Act of 1705 forbidding the import of Scottish products and requiring all Scottish nationals to be treated as Aliens, making estates in England owned by Scots alien property. There was a provision that this legislation would be suspended if Scots agreed to enter negotiations on the proposed union with England. The year 1707 was also a key date in imperial expansion in India, as it marked the death of the powerful Mughal emperor Aurangzeb, the decline of Mughal power, and the ascendance of the East India Company.

As the British Empire consolidated and expanded, the rights of movement of people from England/Britain around the world to colonize, make war, explore, and conduct business were not at issue for government in London. This was not only a movement of the privileged, and there was a considerable trade in labour from the United Kingdom, notably of indentured servants, and, following the 1718 Transportation Act, of transported convict labour (Morgan 1985; Steinfeld 1991).[1] Approximately 50,000 felons were transported to the American colonies in the century following this Act, accounting for around one-quarter of British immigrants to colonial America (Bleichmar 1999).[2] As discussed in the previous chapter, many of these had been criminalized through vagrancy laws, and the enforced mobility that was a consequence of this criminalization became an important means of securing labour for the colonies. Thus vagrancy became one of the ways that the poor could be turned into the building blocks of Empire. Via transportation, 'Thieves became soldiers, prostitutes became wives, and orphans became apprenticed artisans' (Ocobock 2008: 12). The same might be said of contracts of indenture and debt-financed emigration.

---

[1] There was in the later years of the eighteenth century some hostility to the importation of convicts—Benjamin Franklin reportedly remarked that rattlesnakes would be a suitable gift in return for the convicts dumped by Britain in its colonies.

[2] Following the Transportation Act, transported felons were more likely to be women than before its enactment. This was because the Transportation Act allocated funds for transportation, which had previously been left to private interests. These private interests derived profits from selling convicts as indentured labourers, and able-bodied men were therefore more likely to be transported, while women would be left in jail.

In the same way that not all those residing on a territory were necessarily subjects or aliens, so also for those who moved. The forced movement of African slaves was not imagined as the movement of either subjects or aliens, and children born to slaves on British territory, were not considered subjects. The first US Naturalization Law, passed in 1790, declared that naturalization was open only to 'free, white persons', and the Federal Militia Act of 1792 stated that only 'free able-bodied white male citizens of the respective States' were to be subject to military service (Welke 2010: 35). The trade in slaves was abolished in 1807 in the British Empire, and following the British Emancipation Act of 1834, slavery was gradually abolished in the colonies. This did not mean an end to forced labour for former slaves, and among other mechanisms of coercion was the extension of vagrancy laws to compel their labour (Cohen 1997). In post-emancipation colonial economies, vagrancy laws were deployed to force non-Europeans 'deemed wandering or idle' to work for private companies or on government projects (Ocobock 2008: 14). Emancipation was also followed by a massive transcontinental movement of indentured labourers from Asia, primarily from China and India, and this raised two questions: how this labour was to be constituted as the movement of 'free' subjects? And how to control the labour of non-indentured negatively racialized British subjects?

The changing ways in which the employment/service relation was imagined, formalised and constrained between the fourteenth and nineteenth centuries in England and in the USA has been described by Robert Steinfeld (Steinfeld 1991; Steinfeld 2001). He describes how throughout the eighteenth century in England, unauthorized departure from service continued to be subject to penal sanctions, even as the relation was imagined as more contractual. The American Revolution did not mark any call for an end to indenture, but rather indentured servitude continued to be seen as a form of contractual freedom. He argues that the spread of markets, though limiting the authority of masters to 'physically correct' their servants, in practice further limited the liberty of labour rather than undermining traditional restrictions (Steinfeld 1991). The stark distinction between indentured servitude and free wage labour that currently pertains (with migrants an important exception) cannot be read back into earlier periods. By the nineteenth century, however, following vociferous anti-slavery campaigns, it became important to distinguish between indentured labour and slavery, particularly in the light of the British Empire's 'civilizing mission'. Kidnapping and maltreatment were not endorsed by Westminster, and labourers were impelled not by direct physical violence but rather by the undermining of village economies, indebtedness, and the need for cash income (Miles 1987).

While planters and other commodity producers were the source of demand for indentured labour, the movement of 'free labour' was not welcomed. As a colonial official in Natal put it: 'Because we want indentured labour for agriculture it is no reason why we should be swamped by black matter in the wrong place—namely storekeepers etc.' (Goldberg 2002). This is but one example of the ongoing and considerable hostility to the movement of people from the 'New Commonwealth' to the 'Old Commonwealth'. White settler colonies, or the Old Commonwealth, were far more autonomous than the New Commonwealth countries. While New Commonwealth countries were ruled by people sent out from Britain, Britain's ability to veto legislation in Old Commonwealth countries was more limited. The difficulty was that to limit mobility of 'Europeans' was unthinkable, yet any mention of 'race' could threaten to undermine assertions of equality and benevolent rule. This was particularly tricky in the case of India, in the context of Queen Victoria's Proclamation to the Princes, Chiefs and People of India in 1858, undertaking that 'we hold ourselves bound to the natives of our Indian territories by the same obligations of duty which bind us to all our other subjects'. As Joseph Chamberlain said in 1896:

> We quite sympathise with the determination of white inhabitants of these colonies which are in comparatively close proximity to millions and hundreds of millions of Asiatics that there should not be an influx of people alien in colour...
> An immigration of that kind must, I quite understand...be prevented at all hazards...but you must also bear in mind the traditions of the Empire which make no distinction in favour of, or against race or colour. (Cited in Dummett and Nicol 1990: 118)

The British Government, with very little demand for labour within the territory of the United Kingdom and facing growing challenges to imperial rule, promoted common British subjecthood, but the governments of white settler societies wanted to restrict entry of some British subjects. The question was how to stop the mobility of free Indians without either impeding the mobility of white Europeans and the entry of indentured Indian labour, or undermining notions of shared British subjecthood. How could the requirements of colonial governments to make the mobility of some easier than others be accommodated?

The case of Indians in Natal is illustrative of the ways in which imperial governance that posited the equality of all subjects, irrespective of the colour of their skin, responded to these challenges. Natal had been declared a British colony in 1843, but under the fundamental condition that 'there should not be in the eye of the law any distinction or disqualification whatever, founded on mere difference of colour, origin, language or creed' (Despatch 13 December 1842 from Lord Stanley to Sir George Napier quoted in *Encyclopedia Britannica* 1911: vol.19, 260). It had been granted 'responsible government' in 1893. The Immigration Restriction Act of 1897, passed by the government of Natal and not reserved by London (unlike similar legislation attempted by New South Wales in 1888), appeared the perfect solution. It explicitly emulated the American Immigration Restriction Act of 1896 (later vetoed by President Cleveland) which had required all immigrants to be literate in order to facilitate the exclusion of people from eastern and southern Europe where there were very low levels of literacy. Thus the Act did not discriminate on paper, but in practice the consequences were grave for particular populations. Similarly the 1897 Act had the appearance of not distinguishing between free Indians and Europeans. Qualifications for entry were based on property (first, the holding of £25, and later, a restriction on paupers and those likely to become a charge on the public purse, or, in the words of the 1662 Poor Relief Act 'likely to be chargeable'), and on knowledge of a European language. The immigration entry officer was free to choose the European language in which he could expect competence, so an 'Indian' English speaker, for example, could be presented with a form in German. In practice this meant that Europeans were able to enter, and that non-indentured Indians found it extremely difficult but the law could not be said to be distinguishing between people on account of their colour. Effectively there was no discrimination in the letter of the law, but in practice, most Europeans were eligible to enter Natal, while virtually all non-indentured Indians were not. This was possible while retaining British subjecthood. The Prime Minister of Natal informed the legislature:

> It never occurred to me for a single minute that (the Act) should ever be applied to English immigrants...can you imagine anything more mad for a Government than that it should apply to English immigrants? The object of the bill is to deal with Asiatic immigrants. (Cited in Dummett and Nicol 1990: 19)

The element of discretion with respect to which European language to require was explicitly created to enable individual officers to discriminate. It was not that miscreant officials wilfully or inadvertently misinterpreted an otherwise even handed objective approach. The letter of the law was 'raceless', but in effect, the law created a racial category that could be refused entrance, and its consequences and its implementation were charged with racism. There were many other examples of self-governing colonies passing legislation that made negatively racialized subjects. In 1901 for instance the Parliament of Australia passed the Immigration Restriction Act, based on the 1897 Natal Act and this later formed the basis for the infamous 'White Australia' policy.

Attention to the government of mobility within the British Empire then reveals that British subjects were racialized and that ownership of property and education was an important mechanism for managing the contradiction between claims for the equality of subjects on the one hand, and racist hierarchies on the other. The question of property ownership and its relation to race reminds us that 'race' is constructed and contested, and not a natural category. It is a 'constellation of processes and practices' (Frankenberg 2001: 73) not a simple empirical description of skin colour. The laws governing the movement of subjects within the Empire were an important means of manufacturing the category, and the category was not 'stand-alone' but related to both gender and class. The role of gender in this process will be discussed in greater detail in Chapter 8.

2.3 Race and the State

The role of the law (and not only immigration law) in the creation and hardening of the conceptualization and categorization of 'race', points to the importance of the relation between race and the nature of the state. It is relatively uncontroversial to hold that 'modern states—particularly those in Europe—were built on notions of shared identity and values, constructed or otherwise' (Phillips 2011: 47). But the important question is how race and ethnicity mapped and maps on to these notions (that is, imaginings) of 'shared identity' and nationhood. The fiction of race became an ordering principle at a time of expanding social mobilities, when state forms other than the national were competing with nation states for dominance (Balibar 1991: 89). Goldberg (2002) reminds us that the 'state of nature', the founding myth of the state for social contract theorists from Hobbes to Rousseau, is conceived in racial and in gendered terms. While race is morally irrelevant, its great thinkers are 'fixated' on it (Goldberg 1993). He has convincingly argued that the modern state is unavoidably racial. Race, and its intertwining with gender, he claims, is integral to the emergence and the development of modern states. The imagining of an age of homogeneity, and the writing out of what is now perceived as racial difference, is a part of that construction. This writing out is countered by 'emphatic foregrounding', that effectively emphasizes extraordinariness. Evidence of Asians or Africans living in pre-twentieth century Britain is frequently treated with surprise. The discovering of an African woman's body in York buried in Roman times, the discovery of a gene linking the people of North Wales to the eastern Mediterranean, the expulsion of the Moors from Elizabethan England,[3] these are rediscoveries of an old, heterogeneous past. The development of the modern state 'depended

---

[3] In a fascinating paper, Bartels (2006) examines the official letters issued by Queen Elizabeth between 1596 and 1601, and the move from deporting particular and specified groups of 'blackamoors' as an expedient response to the Anglo-Spanish conflict (mutual exchanges of prisoners of war for instance) to the presentation of a racialized threat to the people of England.

on the ideological work of manufacturing sameness' and this sameness was built on ideas of race (Comaroff 1997: 16).

Colonizing European states, with Britain amongst the foremost, were concerned with constructing an 'internal' racial homogeneity and the constitution and maintenance of whiteness, but related to this, they were also concerned with the management and regulation of heterogeneity outside of the 'motherland'. As Radhika Singha puts it in her description of identification practices in colonial India: 'One way of conceptually subduing the social flux unleashed by British paramountcy was to build up ethnologies distinguishing between those who provided good material for productive, revenue-generating subjects from those whose way of life was inimical to this endeavour' (Singha 2000: 154). This fixing of racial/ethnic identities was intricately related to the control of mobility within imperial territory. Huge efforts were expended to assert orderly movement within territories, ordering people through systematic ethnographies, and controlling them accordingly. Natives were classified, placed in a hierarchy, placed in their territories, differentiated by culture and race, personality and intelligence, declared 'indigenous', 'tribal', and 'urban', with ethnicities tied to territories (Nzongola-Ntalaja 2002; Mamdani 2011).

Colonialism was key to the creation of 'race' and racial categories (Stoler 1995) and whiteness 'at home' was intimately and inextricably related to blackness 'abroad'. Empire helped to 'whiten' the urban poor who, when they were 'at home' were, as discussed in the previous chapter, associated with degeneracy, turpitude, and degraded races. 'Colonies elevated the European proletariat to the property of whiteness by making at least the semblance of privileges and power, customs and behaviour available to them' (Goldberg 2002: 172). Colonialism was key to the creation of whiteness as a *national* identity. The whiteness that distinguished the colonizer from the colonized was a social construction that was not concerned simply with skin colour, but with what that signified in terms of disposition, culture, and habits. Key dispositions, fostered in the bourgeois family, were self-discipline and self-control, but it was self-mastery that marked the 'truly European' (Stoler 1995), and pigmentation was not sufficient to distinguish the properly white. Self-mastery requires self-ownership or property in the person, and so the borders of whiteness are particularly (im)permeable for working-class women. While Empire and colonialism whitened the urban poor in Britain, there was the ever present danger that they might revert to type because of their genetic and cultural inadequacies.

Thomas Carlyle infamously compared Irish peasants and English seamstresses and English working classes to 'negroes' (Carlyle 1849). The Irish, early subjects of English domination, exemplify the contradictions and tensions within ideas of 'race' and its relation to mobility and to colonialism, and

Ireland was a space where the colonial imaginary was both domesticated and exported. The skin pigmentation of the Irish may have been 'white', but they did not own proper whiteness, and were depicted as feminized, lazy, and disorganized. Anne McClintock suggests that 'the inconography of domestic degeneracy was widely used to mediate the manifold contradictions in imperial hierarchy—not only with respect to the Irish but also to the other "white negroes": Jews, prostitutes, the working-class, domestic workers, and so on, where skin color as a marker of power was imprecise and inadequate' (McClintock 1995: 53). Certain groups, like the Irish and Jews, have moved in and out of 'whiteness'. Whiteness is graduated, with internal boundaries between the more and the less white. This is not to deny that those who are 'white', however degraded, are nearly always salvageable in contrast and relation to those who are not, but it indicates the motility and contingency of racial categories.

2.4 From Subjects to Citizens

While the dominions were concerned about the entry to their territory of negatively racialized British subjects who were not indentured labour, when it came to the British mainland the concern was with the entry of aliens. The system for the monitoring of alien entry established in 1793 was centralized in 1816, but the first substantial control over the entry of aliens came with the 1905 Act. This was aimed particularly at Jewish people who were entering London in considerable numbers having been expelled from Russia and Eastern Europe. The Act stipulated that non-British subjects could only enter through specified ports, and that immigration officers could deny access to those classified as 'undesirable immigrants'. A person could be so classed on the basis of poverty ('If he cannot show that he has in his possession or is in a position to obtain the means of decently supporting himself and his dependents' (Aliens Act 1905: 1(3)a)) or sickness leading to a judgement that they were 'likely to become a charge upon the rates[4] or otherwise a detriment to the public' (Aliens Act 1905: 1(3)b), or had a criminal conviction. Thus the Act was aimed principally at preventing the entry of the poor. Notably, there was an early recognition of a group that would now be described as 'refugees' in that it was allowed that the 1905 Aliens Act did not apply to 'An immigrant who proves that he is seeking admission into this country solely to avoid prosecution or punishment on religious or political grounds or for an offence of a political character' (Aliens Act 1905: 1(3)).

---

[4] Note the terminological consistency with the 1662 Poor Relief Act.

In 1914, the British Nationality and Status of Aliens Act defined in statute who was to be considered a British subject (up until then it had been principally enshrined in common law). Subject status was still to be based on allegiance, and acquisition was by birth within the Commonwealth, or by descent within one generation in the legitimate male line (this was later changed to indefinite transmission in a 1922 Act). However, it also allowed for differential treatment between subjects by British Dominions, permitting that legislatures and governments should not be prevented 'from treating differently different classes of British subjects' (British Nationality and Status of Aliens Act 1914: 26(1)). Nevertheless, members of the Commonwealth were urged to comply with a Common Code, and not to undertake substantial amendments without prior consultation (Hansen 2000: 40). The year 1914 also saw the Aliens Registration Act, emergency legislation directed at 'enemy aliens' and giving the Home Secretary powers to deport aliens and to control their movements in British territory. This emergency legislation was renewed and expanded for over fifty years until the 1971 Immigration Act.

In contrast, the movement of subjects to the United Kingdom was unregulated but not numerically significant for the first half of the twentieth century. For many years, most of the movement was from the Old Commonwealth, particularly Canada, and what movement there was from the New Commonwealth to the United Kingdom was largely temporary and for the purpose of study (Hansen 2000).[5] After the Second World War, large-scale immigration from the New Commonwealth was simply not imagined and it was anticipated that the demand for labour that was a consequence of reconstruction was to be met by the European Voluntary Worker Scheme (EVWS). The primary concern of the colonial office was not that New Commonwealth British subjects would move to the UK but rather the maintenance of British subjecthood in the face of the moves of former colonies to independence (Hansen 2000). This concern was precipitated in 1946 by the Canadian government's passage of the Canadian Citizenship Act which made Canadian citizens British subjects by virtue of their Canadian citizenship—that is, the relationship between sovereign and subject was now mediated and derivative. It was clear that, if British subjecthood were to survive, it needed to be rethought in the light of the independence of former colonies, and this lay behind the formulation of the British Nationality Act (BNA) of 1948 (Hansen 2000).

---

[5] The exception to this limited movement was the migration from Ireland to England, which had for centuries been a source of cheap migrant labour. As early as 1594 Queen Elizabeth I had attempted to force 'men of Ireland' (many of whom were vagrants) to leave or be imprisoned, and Irish labour was to prove crucial for the expansion of the railways and the canal system in the eighteenth century (Dummett and Nicol 1990: 45).

The BNA divided the people of the world into six groups. Two of these were not subjects: aliens and British Protected Persons. Three groups were subjects: Citizens of the United Kingdom and Colonies (CUKC), Citizens of Independent Commonwealth Countries (CICC), and the residual group of British subjects without citizenship. The Irish British once again were treated as exceptional—an instance of 'fuzzy frontiers' (Cohen 1994)—and they could become subjects should they so request. The concern was not with immigration, but with 'maintaining the formal indivisibility of British subjecthood' (Hansen 2000: 55). While it has been characterized as 'one of the most generous and liberal immigration policies in the world' (Freeman 1994) this was NOT an immigration policy per se, but a nationality policy with immigration consequences. It was the BNA that effectively continued 'open borders' rather than a migration policy per se. The migration that was anticipated (and valued) was migration from the dominions, which had formed the bulk of internal movement in pre-war years. Freedom of movement for New Commonwealth citizens was imagined as being of minor importance and largely temporary. It was viewed as a small price to pay to preserve British subjecthood and the Commonwealth even as independent commonwealth countries adopted their own national citizenship.

From 1948 until 1962 what we now call 'migration' to the UK from colonies was in fact the mobility of subjects.[6] As with the immigration of Eastern Europeans post-2004, the movement of people resulting from nationality/citizenship rights, was considerably greater than anticipated. Like European migration today, because it was based on nationality/citizenship, it proved difficult to counter without dismantling the edifice of nationality/citizenship that it was built on, although there were explorations of ways in which 'coloured people' could be prevented from migrating (Dummett and Nicol 1990).

This was the nettle that was finally grasped in 1962 with the Commonwealth Immigrants Act. In post-war social practice, 'immigrant' was already a racialized term, but this was the first time in law that the term 'immigrant' was used to refer to British subjects, as previously its application had been restricted to aliens. The Act did not change the architecture of British subjecthood in that all those formerly considered subjects continued to be subjects, but it did restrict rights of entry and settlement in the UK to citizens of the UK and Colonies only. In effect, it recognized different classes of British subjects by differentiating passports. The Act distinguished between CUKC passports

---

[6] This is not to say that there weren't attempts to limit migration from the New Commonwealth when it became apparent that this was to be larger than expected. The first discussion about limiting rights of access of some British subjects was only a year after the BNA, and interestingly, although dealing with West Indian migration, the initial focus of concern were Canadian members of the Communist party who had been fomenting the London Dock Strike of 1949 (Hansen 2000).

issued under the authority of the government of Britain, whose holders were not subject to immigration controls, and CUKC passports issued under the authority of a colonial government, whose holders were British subjects but whose British passports did not guarantee entry to the United Kingdom.

Work permits, which were held by aliens, were subject to a strict labour-market test, but CUKC colonial subjects and CICCs were given preferential access to the labour market. They were eligible to enter to work in the UK under a quota system with employment vouchers. Employment vouchers were available without a labour-market test in three categories: a pre-arranged job, special skills, or where there were specific domestic needs for unskilled workers. However, eligible CUKCs could be refused entry on the grounds of mental illness, criminality, and national security. These restrictions were developed from restrictions previously experienced by aliens, and this Act marked the first time that some British subjects were dealt with in ways similar to aliens. It also marked the beginning of the merging of the Alien and colonial Subject into the Immigrant, and from then on, nationality and immigration began to develop as discrete areas of law.

The 1962 Act was modified in 1968 when the Labour government restricted the entry of Kenyan Asians, fleeing the increasingly repressive policies of Kenyatta. They were CUKC passport holders—passports issued by the High Commissioner, the UK's direct representative in independent Kenya. This meant that they had a right to enter the UK, a right that they were exercising in increasing numbers. In 1968, specifically as a response to this, the UK passed a bill that introduced a requirement that those who held the right passport needed also to have been born, or to have a parent or grandparent who had been born, in the United Kingdom. In 1971 this was described as 'patriality' and served as a mechanism to facilitate the entry for white Australians, Canadians, and New Zealanders but not other Commonwealth citizens.

The 1971 Act also introduced 'settlement', giving non-citizens with certain types of immigration status the right to remain indefinitely in the UK. This meant they had the right to live and work without restrictions, and the right to apply for citizenship. Indeed, for most non-citizens, a period of settled status became a condition of citizenship acquisition. Under certain circumstances, settled migrants could still be deported and settled status could be revoked, so ultimately they were still, to use De Genova's (2002) phrase, 'deportable'. However, the status indicates an important acknowledgement of belonging or membership that is not entirely congruent with legal citizenship (Ryan 2010; Sawyer 2010).

The 1981 British Nationality Act abolished CUKC and all but abolished British subject status apart from a few residual categories. It introduced British citizenship with the bounded territory of the UK, and all holders of British citizenship, unlike British subjects post-1962, had the 'right of abode' in the

UK. However, birth on UK territory was no longer sufficient to obtain British nationality and at least one parent had to be born or settled in the United Kingdom. The act also decoupled nationality and immigration laws. Immigration and citizenship were to be governed by different legal regimes, and this continued to be the case for over twenty years.

2.5 Racism and Immigration Controls

Whether this history of movement from subjects/aliens to citizens/immigrants is a history of institutionalized racism has been the subject of heated academic and public debate. It has been argued that in post-war days, immigration restrictions were deeply racialized, although as argued above, since the Natal Immigration Restriction Act of 1897, considerable effort has been made to create 'raceless' policies (Layton-Henry 1980; Solomos 1993; Hansen 2000). Contemporaneously, it is argued that 'we' can have a 'sensible' debate about immigration, where 'sensible' indicates avoiding extremes, rationality (often expressed through the use of statistics), and most emphatically does not involve the hurling round of accusations of racism. Having created and codified 'race', modern liberal democracies now claim to move beyond it. The horrors of imperialism and colonialism, the Holocaust, and war in the Balkans hark back to a past that modern Europe has moved beyond. The aspiration is to 'racelessness' where race is made invisible and no longer matters. The erasure of imperial history further entrenches ideas that Britain is a highly desirable placed to be. It means that the reasons why people from Zimbabwe, Sri Lanka, Kashmir, and other former colonies, 'choose' to come to the UK reflect the UK's dehistoricized present rather than post-colonial legacies. The asylum seeker is a victim of senseless violence that is historically disconnected (Mamdani 2011). Thus in the same way that raceless policies mean that the black becomes the Criminal and the junkee (Goldberg 2002), they turn the Migrant into the poor and the desperate.

The political claim that immigration policies are raceless, not designed to keep out black people, is not paralleled by any claim that 'immigration controls are not designed to keep out the poor'. Indeed, it is the poor, in their guise as 'low skilled', 'low waged', and 'poorly educated', that have long been the target of respectable controls. In 2010 Damian Green, the incoming immigration minister, quipped that the 1905 Aliens Act had 'some fairly obvious loopholes. First class passengers were entirely exempt from immigration control' (Green 2010). Nevertheless, at the same time as toughening controls for the vast majority and significantly limiting access to settlement, his government relaxed restrictions on the wealthy. In the same way as those people who were able to pay £10 a year rent on their tenement were permitted to 'settle' in

UNIVERSITY
OF SHEFFIELD
LIBRARY

post-1662 English parishes, and, following the 1893 Act people who wanted to move to Natal could do so if they had £25, in 2012 all those with more than £2 million to invest in the British economy had accelerated access to the rights of settlement. Similar differences are made when it comes to immigration enforcement. Guidelines in 2007 were relatively explicit about this: over-stayers from a country with a high gross domestic product (GDP) were unlikely to be a problem as in the end they would return; they should not therefore be a priority for enforcement action. In contrast, overstayers from a country with a low GDP, might make a false asylum claim and so were suitable for targeted enforcement (Home Office 2007b: 10).

The claim to racelessness is not paralleled either by a claim that immigration policies are not designed to keep out certain nationalities. The equation of race with nationality is precisely the homogenizing process in which colonial histories are so implicated but which is now disavowed by the British state. It is facilitated by the system of 'ministerial exemptions' permitted by the Race Relations (Amendment) Act of 2000.[7] This extended the remit of the Race Relations Act of 1976 to public authorities including central government but the Home Office was given an exemption in the administration of immigration, asylum, and nationality law. Officials may only discriminate on the grounds of race or colour on the grounds of national security. They can discriminate on the grounds of nationality, or ethnic, or national origin when required by specific legislation or expressly authorized by a minister. The distinction between lawful discrimination on ethnic and national origin on the one hand, and unlawful discrimination on the grounds of race on the other is of course extremely unclear in practice (Dummett 2001) because of the racialized nature of modern states. The reports of the Independent Race Monitor between 2003 and 2008 on the consequences of ministerial authorizations to discriminate provide interesting insights into enforcement and nationality at port of entry:

> It seemed to me that passengers from certain nationalities with a record of refusals or of immigration breaches were less likely to be given the benefit of the doubt when compared with passengers from nationalities with a good record. What in some nationalities is viewed with skepticism will be accepted in others. To this extent the use of information on adverse decisions and breaches may become self-reinforcing. (Coussey 2004: para. 11)

Concern that caseworkers were becoming 'case hardened' when it came to certain nationalities was fuelled by the high rate of allowed appeals for claimants from all African nationalities.

---

[7] Consolidated by the Equality Act 2010.

Race and nationality are also interrelated with poverty. The incomes of nationals of some states are lower than those of others. While political theory assumes that nation states are equal, this does not hold in political fact. Moreover, these states are not unequal simply because of bad luck, but often precisely because of the colonial history that racelessness erases. Race, nationality, and poverty are not independent variables. This poses some challenges for raceless policy. In 2007, the Home Office commissioned a research report into race and the decision-making of immigration officers (IOs) on the entry of non-EEA passengers arriving at UK ports. This found that IOs did not stop a disproportionate number of non-white passengers *once one controlled for economic differences* between different nationalities—that is, the relation between race, nationality, and poverty is critical. It might seem as if there are a disproportionate number of non-white passengers stopped, but this is because of their economic status rather than their race or their nationality. The relationship between ethnicity and economic status was acknowledged by IOs as difficult to manage, but the categories of race and economic status were still treated as fixed rather than mutually constitutive, allowing for the assertion that it was economic status, NOT race or ethnicity, that accounted for apparent discrepancies. Interestingly, there was an exception made for Canada and South Africa (though the sample size was small). For Canada, stopping rates were four per 10,000 white passengers and thirty-five per 10,000 for non-white passengers. One might expect adjusted rates allowing for socio-economic factors to make the discrepancy smaller (as proved to be the case with respect to US citizens), but for Canadian nationals they increased to fifty-four per 10,000 for non-white passengers. For South Africans the stopping rate was fourteen per 10,000 for white passengers, and 148 for non-white, rising to 254 for adjusted figures (Woodfield et al. 2007: 31). This suggests that for South Africans and Canadians, (but not US nationals), *not* being black and poor constituted grounds for suspicion.

In 2010, the Chief Inspector of the UK Border Agency found evidence of potential discrimination against particular nationalities; more specifically, that applicants from Pakistan were subject to higher evidential requirements than applicants from Abu Dhabi, Bahrain, and Dubai. This association between nationality, credibility, and refusals has now been formalized. Fast-track passport queues were to be introduced in the second half of 2012, principally to facilitate the 'airport experience' of Old Commonwealth nationals (Travis 2012). In a little-noticed announcement of January 2011, the immigration minister authorized UKBA to give greater scrutiny and priority to particular nationalities when it came to entry and enforcement. UKBA was also authorized to refuse people entry on the grounds of their nationality alone (Green 2011). The list of nationalities was to be personally approved by the minister on the basis of 'statistical evidence' (that is, it was to be 'rational' rather than discriminatory). However, it was also to be kept secret, it was claimed, because of concerns that the states on the list might thereby withdraw from cooperation with the UK on migration and on other issues, and because passports from states that are not on the list might then be used by organized criminal gangs. IOs were not to disclose their use of the list in the grounds for refusal given to applicants.

2.6 Racism and Migration from Eastern Europe

One of the arguments evinced to support the notion that anti-immigrant feeling has no relation to racism is that post-2004 EU Enlargement, there is hostility to Eastern European migrants who are 'white'. It is claimed that this suggests public anxiety is about immigration per se rather than opposition to the 'coloured immigration' of the post-war years. Indeed, the claims go, many of the previous 'coloured immigrants' object to these new white incomers, and one cannot label their concerns racist because they themselves have been victims of racism. In this way it is argued that concerns about immigration are not racial per se, but are to do with culture, values, and 'sustainability'. The involvement of settled migrants brings to the fore the importance of ideas of competitive autochthony—the assertion that 'I was here before you' in the claim for privileges of membership. The 'I' here can refer to parents, grandparents, and ancestors as well as the claims of an individual—that is, it is related to the question raised at the end of the previous chapter about how we understand our relation to the past and how this inflects attitudes to the nation.

Arguments about sustainability will be discussed in the next chapter, but for now there are three points to make with reference to this argument. The first is straightforwardly that as discussed above, considerations of race and of immigration are not so easy to separate, and even when policies are raceless, they have racial implications. 'Migrant' is far from a value-free description of a person who has crossed an international border. In opinion-poll data, which are often cited as evidence of British people's concern about immigration, it is almost always unclear what the respondents mean by the term 'migrant' or 'immigrant'. Some surveys do not define their terms, leaving respondents to answer questions based on their own implicit definitions. Other surveys define an immigrant as someone who has come to the UK 'to live' (Ipsos-MORI) or 'to settle' (National Centre for Social Research 2003), neither of which fit the definitions in law or in data. When the British Election Survey began questioning the public about immigration in 1964, they did not ask 'coloured' respondents (Blinder 2011b) indicating a racialized framing of the issue on the part of the survey designers if not of the respondents. Similar assumptions seem to lie behind the current Ipsos-MORI coding scheme, which assumes that public concern about 'immigration' can be equated with public concern about 'race relations'. There is some evidence that suggests that respondents too are particularly concerned with racialized groups: negative attitudes towards immigration are more common when migrants are defined as coming from the Caribbean and 'Indian sub-continent' than when they are from Australia and Europe (Blinder 2011c).

Secondly, post-2004 Eastern Europeans present a 'degenerate' whiteness. While they may be 'white' for the purposes of immigration categories, they are nevertheless not 'properly' white. Like the Jews and the Irish before them, they represent a contingent and degraded form of whiteness. Media coverage refers to 'cultural differences' and law-breaking, particularly with reference to Polish and other Eastern Europeans. While, as EU citizens, they cannot be 'illegal' in terms of immigration status, they are frequently represented as engaging in illegal activities. They are depicted as poor, living in sheds and off handouts. To give one example, in 2010 the *Daily Mail* warned that Eastern Europeans were 'raping and pillaging a river' by illegally fishing and catching swans with 'barbed snares' and then clubbing them to death (Levy 2010b).[8] The article helpfully explains that these people are not wantonly breaking the law, but are just acting according to a difference in culture 'they are simply unaware that the rules here are different to the ones in their homelands'. As discussed above, race and 'culture' are ever imbricated. To shift the discourse from race to culture does not decentre the 'truly European', but it does help to emphasize that Polish and others do not have the self-mastery that enables the truly European to escape from 'culture' (Brown 2006).

Reference to the concerns of black and minority ethnic (BME) groups about immigration in order to demonstrate that anxiety about immigration does not mean that one is racist are interesting, partly because they run against a current of public discourse that argues that BME people are racist; for instance, that 'Asian gangs' racially abuse white youth and sexually groom white girls, and that this goes unrecognized because of political correctness. It goes along-side the claim that the white working class are also objecting to immigration. The idea that immigration has been foisted on working-class people by policy makers who are far more liberal than the electorate is longstanding (Hage 2000). The relation between immigration policy and illiberal public opinion has been the subject of considerable debate in political science (Joppke 1999; Joppke 2004; Boswell 2007).

The conundrum thus posed then is scarcely new. However, what is new is the extent to which this claim has been reiterated by many who might indeed

---

[8] The killing of swans is a regular trope in tabloid coverage of Eastern European migration, pre-dating EU enlargement in 2004. In this and other coverage, they are associated with 'our heritage', perhaps because of the mix of related ideas: whiteness? The Queen? A nation of animal lovers?

be called 'the metropolitan elite' who have come forward with *mea culpas*. One author from a prominent leftist think tank even suggested that challenging this strain of public opinion might be undemocratic: 'Today's social democrats may have to admit that there are limits to the tolerance and understanding of ordinary people and recognize that it is fundamentally undemocratic, as well as unrealistic, to stretch things beyond that limit' (Bale 2011: 12). This type of argument claims that to say hostility to immigration is racist is simply a patronizing middle-class dismissal of the white working class and that it is the white working class who compete for jobs and services, not the elite. One might equally add that it is those on benefits and low incomes, whatever their race, who are likely to be hardest hit by immigration controls that require, for instance, that one earn above a minimum income threshold before being allowed to be joined by a foreign spouse. Indeed, it is notable that while class has largely disappeared from public discourse, it has re-emerged in a critique of multiculturalism and immigration through the claim that there has been a prioritization of race over class (Garner 2010). While the white-ness of the middle class and policy makers is empty except in so far as it makes visible other ethnicities, the whiteness of the working class is worthy of note. Their whiteness and the whiteness of Eastern Europeans is racialized; it is not a simple marker of privilege but revealed as contested and unstable, unsettling and subject to internal hierarchies. So precisely at the moment when immigration debates have made the race of white UK working-class citizens and Eastern European nationals (but not the white middle class) more visible, they are characterized as raceless.

As well as visible whiteness there is increasing differentiation between those in the UK who are designated 'native' or 'indigenous' and the rest (see 2012 Migration Advisory Committee Impacts of Migration Report). This terminology is also racialized and in the past was used to describe 'uncivilized' peoples living on imperial territory who required of special protection because of their tribal rather than citizenship status (Sharma and Wright 2008). It designated those who were not yet ready for self-government, but it now summons the claim to authenticity and belonging in the spirit of autochthony.

2.7 Conclusion

Immigration and citizenship policy claim to be 'raceless', yet their consequences seem to be unavoidably 'race-ful'. This is not just to point to the multiplicity of examples of racism in the treatment of people under immigration regimes, in the popular press, and in public discourse about immigration and asylum. Immigration controls are not simply the consequence of the policies of individual racist bureaucrats, and neither, come to that, are they a consequence of the racism of British citizens, if by 'racism' we mean an individual's belief in biological difference and hierarchy on the basis of skin colour. To analyse them thus is to risk underestimating their persuasive power, and the ways in which they are rational to many of those who take a strongly anti-racist position in non-immigration politics. It is to risk missing that the modern state is a racial project, bound up with the making and maintaining of racial difference, and immigration controls are deeply implicated in this project.

The claims that it is now possible to have a sensible and non-racist debate about immigration demonstrate the need for a more nuanced analysis of race, class, belonging, and immigration controls. It requires an understanding that 'race' is more nuanced and complex than skin pigmentation, at the same time that it is always reducible to it. Introducing this into public debate may sound ambitious. However, the urban poor today, as in Victorian times, can be presented as erupting into disorderly blackness. Historian David Starkey, commenting on the urban riots of summer 2011 remarked in an interview for the BBC television current affairs programme, *Newsnight*:

> A substantial section of the chavs has become black. The whites have become black. A particular sort of violent, destructive, nihilistic gangster culture has become the fashion. Black and white, boy and girl, operate in this language together. This language which is wholly false, which is a Jamaican patois, that's been intruded in England, and this is why so many of us have this sense of literally a foreign country. (YouTube 2011)

This is the community of value that is both raceless and 'race-ful', threatened from without and from within, by people whose skin colour may be 'white' but whose debased 'culture' is black. The implication is that this is not about race in the sense of skin colour (nor is it about gender), but it is about an uncivilized foreignness that leaves the Good Citizen beleaguered and excluded from 'his' country. Race, with all its contradictions and malleability, has not been left behind but is invoked with new inflections in the present.

3

Migration Management: Ending in Tiers

Chapter 1 described how the struggles over vagrancy were struggles for control over the mobility of labour which were also manifest in the development of the organizing of poor relief around ideas of settlement and merit. Chapter 2 discussed how the emerging British state was a colonial/imperialist state that facilitated the massive movement of people for labour through slavery, transportation, and indenture. The contemporary mechanisms of control and disciplining of labour 'at home' and 'abroad' and their relation to mobility are related to these histories and to each other.

This chapter will examine the development of 'managed migration', a process that builds on the law and social practices that have their roots in vagrancy, settlement, and contracts of indenture. It examines the ways in which Britain, thought of as a community of value, is promoted through ideas of who is allowed entry, for what purpose, and under what conditions. Immigration controls give legal significance to certain characteristics such as age, marital status, nationality, earnings, education, etc., which means that they can facilitate or prevent legal entry. What characteristics matter, and the weight that is given to them, often depends on putative reason for entry. Those entering under labour routes are envisaged as rational utility maximizers whose skills and earnings can be measured to determine how they benefit Britain. In contrast, to be recognized as a spouse, an applicant must present as being motivated by emotion rather than reason. Plans for a life-long monogamous relationship must be driven by feeling rather than calculation, and utility maximization suggests a relationship is not genuine. How these categories are governed reveals the ways in which workers and spouses are imagined more generally and not just in terms of immigration policy. Regulations governing asylum, family migration, and labour can be used deliberately as well as by default, to delineate the community of value, to demonstrate what kinds of family relations, what kinds of work, and what kinds of politics are valued and deemed desirable, and what not.

The chapter begins by considering the political context of debates and in particular the current focus on 'net migration'. This throws into relief the policy tension between the technocratic (the assessing of relevant characteristics, measuring impacts, counting) and the political (the Migrant as indicating the borders of the community of value). It is useful to distinguish between the Migrant as a political figure, and the Migrant in law and in data. These different manifestations of the Migrant do not map on to one another and this is a problem for migration policy in general, but the issues raised are particularly clear in a policy that concerns itself with net migration. The chapter goes on to examine the development of policies of asylum, labour, and family migration from the post-Second World War to the present day, starting with the refugee and the immigration/asylum-seeker pairing, noting the shift from the good asylum seeker—bad economic migrant binary opposition, to the rhetoric of the 'brightest and the best'. It discusses the economic migrant and the development of the points-based system, with particular reference to ideas of 'skilled' labour and how this is defined. It then turns to the regulation of family migration, and the ideals of what constitutes a family as manifest in immigration law and policy.

3.1 Immigration by Numbers

Since polling on the question began in 1964, public opinion has consistently been reported as reflecting the view that there are 'too many' migrants (Blinder 2011b). This is not the same as identifying migration as a significant problem, which is far more recent. Ipsos MORI conducts a monthly poll asking respondents what they consider the most important issues facing 'the nation'. Until 2000, immigration/race relations (as discussed in Chapter 2, these are usually elided in opinion data) was rarely considered an important issue, and in 1999 only 5 per cent of the polled population felt that it was a priority matter (Blinder 2011). Eight years later in December 2007, this had risen to 46 per cent. The reasons for this massive increase in salience are not clear. Although much is made of media coverage causing negative attitudes to immigration, newspapers argue that they are reflecting the opinions of their readership as much as shaping them. Moreover, while there are claims that policy is driven by media coverage, media coverage also feeds on government press releases. Notably, a significant proportion of UKBA news feeds, at both local and national level, are to do with the capture and conviction of undocumented migrants. The relations between the media, policy, and public opinion are further complicated by the unmeasurable potential 'observer effect' of opinion polls—if I see that other people are concerned about immigration, then there is the potential for this to make me worried too.

There are four key post-war periods that set the context for UK migration policy in the second decade of the 2000s. The first is beginning 1989, the end of the Cold War and increasing accessibility of global mobility, acting together as the catalyst for a significant shift in the policy and rhetoric around refugees and asylum. The second is the election of the Labour government in 1997, and the instigation of a more open attitude to labour migration—although arguably this had also been the way that the previous administration had been headed. The third is EU Enlargement in 2004, when Britain opened its labour market to nationals of the new member states, leading to significant migration of young people, particularly from Poland, to a range of low-waged jobs all over the UK (that is, not only in urban centres). The last is the period beginning with the election in 2010 of the Conservative-Liberal Democrat coalition government, and a focus on the control of 'net migration'. These four periods have also to be seen in conjunction with the workings of the economic cycle (most obviously, the 2008 crash and subsequent recession) and the UK's changing labour market, both of which will be discussed in more detail in Chapter 4.

From 2010 British immigration policy has had as a priority decreasing 'net migration'. This is a number obtained by taking numbers of arrivals from numbers of departures. It was a figure that had previously been produced and published in annual immigration statistics, but had not been taken up for policy purposes until the Conservative-Liberal Democrat coalition came to power. Damian Green, the incoming Immigration Minister, announced in 2010 that 'The Prime Minister has identified the sustainable level of immigration as an annual rate of net migration in the tens of thousands rather than the hundreds of thousands' (Green 2010). Imprecise as this is, it marked the first time a numerical target, however vague, had been set for all migration rather than for particular categories. The terminology of sustainability indicates a concern with limited resources that parallels that of previous eras, including those related to the parish incomers of the late seventeenth century and the Malthusian logic of the nineteenth. But although we are told (roughly) what the sustainable number is, the thinking behind the number is opaque. What does sustainability mean? Whether the anxiety is about demographic, economic, or public service sustainability, what can be said meaningfully about sustainable numbers if all migrants are treated as homogeneous, and if this is the only part of the population that counts?

The policy aim of lowering net migration is hampered by three interrelated factors: the tools to count 'migrants' use incompatible definitions; the levers to manage migration cannot be applied to all those who count as migrants; and the public debate about migration does not straightforwardly map on to those whose movement can be controlled. These kinds of problems are in fact built into all attempts to manage 'social problems' numerically, but the contradictions have been made particularly apparent in the setting of the net migration target.

Net migration measures the flows of 'migrants' across borders, rather than the numbers within the country. This is in tension with the language of sustainability, which one might expect to be more concerned with how many migrants remain within a state's borders. For net migration, what matters is the relation between outflow and inflow. As long as this is balanced, the country could have an 'unsustainable' stock of one hundred million migrants, or a 'sustainable' stock of five migrants, the net migration figure in both cases would still be zero. Its association with flow also means that net migration is a peculiar number in that it is not a count of individuals. Two people can enter and stay and a different person leave, resulting in a net migration of one—that is, none of these three people is a 'net migrant'. A 'migrant' for the purposes of this policy is defined in accordance with the UN definition of a 'long-term international migrant' (LTIM) as 'A person who moves to a country other than that of his or her usual residence for a period of at least a year . . . so that the country of destination effectively becomes his or her new country of usual residence'. The time frame of one year is arbitrary and a change in the length of intended stay has a dramatic effect on the numbers. If, for example, one chooses to define a 'migrant' as a person intending to stay (away) for four years or more (residence of a minimum of five years is necessary for most people before they can apply for settlement in the UK), Britain has been experiencing *negative* net migration for many years.[1]

The numeric policy goal set by net migration is not only 'raceless' but 'citizenship-less': the citizenship of any of these people has no consequences for the number. A UK national who has lived abroad for a time and made another country their 'usual residence', and who returns to the UK with the stated intention of staying for a year or more, is, according to this definition, an incoming migrant, and similarly, a British national leaving the country to stay abroad for a year or more is an outgoing 'migrant'. But the public is not imagined as clamouring for (white, non-criminal) British-born citizens to leave or be forbidden entry to the UK in order to achieve the net migration target. The fact that encouraging British nationals to leave and discouraging them from entering is one way of achieving this policy goal indicates that it

---

[1] In 2008, the Office for National Statistics estimates that 162,000 people arrived in the UK intending to stay for more than four years, while 267,000 left the UK intending to stay away for more than four years, resulting in a negative net migration of 105,000 (Anderson and Blinder 2011: 6).

does not in fact deal with the normative 'migrant' that is the subject of public anxiety.

A further challenge for policies fixated on the control of numbers is that immigration policy can only affect a certain proportion of those who count towards the target. Public opinion data suggest that asylum seekers are the main group of migrants that those polled are concerned about even though they only comprise 4 per cent of new entrants (Migration Observatory 2011), but international obligations mean that the government cannot completely close down the asylum route. More critically for the numbers, the British state currently has very limited control over the entry and exit of UK nationals which has significant consequences for net migration figures. In 2009 total net migration increased even though the net migration of non-UK nationals decreased because more British people came to the UK and fewer left. This was completely outside the government's control. Furthermore, however tight the immigration policy, it does not apply to EU nationals (many of whom, usually excluded from the community of value, *do* count as migrants for the purposes of public debate), but it does apply to others such as (white) US academics (who, although generally included in the community of value, *do not* count as migrants for these purposes). This becomes a problem for government because groups like the latter are squeezed when entry controls are tightened, even though these may be regarded by business and state interests and in public debate as unproblematic, even desirable, entrants. It also becomes a problem for individual (white) British citizens who are accustomed to being a part of the community of value but who are married to non-EU citizens. The Family Immigration Alliance for instance, was launched by a white male research executive whose New Zealand wife's spousal visa was rejected on the grounds that they had not proved a genuine relationship (Family Immigration Alliance 2011).

This disjuncture between the Migrant as managed by policies (the Migrant, in law) and the Migrant in public debate (the Migrant, in politics) is not new, and pre-dates the net migration policy. It is compounded by a further disjuncture between these two migrant figures, and a third, the Migrant, in data. This is a significant problem for policy that sets itself up as 'evidence based' and uses data to inform and measure its success. For example, analyses of the impacts of migrants on the UK economy usually define migrants as 'foreign born', principally for reasons of consistency, as a person cannot change their place of birth.[2] However, like LTIM, this definition disregards British citizenship: a person may be 'foreign born' and nevertheless be a British citizen by naturalization, or be a British citizen born abroad by, for example, being a

---

[2] Although obviously the 'country' of birth can change as borders shift, so the same person can be born in both Georgia and Russia depending on the date that they are asked.

child of a parent serving in the British armed forces. Foreign-born British citizens and EU nationals are not subject to immigration controls and, unlike those who are so subject, cannot be discriminated against for the purposes of employment on the basis of their country of birth. Thus labour migration policies may be evidence-based, but they are informed by data that uses a definition of 'migrant' that is different from the population on which the policies are enacted.

In terms of immigration policy, the definition of 'migrant' as foreign national may be more satisfactory as foreign nationals do not have the right of abode in the UK, and although some are not subject to immigration controls (most notably EU nationals), there are some occasions when they can be deported. To define migrants as foreign nationals brings numbers down dramatically. At the end of 2009, an estimated 11.3 per cent of the UK population was born abroad, but this includes 4.6 per cent who are UK nationals, so 6.7 per cent of the population was both foreign born and of foreign nationality (Anderson and Blinder 2011: 6). Quantitative analysts can be more reluctant to use the foreign national definition because nationality can change and also, if self-reported, nationality may be interpreted as describing an elective affinity dependent on social and cultural factors and personal feelings, rather than legal status. In this sense it is akin to LTIM, as the reports of intention of length of stay that LTIM depends on are also notoriously subjective and of limited use in discovering what migrants actually do (Jaya-weera and Anderson 2008). Migration figures are beset by uncertainty and ambiguity. Policy aims for technocratic 'sensible' solutions (who could argue for a policy that is not sensible?) to what is, in the end, a politically con-structed problem.

The politics of immigration haunts attempts to manage migration through entry controls. Post-war immigration controls are structured in a way that imagines the economic and the political as fundamentally separate, and both are divided from the private world of family relations. Accordingly, non-citizens are divided into three broad categories of entrant: workers and refu-gees/asylum seekers, and family members. Each type of entrant is differently imagined, and if an 'asylum seeker' (that is, a person who has applied for asylum) is seen as *really* a worker or family member rather than an asylum seeker, for instance, this serves as grounds for refusal of entry or removal. National policy on asylum and family reunion is constrained by international treaty obligations which mean that neither can be abolished as a category of entrant. The following sections examine how different entry controls work, and what this reveals about the community of value, and ideals of family relations, work, skill, and the exercise of politics.

3.2 Migration Binaries and Shifting Sympathies

It is commonly observed that immigration policy and research rest on a fundamental distinction between asylum and immigration, between those who are fleeing persecution and those who are seeking employment or to better their lives in some way. This in turn rests on the distinction between the political and the economic, and it has often been noted that such a binary, between forced and free, political and economic, and refugee and migrant is not at all clear cut. Even at the most obvious level, conflict zones are usually not good places for economic as well as political survival, while 'persecution' is an indeterminate concept (Francesco 2008).

As observed in the previous chapter, the idea of fleeing from persecution has long been recognized as a reason why people might seek to move. The two instances most commonly referred to in Britain are the historical migrations of the Huguenots and the Jews (Morgan 1985). While these are often given as instances of the openness of England to those fleeing persecution, some historians suggest we should be more sanguine. The Huguenots affirmed the attraction of Protestantism and England over Catholicism and France, and also brought to Britain much-needed artisanal and craft skills, such as weaving, but this did not mean that they were welcomed at the time (Gwynn 2001). The possibility of Huguenots naturalizing as a group was rejected until 1709 and in 1711 the Act for Naturalising Foreign Protestants was repealed because it was felt that too many people were taking advantage of it. Similarly, many Jews who arrived in the early twentieth century were not embraced as the deserving victims of persecution. The emergent socialist movement, and the Trades Union Congress advocated against Jewish immigration (Cohen 2005), and the socialist weekly *The Clarion,* described the 'appalling' numbers of Jewish people as 'a poison injected into the national veins' (*The Clarion* 1906, cited in Cohen 2005: 15). There were also people who opposed anti-Semitic responses to Jewish migration, but these histories suggest that one must beware of falsely representing a troubled past with relation to refugees.

The idea of leaving a place because one's life and livelihood was in danger was recognized in the 1905 Aliens Act, but the oppositional migration/asylum binary did not harden into policy until the 1950s. The European Voluntary Worker Scheme (EVWS) which began in 1946 exemplifies the fragility of the distinction between migrant workers and refugees. It was variously a labour policy, a means of replenishing the population, and a refugee resettlement scheme. The EVWS involved the recruitment of stateless people from Displaced Persons camps established in Germany and Austria, many of whom did not want to live in the states that had been reconstituted as 'behind the Iron

Curtain'. They had the right values which meant that they were capable of being 'of great benefit to our stock': 'Their "love of freedom", as demonstrated by their preference to remain in the West rather than to return to "conditions which were not free", was seen to constitute the "spirit and stuff of which we can make Britons".' (Kay and Miles 1988, citing Hansard HC Deb 14 February 1947, vol. 433, cols 749–66).

Yet as mentioned in the previous chapter, this was also a policy about accessing labour, as in those early post-war years it was not envisaged that labour would come from the (former) colonies. The Baltic Cygnet scheme and the Westward Ho! Scheme facilitated the entry of some 80,000 displaced persons as the 'unskilled', low-waged, and often temporary labour required for the hard physical work of reconstruction (MacDowell 2005). The scheme tied workers to specific sectors, and they could not leave their jobs without official agreement, but their statelessness meant that it was difficult to repatriate them,[3] This was perceived to be a disadvantage of this labour source compared with other European workers who, if they were 'undesirable types or misfits could be sent back to their homes' (Kay and Miles 1988: 218).

From 1951, EVWS workers who had lived in the UK for over three years were freed from their restrictive employment conditions, and newcomers from Central and Eastern Europe began entering under the new refugee regime. This was governed by the 1951 Geneva Convention which established the principle of the international governance of asylum. As a signatory, the British government was (and is) obliged to consider whether an asylum seeker is eligible for protection, and to accept as bona fide certain grounds for persecution. Drawn up at the time of the Cold War, the Geneva Convention framed the concept of the 'refugee' (a term first applied to the Huguenots) as the liberal individual fleeing Communist oppression (Newland 1995; Gibney and Hansen 2003b). The refugee was the embodiment of liberal polity, not only fleeing persecution but practising liberal politics, both a subject of human rights violations and one who is explicitly demanding human rights.

Until the 1980s there was a (relative) openness to refugees and a sympathetic public response to them. As Gibney and Hansen put it, 'When the public thought about refugees, to the extent it thought about them at all, it associated them with Hungarian freedom fighters or Soviet ballet dancers, both of which were popular figures' (Gibney and Hansen 2003a: 1). One could add that these associations have strong class associations. During the Cold War the political refugee was the symbol of an educated choice for freedom over communism. Refugees from the Soviet Union were seen as confirming the values of Western liberal democracies. During the Cold War

---

[3] This is not to say that EVWS workers were not returned, and for a period those people who had tuberculosis or were mentally ill, could be returned to Germany on medical grounds.

the contours of the community of value were shaped by appeals to human rights. Even as human rights purported to be a universalist discourse, it also helped to delineate the borders between 'us' and 'them'.

Numbers of recognized refugees were small partly because of emigration restrictions. In the 1970s the total number of asylum claims across 'Western Europe' averaged 13,000 annually (Gibney 2001: 3). In 1980 there were 2,352 applications for asylum in the UK, for instance, with over half of them (1,421) coming from Iran (UNHCR 2001: 16). Numbers claiming asylum began to grow steadily in the 1980s, and difficult questions within the Geneva Convention, such as whether persecution could be conducted by private parties, and whether a person had to be individually targeted, came to the fore with the end of the Cold War. This happened at the same time as the number and intensity of conflicts and state breakdowns in law and order increased, and international travel became easier. Hence the numbers of people claiming asylum increased throughout the 1990s and there was a move from the figure of the white political refugee fleeing the oppressive Soviets to the black asylum seeker, running away from a failed state, or the Eastern European criminal looking for a better life, both likely to be 'bogus' and not political refugees at all. Contemporary asylum seekers are often imagined as seeking to enter the UK not because they share liberal values, but because they are in search of work or benefits rather than practical ideals like freedom of speech. Rather than affirming the superiority and desirability of liberal values, they threaten them, and the community of value is confirmed by their rejection rather than by their inclusion.

By the early 2000s the British tabloid press was running vociferous anti-asylum stories. The Labour government initiated an approach that was increasingly harsh on asylum seekers driven by Prime Minister Tony Blair who had over fifty meetings on the subject between 2001 and 2004. Arguably in 2004, Blair anticipated the net migration agenda by setting a 'tipping point', and announcing that every month, more failed asylum seekers should be removed than new claims made (it proved impossible to meet). However, asylum policy claims to be driven by a human rights agenda, and so even though the concern was principally with numbers, the clamp-down was framed in terms of false claims and 'bogus asylum seekers'. Visa requirements and carrier sanctions made it ever more difficult for people who wanted to claim asylum to reach the UK; decision-making was sped up in an attempt to cut rights to appeal, levels of detention increased, and access to work and welfare support was curtailed (Spencer 2011). There was periodic talk of pulling out of the Geneva Convention and a marked increase in hostility to asylum seekers. Hostility it seems is not only to do with arbitrary designations of 'too many' as it shows no sign of diminishing to this day, even though the numbers of asylum seekers dropped dramatically from over 84,000 in 2002 to just under 18,000 in 2010.

For a period beginning with the Labour government in 1997, entry controls became more liberal when it came to economic migrants, and a pilot 'low-skilled' migrant entry scheme was initiated. In 2003 Don Flynn argued that this bifurcated approach, harsh on asylum, more liberal on labour, far from being contradictory, was entirely consistent, and that it heralded an era of managed migration based 'almost exclusively on utilitarian principles... guided... by the economic objectives of growth and modernization' (Flynn 2003: 2). He claimed that this was informed by an attitude to mobility and globalization and that:

> In the new world of globalised reality, the concept of 'rights', if it is applicable at all, should be reserved for those who have made themselves useful to the needs of a growing and dynamic world economy, and who are actively contributing to its further development. (Flynn 2003: 2)

This cast economic migrants, in contrast to needy and criminal asylum seekers, as social contributors. In this post-Cold War, globalized world, it was economic value rather than political values that was becoming the measure of worth.

This relative openness to labour migration when compared to previous decades was to change in the mid-2000s. Policies on labour migration became much more restrictive after EU Enlargement in 2004. Unlike many other EU states, the British government had chosen not to impose 'transitional measures' on the citizens of new member states but allowed them to access the UK labour market with limited conditionality (Anderson et al. 2006; Currie 2008). Numbers significantly exceeded the original estimate of 13,000 (partly because of other EU states unexpectedly imposing transitional measures relatively late in the day). Headlines like 'Halt the tide of EU migrants' (*Sunday Express* 2006), and 'East Europe migrants help take jobless to six-year high' (Barrow 2006) contributed to the presentation of the Labour government being reckless in its labour immigration policy. In response, the Labour government became increasingly tough when pronouncing on immigration. Infamously, Gordon Brown coined the slogan 'British Jobs for British Workers' at the Labour Party Conference in 2007, a slogan that was used as its electoral strap-line by the far right British National Party in the 2010 election. The binary opposition of good refugee/bad economic migrant which had moved in the late 1990s and early 2000s to bad asylum seeker/good economic migrant, then became bad asylum seeker/bad economic migrant. However, what remained constant, and continues to frame policy documents independently of the political affiliations of the minister introducing them, is the rhetoric of good *genuine* refugee and good *highly skilled* migrant.

3.3 Labour Migration Policy: 'The Brightest and the Best'

Labour migration policy is underpinned by the division of labour migrants into 'skilled' and 'unskilled'. It is acknowledged that some types of 'skilled' labour (although they might not be conventionally thought of as 'labour', as they include, for example, bankers, doctors, and ballet dancers) will always have to brought in from 'outside'. There is a global labour market for certain types of talent that are needed for the economy. In 2000 the Labour Immigration Minister, Barbara Roche, announced: 'We are in competition for the brightest and the best' (Roche 2000). Over a decade later the rhetoric continues despite a change of government. The Conservative Home Secretary's introduction to the 2011 Settlement Consultation offered the 'simple message': 'We want the brightest and the best' (Home Office 2011a: 3). The race for the brightest and the best (which, like 'sensible' immigration policy is difficult to contest—who would not want the brightest and the best?), leaves hanging the question of who comprises the not-brightest-and-best, and what is to be done with them. The 'unskilled' may be needed in times of acute labour (but not skills) shortage, but they are presented as potentially undermining the conditions of 'local' unskilled workers. The assumption is that unskilled work can be done by anyone, and unskilled workers are easily replaceable.

In recent years there has been some acknowledgment of the limitations of a framework for valuing work that is organized around 'skills'. Some jobs which are deemed 'low-skilled' may demand aptitude for personal relations, organization, facility with the internet, etc. These skills are not specialized and often they are not reflected in a formal qualification but in generalized 'experience'. They are particularly important in sectors where social relations with customers, clients, and/or service users are important to the delivery and quality of the work, and where employers require that the job is done in a way that contributes to a good service experience, rather than simply to complete the task. In these kinds of occupations employers may make great claims for the skills set of their workforce without this equating to higher pay or status. In low-waged work, employers can demand particular personal qualities (enthusiasm, friendliness, caring, etc.), and experience, and designate these as 'skills' even if they do not require formal qualifications and are not financially rewarded. For example, service users in health and social care often actively express a preference for personal qualities or experience over formal qualifications (Cangiano et al. 2009; Anderson and Ruhs 2010).

The shift to services has meant that in the UK, the population has been encouraged to broaden its ideas of skills and to think of skills acquisition as constant and ongoing. There has been increasing attention paid to 'soft skills', a category which covers a broad range of competences transferable across occupations, such as customer handling, problem-solving, and team-working (for example, see Learning and Skills Council 2007). However, this broadening of meaning (partly to confer value) has been critiqued as enabling policy-makers to claim a trend of workers increasing their skills 'while also allowing a convenient veil to be drawn over the dull, monotonous reality of much service sector work' (Lloyd and Payne 2009: 631).

These sorts of claims reveal that the meaning of 'skills' is highly contested. Some skills can require years of specialized training; others a one-day course. Some skills like basic literacy and numeracy are supposed to be 'produced' by national educational systems and require long-term state investment; others may be obtained through further education (that is, a combination of state and individual investment), and others may be firm- or industry-specific (as in the financial services or information technology sectors), in which case they may be principally the responsibility of employers. These systems are usually interdependent—for example, an IT worker may have to demonstrate numerical competency and have a good degree to qualify for further training paid for by an employer (Wickham and Bruff 2008: 31). Some skills come with credentials, but what is and is not rewarded with credentials changes, and jobs can shift from being classified as 'low-skilled' to 'skilled' and vice versa without necessarily changing in their content (Anderson and Ruhs 2010). There is also a complex relation between skills, experience, and their embodiment. For example, in the restaurant sector, some employers say that familiarity with the cultural background and exposure by 'ethnic chefs' 'in their formative years' (Migration Advisory Committee 2008: para. 9.128), means that their skills cannot simply be acquired through a formal training programme. Similarly employers claim that 'unskilled' jobs such as waiting at table require certain racialized bodies because that is part of the service experience. For example, owners of 'Indian' restaurants argue that clients expect to be served by South Asian waiters. The matching of workers to jobs is part of a range of complex social processes that cannot be reduced to individual employers' discriminatory practices, workers' skills levels, or indeed to an individual's simply 'refusing' to take a job.

The centrality of the skilled/unskilled distinction to these kinds of debates and to work hierarchies more generally is extremely limiting. Loosening the language of skills and applying it across a broad spectrum of human dispositions and attributes risks making the term so generic that it becomes meaningless (Lloyd and Payne 2009), and overlooks the ways in which work and jobs are socially constructed, imagined as suitable for different races and genders. Yet despite these problems, the allocation of skills levels continues to be central to labour migration policy. Labour migration to the UK is now structured by the 'points-based system' (PBS), introduced by the Labour government in an attempt to simplify the proliferation of entry routes, and designed to restrict entry to those migrants identified as having the skills to benefit to the British economy. How 'skills' can be recognized and measured was considered at some length by the Migration Advisory Committee (MAC). This is an advisory body established by the government at the same time as it initiated the PBS. It is comprised of five economists tasked with giving 'transparent, independent and evidence-based advice to the Government on where shortages of skilled labour can sensibly be filled by immigration from outside the European Economic Area' (Migration Advisory Committee 2008: 11).[4] The MAC set as indicators of skill for the purposes of immigration: the skill levels defined in the Standard Occupational Classification (SOC) hierarchy, formal qualifications, and earnings. These are supplemented by two further 'softer' considerations: on-the-job training/experience, and innate ability required to carry out the job to an appropriate level (Migration Advisory Committee 2008: para. 6.15). This last was to capture 'skills that cannot be readily taught or learnt' like dancing (Migration Advisory Committee 2008: para. 6.26).

From May 2008, with the exception of asylum seekers who fall under refugee law, those subject to immigration control and seeking to enter on their own account (that is, not as family members), have been allocated points on the basis of education, prospective employment, and earnings. Only those with sufficient numbers of points are admitted. They also have to satisfy a requirement to have basic competence in English and hold funds sufficient to support themselves (and any accompanying dependants) before their first pay cheque (that is, they have to have access to some property). Successful entrants are now admitted under one of five 'tiers'. The only tiers available for long-term employment are Tiers 1 and 2 (highly skilled and skilled), open to those who exceed a certain number of points, garnered by a combination of qualifications, prospective earnings, and sponsorship offers. Tier 3, for 'low-skilled' workers has been suspended since its inception on the grounds that EU nationals can fill low-skilled posts; Tier 4 is for students, and Tier 5 for temporary workers and youth mobility. In practice many of the categories under the previous system ended up in Tier 5, particularly those where formal definitions of skill and models of employment are difficult to apply: religious leaders, sports people, entertainers, au pairs, business people, etc. (many of whose 'skills' might fall under the criteria of 'innate ability'). Tier 5 applicants must have a sponsor who would be the employer, educational institution, or, for youth mobility scheme applicants, one of seven sponsoring states of origin (Japan, Australia, New Zealand, Taiwan, Monaco, Canada, and, from June

---

[4] Although principally focused on the labour market, their remit also includes advice 'from time to time' on other migration issues.

2012, South Korea). These sponsors are subject to rigorous checks, and if found to be in breach of their obligations, they are de-recognized. This system was held to be transparent, efficient, and 'objective'.

Despite claims to objectivity, the terminology of 'the brightest and the best' indicates that skill is not purely a technical term but is bound up with social status and social relations. Skilled labour is honourable, unskilled is drudgery (Brace 2004). The five-tier system signified quite literally differentiated inclusion, organized by skills level. Only the top tiers were eligible for settlement, the others were tolerated, effectively permitted entry to the territory but not into permanence, with no possibility of acceptance into the community of value. The PBS has had very different implications for women than for men. In 2009 two-thirds of applicants were male, and over three quarters of Tier 2 applicants were male (Murray 2011).

3.4 Family Migration

One of the consequences of the migrant/asylum-seeker dichotomy structuring migration policy and analysis is that it has obscured family migration which is less easy to fit into the free choice/forced movement binary. Family migration, gendered as female, was for many years imagined as secondary to labour and asylum migration, both gendered as male. It received little policy attention, although for many years it has been a significant contributor to settlement numbers—in 2010, 56 per cent of the total of all grants of settlement were on the basis of family and dependence (Migration Observatory 2012). The numerical target set by net migration drew attention to family migration and students, both categories that had previously not been of much interest but that accounted for a substantial proportion of entrants. Student visas were incorporated into the points-based system, but this was not possible for family migrants. The right to private and family life is a fundamental liberal principle and policy on family migration is therefore, like asylum, constrained by international human rights law. However, the argument that a family can choose to live together abroad means that there has always been some considerable scope for policy to become harsher. As Enoch Powell put it in his infamous 1968 'Rivers of Blood' speech, 'It can be no part of any policy that existing families should be kept divided. But there are two directions on which families can be reunited'.[5]

This parallels the 'safe third-country rule' that enables asylum seekers to be returned to the first 'safe' country in which they arrived after leaving their

---

[5] Full text available at <http://www.telegraph.co.uk/comment/3643823/Enoch-Powells-Rivers-of-Blood-speech.html>.

country of origin. Both rest on the logic that liberal states can acknowledge a right (to asylum or to family life) without this meaning they therefore must permit its exercise on their territory. In practice, Powell's observation has characterized the development of family migration policy since the early 2000s, and the family route has become ever more restrictive, through tightening definitions of family, limiting who can be joined by family members, and through measures ostensibly designed to prevent 'false', 'sham', and 'forced' marriages (Spencer 2011).

Family migration does not describe an immigration route that is open to families who simply decide to migrate and who are allowed to enter because they are families, but is applied to a group of people whose entry is permitted because of their recognized familial relation to other people. Non-citizens who enter under the family route may be family members of settled migrants or of British/EU nationals. They can also be 'dependents', family members entering with workers who are themselves temporary.[6] The distinction, while important in policy terms because the latter are less likely to settle than the former, is somewhat arbitrary, in that all family members are cast as 'dependent'. In contrast to the independence and self-sufficiency of the worker, dependence is perceived as a fundamental characteristic of family life (for example, see European Court of Human Rights 2010, para. 43).

As immigration policies are constructive of certain types of subjects, the rules governing their construction are intensely ideological. The ideal family migrant is described in the 2011 Family Migration Consultation thus: 'Those who want to make a real life here with their family, who want to work hard and contribute to their local community and who are not seeking to abuse the system or the rights of others. That is the type of family migration to the UK that we want to see' (Home Office 2011b: para. 5.1). The relationship of the family to society is ambivalent: the real family must demonstrate its integration into society yet if the partnership really is genuine, the family must also be prepared to up sticks and live somewhere else. These ideal families are foundational to society at the same time as being curiously separated from it, and they must be able to support their members 'without recourse to public funds'—that is, they cannot claim a wide range of income-related benefits or housing and homelessness support.

Legislation governing family migration reflects deeply held assumptions about the nature of the family and the nation, and is unavoidably inflected with notions of race and gender. This will be discussed at greater length in Chapter 5, but here I would simply draw attention to the ways in which public discourse is fraught with anxieties about the fecundity of immigrant women

---

[6] There are also family members who enter temporarily on a family visit visa.

and the dangers 'too many children' pose to schools, hospitals, and midwifery services (Walters 2006; Slack 2007; Jones 2009; Pandya 2012). These are usually put in 'raceless' terms, increasingly, in fact, to do with 'sustainability', but this can mask a concern with the 'stock' of the racialized nation. Coleman, for instance, warned that because of the increase in immigration 'white Britons will be a minority by 2066' (Coleman 2010). This indicates not simply a concern for racial homogeneity, but for a *white* nation. Yet liberal democracies must also respect family life, and however hermetically sealed the state is to the trailing spouses and dependants of new arrivals, there are always British citizens who wish to marry non-British people, whether this means marrying them in the UK or bringing in spouses from abroad. Some degree of family migration is inevitable unless the right of citizens to marry whom they wish is completely curtailed.

Policy determines who counts as a family member and who can sponsor family members, and it guides immigration officers in their considerations of what constitutes a genuine relationship. Who has the right to sponsor family members, and who counts as a family member are matters which have long been contested and the regulations governing this have become increasingly restrictive (Spencer 2011). A family's definition of membership is not enough to warrant recognition by the state, and those permitted to enter with or join relatives in the UK have been increasingly limited to the monogamous nuclear family, with the definition of 'child' restricted to under-eighteen-year-olds. Only in 'the most exceptional compassionate circumstances' of 'illness, isolation and poverty' are relatives such as parents aged over sixty-five permitted entry (Immigration Directorate 2011). This was further tightened in June 2012 when, among other restrictions, sponsors were required to demonstrate that they could care for a dependent relative for five years without recourse to public funds.

1997 saw some exceptions to the increasing restriction that characterized post-war policy on family migration. One was the abolition of the infamous Primary Purpose Rule in 1997. This had required applicants to prove that the primary purpose of marriage was not to obtain entry and settlement. This rule was one of a number of provisions whose implementation had a particular impact on men from the Indian subcontinent, even those this group were not specifically referred to in the guidance (Dummett and Nicol 1990; Spencer 2011). Applicants were required to prove a negative; that their main reason for getting married was *not* because they wanted to live together in the UK. But they also had to prove that they genuinely did intend to live together. Immigration restrictions over family members also appear to have been relaxed with respect to same-sex relationships. In 1997 a concession was introduced allowing entry on the basis of relations within a same-sex couple and this was formalized in immigration rules in 2000. This does not mean that the law has been queered. The ideal is still uncontrovertibly heterosexual marriage (Simmons 2008) and couples must have lived together for a period of a minimum number of years and plan to be together permanently 'in a relation akin to marriage' (UK Border Agency 2012: para. 10). Moreover, not only did the concession require that in order to qualify for entry, the same-sex couple had to be legally unable to marry in their country of origin, it also applied the same requirement to unmarried couples. This meant that at the same time as heterosexual cohabitation was becoming increasingly common in the UK, marriage was still being enforced at the border, and until 2003 heterosexual couples had to marry in order to be permitted family reunion. Cohabitation and same-sex relations may be tolerated as long as they do not undermine the primacy of marriage.

Unmarried and same-sex partners are grouped together in the immigration rules and separated from married partners yet the marriage relation is not simply a formal legal status. In the same way as formal citizenship is not sufficient to mean membership of the community of value, so formal marriage does not mean that couples have formed a 'genuine relationship'. The legal contract of marriage is a symbol and not the substance of the relationship, and the marriage of some couples can be designated a 'sham marriage'. 'Family migration must be based on a genuine and continuing marriage or partnership. Those involved in sham marriages undermine our immigration system, and damage the institution of marriage' (Home Office 2011b: para. 1.12). Like those marriages refused under the primary purpose rule, marriages are considered sham if they are judged as undertaken for the purposes of gaining a right of residence in the UK. Unlike primary purpose rule marriages, the weddings for sham marriages are depicted as conducted in the UK. In this way the emphasis on sham marriages marks a shift from enforcement at the UK border to enforcement on UK territory that will be discussed in Chapter 6.

Because it is principally concerned with marriage as a response to immigration controls, the distinction between a genuine and a sham marriage is not one that is maintained so straightforwardly for marriages where both parties are British citizens. Perhaps the nearest equivalent is when marriage relationships are annulled which is still a relatively rare procedure. In 2004, for example, there were only 492 annulments as compared to 167,193 divorces (National Statistics 2007). Rather than sham marriage as manifest in annulments, the problem when it comes to British nationals could better be expressed as the opposite one of 'sham singles': that of people claiming benefits as lone parents or single people when they are in fact living as or with a partner.[7] In the case of sham singles, sexual relations and shared

---

[7] See speech delivered by Iain Duncan Smith (2011).

household tasks are held to indicate that a couple is in a relationship, whatever plans the couple has for the future. This is not sufficient when it comes to evidence for establishing a genuine marriage for immigration purposes. Immigration requirements demand that a marriage be characterized by an intention to remain together, and this is also key to the entry of unmarried and same-sex partners. Immigration Rules stipulate that 'The intention of the Rules relating to unmarried and same sex partners is to allow *genuine long-term relationships to continue.* It is not an open door to couples who are in the early stages of a cohabiting relationship' (Immigration Directorate 2006: para. 2, emphasis in original). This is about long-term monogamy, in contrast to the understanding underpinning claims of benefit fraud, which recognizes a wide range of arrangements as partnerships for the purpose of denying people benefits.

Those who are claiming benefits, even if they are in a 'genuine long-term relationship' are discriminated against for the purposes of family reunion. Those on low incomes are potentially more vulnerable generally to accusations of sham marriages: under the headline 'How to spot a bogus wedding', a UKBA enforcement officer suggested that people with 'labels of Primark (a famously low cost clothing outlet) suits still on their clothes' might give cause for suspicion (*Halifax Courier* 2011). For many years, sponsors have had to prove that they can maintain and accommodate their incoming family members 'without recourse to public funds'. In England this kind of restriction has its historical antecedents. Steve Hindle writes of the 'quasi formal inhibition of the marriages of the poor' (Hindle 1998: 91) in the seventeenth century through which parishes sought to limit their responsibility for poor relief. Moreover, Malthusian requirements that a man should be able to support a family before being permitted to marry are coming back into fashion for unemployed and low-waged citizens.[8] These sorts of restrictions have been long-standing for those wanting to marry non-EU nationals, but have been significantly tightened in recent years, and in June 2012 the government announced that the income threshold was to be raised above the previous level of the basic welfare benefit. Sponsors should be able to support their dependents 'at a reasonable level that helps to ensure that they do not become a burden on the taxpayer and allows sufficient participation in everyday life to facilitate integration'. The sponsor's income alone was to count, and, following a consultation with the Migration Advisory Committee, the threshold was set at a minimum of £18,600 in order to be able to sponsor a partner, £22,400 for a partner and one child, and an additional £2,400 for every other

---

[8] In July 2012 the Prime Minister announced that the government was considering refusing Housing Benefit to the under-twenty-fives. 'A couple will say, "We are engaged, we are both living with our parents, we are trying to save before we get married and have children and be good parents. But how does it make us feel, Mr Cameron, when we see someone who goes ahead, has the child, gets the council home, gets the help that isn't available to us?"' (Walters 2012).

child. As *The Economist* pointed out, £18,600 is half again as much as someone would make working forty hours a week, fifty-two weeks a year if they are paid the minimum wage (*Economist* 2012). Of all British citizens in employment, 47 per cent would not qualify as a sponsor, and of British women in employment, 61 per cent would not qualify.

At the same time as asserting that 'British citizens should be able to marry or enter into a civil partnership with whoever they choose' (Migration Advisory Committee 2011: 3), these kinds of proposals indicate that the choice of who to marry is in practice heavily constrained for those on low wages, and it is virtually impossible for unemployed or disabled people on benefits to marry a person from outside the EU. Marriage or partnership to a non-national requires a person to demonstrate a greater degree of independence from the state than is required from those who marry UK citizens. Those who wish to enter as, or sponsor the entry of, family members must demonstrate the right type of relationship, but the individuals contracting the relationship must also be of a certain type. The UK-based sponsor must be a worker earning a minimum income, and the person from abroad must successfully pass an English language test, even if they do not speak English to their partner, and have had no opportunity to learn the language because they have been living abroad.

A further requirement of the marriage relationship is that it must have been entered into 'freely'. Despite the long-standing immigration *requirement* for couples to marry in order to merit entry to the UK mentioned above, free (unconstrained) consent is considered a key characteristic of a genuine marriage:

> Marriage must be based on the free consent of both parties. There is no place in British society for the practice of forced marriage—of forcing a young woman or man into marriage against their will, or family advantage, or out of fear of bringing shame on the family or perceived notions of family honour. There can be no justification—cultural, religious or otherwise—for marriage without free consent. It is a breach of human rights and a form of violence against the victim. That must be made clear, here and to those overseas who may be planning such marriages. And we must do as much as we can to protect the victims and potential victims, of this terrible practice. (Home Office 2011b: para. 4.1)

Forced marriage is singled out as a cause of concern, although policymakers are more cautious in differentiating forced and arranged marriages than they have been in the past. It is, as is apparent from the quotation above, associated, in terms of immigration, with the importing of non-liberal traditions from overseas. Most of the research and policy on forced marriage has been focused on South Asian and Muslim communities (Ehrkamp 2010). Research on family migration more generally has tended to focus on these groups, but the emphasis on forced marriage is perhaps partly also because the well-organized and politicized nature of some South Asian feminist groups that have challenged gender relations and immigration controls within the UK (Chantler et al. 2009).

Consent indicates the free choice of a radically individualized liberal self however, it is extremely difficult to maintain the notion of the radically individualized liberal self of contracts and markets when it comes to marriage, which is a relation of status. The difficulty of distinguishing between coercion and acceptable pressure can mean that 'force' occurs only as physical violence.[9] But families can use a combination of sanctions and psychological pressures that do not amount to physical force in order to convince a young person to marry, particularly if there are fears about the sexuality of the young person, for example, or if they are pregnant and unmarried (Chantler et al. 2009). Put like this, the problem of forced marriage becomes more recognizably related to difficulties experienced by some young people in the UK more generally, and associated with parental responses to them going 'off the rails' rather than the importing of backward traditions. The challenges posed by compulsory heterosexuality, and female sexual propriety are not confined to migrant communities.

One of the solutions to the problem of forced marriage, conceived as effectively the importation of uncivilized practices, has been to raise the age of marriage visa applicants, first to eighteen and then to twenty-one. This is on the grounds that greater maturity and independence make it easier for those vulnerable to forced marriage to refuse though there is no evidence this is in fact the case (Chantler et al. 2009). Once again these regulations have a particular impact on those with South Asian (especially Pakistani) backgrounds who are more likely to marry at a younger age than many other (Home Office 2011c). This does not seem to have solved the problem, and in June 2012 Prime Minister David Cameron announced that forcing someone to marry was to be made a criminal offence. This was only days before the announcement on family migration, which included an increase in the spousal probationary period from two to five years 'to test the genuineness of the relationship' (Home Office 2011b: para. 2.34). However, if one is not able to claim welfare benefits independently, has to live with a person, and is dependent on their sponsorship for a right to remain in the UK, the sponsor can operate considerable control over the family member. This raises important questions of exit that have their parallels with issues of slavery, contracts of indenture, and labour contracts. Does genuine consent only have to be given at the moment of entering the contract, or does it have to be ongoing,

---

[9] A similar process can be observed with reference to smuggling and trafficking as will be discussed in Chapter 7.

and, crucially for migrants, does freedom mean freedom to exit as well as to enter a contract? This is important because, while divorce may be protracted and painful for citizens, for those who do not have indefinite leave to remain it can also mean that they have to leave the UK. Indeed, the Home Office identified one of the advantages of an increase in the spousal probationary period as the possibility for reduction in settlement numbers. Data from the Office for National Statistics (ONS) reveal that 10 per cent of marriages end in divorce after five years and divorced spouses cannot claim settlement. Immigration controls are not neutral, but help shape the constraining conditions within which power and force operate, and in this way could be said to 'force' spouses into remaining in unhappy marriages in order to keep their residency.

The implementation of these policies requires a significant degree of intrusion of the state into personal life. How do immigration officials know whether a marriage is genuine? How do they know whether a sponsor is earning enough to maintain family members? And what regimes of inspection are legitimated and normalized through these processes (Luibhéid 2002)? Applicants and sponsors must furbish officials with all sorts of financial and personal documentation: wedding invitations, property deeds and rental agreements, personal photographs, personal letters, doctors' records, and the like. They must tolerate visits from immigration and local authorities to quiz them about their relationship and living arrangements, and in recent proposals it has been suggested that charities and community groups might also be invited to comment on the genuineness of relations and whether they are suitable for settlement. The impact of immigration regulations on marriage are not just experienced by those people marrying non-citizens. Many of the assertions which frame the policy are about families in general rather than migrant families per se. In one striking proposal in the *Family Consultation*, UKBA commits to exploring the possibility of having a 'designated category of officer' who can conduct marriages and enforce immigration laws, who will be charged with conducting marriages 'in the specific environment of a register office' in so-called hotspots for sham marriages (Home Office 2011b: para.3.13).

Through the rhetoric of family migration policy the British government establishes itself as a state that adopts a liberal attitude towards homosexuality, is supportive of women, and consensual marriage. Policies on family migration, as with immigration laws more generally, affect to be both raceless and genderless. It is striking that in the seventy-seven page *Family Consultation* document, the word 'women' only occurs eight times. Seven of these are with respect to victimhood and abuse, and the eighth is in the title of the Minister signing the foreword ('Home Secretary and Minister for Women and Equalities'). 'Wife' is not mentioned at all. In this sense the policy might be said to be gender blind. However, the fact remains that women comprise the majority of family migrants (Home Office 2011c: 5). One consequence of this genderless policy is that, for all the avowals of equality, it enforces female dependency on husbands for their immigration status. Similarly, although permitting entry on the basis of same-sex relations, the implementation of immigration policies such as the proposal to invite comments on living arrangements from community groups, or the current requirement of statements from third parties verifying relationships, has different implications for same sex-couples. As Simmons notes, 'this is not an option for migrants who come from more severe homophobic environments, where being "out" has severe repercussions' (Simmons 2008: 224).

3.5 Conclusion

Concerns about numbers shape the contemporary political discourse about immigration. This discourse works to homogenize the Migrant, who is turned, literally, into a figure, a number that is susceptible to technocratic manipulations. Policy and practice also work to split migrants into different types of actors (by reason for entry, nationality, etc.) thereby imposing the government's own order on the population of mobile people. This chapter has examined the attempts to control the heterogeneity of migration through the imposition of certain logics and assumptions which separate the Migrant into a political or economic actor, or a family member each differently governed. Legal migration categories are then read as if they are neutral and descriptive, reflecting a person's identity rather than shaping particular types of relations and behaviour.

At the same time, migration categories assert certain values and positions. The Migrant as seen in Chapter 2, is a figure signifying the borders of the community of value—that is, one that is susceptible to *political* manipulation. The kinds of people wanted and not wanted are described in graphic and value-laden terms: 'bogus' asylum seekers, 'sham' marriages, 'low-skilled' workers versus 'genuine' refugees, 'genuine and subsisting marriages', 'the brightest and the best'. This terminology evokes who will be accepted and not accepted into the community of value. The Migrant, like the Criminal is cast as both normative and measurable. As with crime statistics, definitions are contested and have a significant impact on data. Numbers can almost always be presented as rising, and, again as with 'criminals', however many 'migrants' there are, the normative element means that the number will inevitably be too high. In the case of all three categories of entry, it has become increasingly clear that the poor are to be excluded. The asylum seeker is no longer imagined as the educated professor, but the illiterate global poor, while workers are to be refused entry or possibility of settlement if they do not earn enough, and similarly family members now have to not simply be self-sufficient but have a minimum income.

'The Migrant' is a symbolic figure delineating the borders of the national community but taking this separation of Us and Them for granted means that connections and tensions are overlooked. In the chapter we have seen that there are contradictions between ideas of skill and ideals of marriage depending on whether the individual under scrutiny is an EU citizen or not. These raise important questions that go beyond migration. For instance, if the amount of money deemed necessary for non-EU national's 'sufficient partici-pation in everyday life' is set at a rate substantially higher than either benefits or the minimum wage, indeed, higher than that earned by half of the working population, what does this tell us about the participation in everyday life of those on benefits and low wages? Don Flynn's warning that rights would be explicitly linked to those who were contributing to the economy seems pres-cient, and increasingly applicable to citizens as well as migrants.

In all this it is important then to unpack when it is helpful to differentiate migrants from citizens, and when it is more useful to consider the commonal-ities between them. When is a person's immigration or citizenship status relevant and when is it not? This puts migratory processes and immigration controls centre-stage but does not simply assume that they are always and necessarily of relevance. It is necessary to move beyond the taken-for-granted-ness of immigration controls which views them as neutral sorting mechan-isms, and consider them as a factor in shaping actions and processes, productive of certain types of relations. It is this productive nature of immi-gration controls that will be discussed in the following chapter.

4

'British Jobs for British Workers!' Migration and the UK Labour Market

Labour markets are a key site for the construction of 'us' and 'them'. The hardening of national borders and the idea that for non-nationals, work is a right that they do not have, and for nationals, work is a duty that they must perform, set insiders and outsiders against each other in a competition for jobs. The competition is generally imagined as principally between the poor in their guise as the low skilled. There has been increasing emphasis on how welfare benefits contribute to the lack of competitiveness of insiders. Combining anxieties about the economy and anxieties about 'broken Britain's' (white) 'underclass', it is argued that the generosity of benefits and a culture of worklessness mean that, like the valiant beggars of old, people who are perfectly capable of doing 'low-skilled' work refuse to engage with labour markets, effectively allowing themselves to be displaced by migrant labour (Holehouse 2012). The welfare dependence of the unemployed demonstrates their dishonourable idleness. But the Migrant is contrasted, not only with the Benefit Scrounger, but also with the British Worker, whose predicament as unemployed reveals the mercenary nature both of those employers who do not reserve jobs for the national labour force, and of the migrants they employ who take jobs that are not rightfully theirs. Either way, the solution is to tighten immigration controls to protect the national labour market, to encourage employers to do their national duty, and to limit access to welfare benefits.

This chapter will unpack some of the complexities masked by this approach and argue that immigration controls are not neutral sorting mechanisms, but they work with migratory processes and other social and institutional regimes to produce certain types of employment relations. In this way immigration controls, far from protecting workers' rights, contribute to creating groups of workers who are more attractive to employers. Use of migrant labour is part of a highly dynamic interplay between institutions, systems, policies, politics, and individual choices, all of which have feedback effects. The interaction between labour markets and immigration has been considerably researched, but there has tended to be a 'now you see it, now you don't' approach to immigration controls, with them coming to the fore often only when illegality is used as a key explanatory variable for understanding migrants' vulnerability to poor employment. This is evidently not applicable to a significant proportion of migrant workers, most obviously EU nationals, who are not subject to immigration controls. This chapter will therefore focus on workers with legal status—that is, people who are living and working in the UK and not in breach of their conditions of entry (although this category is not easy to delineate, as will be discussed in Chapter 6).

The chapter will begin by examining the call 'British Jobs for British Workers' and ask, who is the 'British Worker' and what is a 'British Job'? These questions inevitably problematize the concept of the 'national labour market', which is not only about where jobs are but, it will be argued, partly constructed by immigration controls and by employment law. Migrants (understood as low-waged non-citizens rather than 'foreign born') are concentrated in very specific jobs within certain sectors. These often fall under the heading of 'precarious work', a concept that highlights the temporalities of labour markets. The chapter will discuss how migratory processes can lead newly arrived migrants to work in precarious jobs, and consider the case of post-2004 European migrants (from the so-called EU8) as illustrative of the ways in which life course shapes engagement in low-waged, insecure labour markets. As well as considering migratory processes, it is important that analyses consider immigration controls and how they interact with these migratory processes. EU8 migrants' experiences of the labour market are no longer directly affected by immigration controls, and the chapter will separately consider the ways in which immigration controls create groups of workers over whom employers can exercise particular mechanisms of control, thereby under certain circumstances, making them more desirable as workers than citizens. They also create groups which are confined to temporary or part-time employment.

In public debates around immigration it is notable how groups that might describe themselves as on the left often justify migrants' presence in terms of their economic contribution, an approach that is more usually associated with the right. In contrast, groups on the right appeal to priority of protecting (British) workers' rights, an aim that is more typically associated with the left. Both of these sets of arguments draw on the ideal of the Good Citizen and the community of value. Situating migration and immigration controls in the context outlined above makes it possible to move beyond both these approaches. It means that, rather than displacing British workers, migrants can be analysed as one of many overlapping groups in the labour force that are part of a continual process of labour market re-structuring.

4.1 'British Jobs for British Workers'

The terms which structure the presentation and analysis of the role of migrants in the labour market is an excellent example of how 'flip-flopping' between different definitions and appeals to symbolic figures, in this case, the British Worker as well as the Migrant, can lead to contradictory and unclear demands. Chapter 3 discussed how immigration policies are concerned with measurement, numbers, and impacts, and how the population that is being measured and counted is not the same as the population that is being controlled through immigration, meaning that the 'facts' are very contested. This has consequences for the public debate on labour migration in particular. Consider the claim that 'Foreigners grab 200,000 British jobs' (Wilson 2009). It is implied that these 'foreigners' greedily grabbing jobs are pushing their way to the front of a queue when it is British citizens who should have priority. But the headline uses 'foreigner' to apply to those designated in the ONS data as foreign born, many of whom, as discussed in the previous chapter, are UK nationals. Analyses of impacts and effects of migrant labour typically use this definition of migrant (Aldin et al. 2010), even though the foreign born are not necessarily subject to the policy levers of immigration controls. Particularly relevant in the case of employment is the fact that on the one hand it is illegal to deny a job applicant work *solely* on the basis of where they are born (which could be considered discrimination), but on the other such 'discriminatory' treatment is a requirement of immigration legislation, and job applicants of British and European Economic Area (EEA)[1] nationality must be given preferential access to labour markets.

Importantly for a debate that is obsessed with numbers and measurement and for a policy that is orientated towards getting numbers down, the 'foreign born' category yields far higher numbers than the 'foreign national'. In 2009, 13.2 per cent of those employed in the UK were foreign born, while 8.2 per cent were foreign nationals. Thus if migrants' share of the labour market is a concern for policy makers, that share appears 60 per cent larger if one considers all foreign-born workers rather than foreign nationals (Anderson and Blinder 2011). Moreover, foreign-born labour is not only used in low-waged work, but is a feature of high paying sectors like high-end financial services. Although often bundled together in the presentation of data, the migration and employment experiences of elite migrants like international financiers are likely to be very different from the majority of low-waged workers. As previously discussed, when used in political and popular debate, 'migrant' is a normative as well as a descriptive term and the

---

[1] The EEA comprises the European Union and Liechtenstein, Norway, and Iceland.

wealthy are often not imagined to be migrants (by migrants' rights advocates as much as by academics and politicians). There is an element of self-fulfilling prophecy in the perception of migrants as concentrated in low-waged work then, as once non-citizens are working in poorly paid work, their being a migrant becomes a distinguishing feature, whilst if they are wealthy, the relevance of them being a migrant seems to diminish.

The problems of definition extend beyond 'migrant' to 'British worker'. This is already implicit in problems of the definition of 'migrant', given that many of those 'migrants' are also British citizens. The instability of definition of one implies the instability of definition of the other. Who is a 'British worker'? Gordon Brown's slogan was famously taken up by demonstrators at the Lindsey Oil Refinery early in 2009, demanding 'British Jobs for British Workers'. A look at the photographs of braziers burning, Union Jacks flying, and demonstrators in the snow, all white, all male, all able-bodied, gives some clue as to who counts. The image conjured is of the beleaguered native, the hard working family man, not the dishonourable benefit scrounger. This depiction of the British Worker masks a much more complex and segmented labour force than one which is simply divided between migrants and British workers. There are many British-born black people and people working in Britain are increasingly likely to be women, as the past twenty years has seen significant growth of female employment and prime-age male inactivity.[2] Many 'migrants' do not join the world of contracted, secure work the day after they obtain their citizenship, but instead continue to be faced with multiple axes of discrimination even after decades of residence in the UK, and for negatively racialized groups, discrimination can continue through to so-called 'second and third generations'. In certain sectors and for certain groups, looking at the labour market experiences and trajectories of foreign-born workers can generate important insights into the relation between migration, racial discrimination, and belonging.

4.2 The National Labour Market

There is also the question of what constitutes a 'British Job'? The phrase invokes a national labour market but this is set within a globalized economy. To take the Lindsey Oil Refinery as an example: it is located in North Lincoln-shire and takes its name from the historic kingdom of Lindsey, but it is operated by a French transnational, Total SA. The work was for an expansion

---

[2] They may also be students, and the expansion of higher education and change in the fee-funding arrangement meant that student employment increased markedly between 1996 and 2006 (TUC and NUS 2006; Atfield et al. 2011).

of the refinery, to be carried out by an American transnational, Jacobs Engineering group, but sub-contracted to an Italian company, IREM. The jobs were 'British' because the work was to be conducted on national territory, rather than because it was work offered by a British company. Yet this emphasis on the territorial can be unhelpful as despite the strong imagining of the national, it has no engagement with the specificities of location. The introduction discussed how the depiction of British communities can be very localized (neighbourhood pubs, churches, schools) but when it comes to debates about migration and the labour market, British workers are depicted, not as living in particular places in neighbourhoods, with relations to others in the community, but as unmoored, ranging across the entire of the United Kingdom in their search for employment. Chapter 1 argued that the hardening of territorial boundaries and the importance of socially sanctioned labour to membership in the community of value make of work a duty as well as a right. The hard-working family man, recognizing his duty, will travel to wherever the work is, but the Benefit Scrounger must be made to get on his bike. To ensure this, the doctrine of less eligibility requires that the benefit dependent must not be better off than the hard-working family man. In 2011, the government announced that those claiming benefits would have to be prepared to take jobs offered that were within one-and-a-half-hour's commute of their home in order to continue to be eligible for welfare. The rhetoric from all political parties is about 'protecting' the labour market (the right to work) for the hard-working family man, but this language of protection, rarely invoked except when it comes to immigration, has a strong disciplinary flipside. As Prime Minister David Cameron stated, 'Immigration and welfare reform are two sides of the same coin' (Cameron 2011).

This is not to deny that in certain sectors and highly specialized occupations, the labour market is national and even international. For example, an offshore drilling engineer on an oil rig will be more limited in one way and less constrained in another in his choice of the physical location where he can practise his skills, than the dishwasher working on the same rig. In specialized occupations where the scale of the (inter)national is reflected in job seeking behaviours, migrant 'competition' is often legitimized and states do not claim to preserve jobs for citizens. If employers want to pay someone over £150,000 annually, they can take on a non-citizen without having to first advertise the job in the UK. Immigration controls are supposed to protect not these highly specialized jobs, but those requiring less 'skill'. Yet for this kind of work, analysing the labour market at the scale of the national is not necessarily helpful. Some of this is recognized in practice and the Migration Advisory Committee produces a Scotland Shortage occupation list which contains additional occupations to those listed for all regions of the UK (Migration

Advisory Committee 2010b: para. 3.3).[3] However, its position that 'even if regional shortages, however defined, exist and can be identified, it is probably not sensible to fill vacancies with immigrants if there is not a national shortage' (Migration Advisory Committee 2008: para. 3.4), indicates that the national trumps the local.

The *national* labour market does not particularly help in understanding the processes that lead to 'hard-to-fill vacancies' in areas of unemployment. Spatial mismatch and geographical immobility have long been recognized as features of the UK labour market (Adams et al. 2002; Murphy et al. 2006). Most 'British workers' do not simply look for jobs anywhere within the nation state territory but rather in a particular neighbourhood, town, or region, in labour markets shaped by local and regional factors. This does not mean that national policies do not help form this context, but these national policies may not be directly related to labour markets. For example, people may need to provide some form of care for elderly relatives within a context where social care provision is extremely limited. Home ownership makes moving for employment difficult, especially at times of a sluggish housing market, or from areas of high unemployment low-cost housing to areas of low unemployment high-cost housing (Murphy et al. 2006). In many regions of the country, public transport systems are poor, making commuting time-consuming and expensive.[4] In this way the scale of the national does have relevance, because that is how people are governed, but it is far more complex than the idea of 'the national labour market' depicts.

The job claimed by the British Worker is kite-marked. A British job is, by virtue of its Britishness, a decent one, suitable for a self-respecting member of the community of value. Yet the quality of jobs in the British labour market is not necessarily that high. Many 'low-skilled' manufacturing jobs have moved to low-waged economies, and there has been an expansion of service sector jobs, some of which have been associated with de-skilling and the proliferation of 'McJobs' in low-waged service occupations (Anderson and Ruhs 2010). The growth of the service economy has led to a 'hollowing out' of the labour market and an increase in good and bad jobs and a decline in the 'middling occupations' (Goos and Manning 2007). The UK has one of the most deregulated labour markets in Europe, and it is consistently one of

---

[3] They also produced a report on whether London weighting should be included in the minimum-earnings requirement for incoming skilled workers and the Scottish government lobbied hard for its exclusion on the grounds that it 'effectively awards additional points for working in or around London, rather than recognising that a potential migrant will be paid less (reflecting the lower cost of living) for doing the same job in other parts of the UK or reflecting the skills that they bring to the economy' (Migration Advisory Committee 2010a: para. 3.4). The MAC recommended against exclusion.

[4] The average daily commute is just under one hour, and 10 per cent of workers journey over two hours (thanks to Dr Ali Rogers for this).

the lowest in the Organisation for Economic Co-operation and Development's (OECD) employment protection league. Although the Labour government introduced a national minimum wage, they did not reverse the legislation on trades unions that constrained the right to strike, and opted out of European legislation setting a maximum forty-eight-hour week. For those working on casual, time-limited, and other types of non-permanent contracts, dismissal is relatively straightforward, and there has been a marked prolifer-ation of 'non-standard' arrangements like agency working. Agency workers are often not directly employed by the labour user, but by an employment business (or 'labour-providing agency'). Use of agencies facilitates flexible and short-term work and agency workers who are employed for less than twelve weeks have significantly fewer rights than those who are directly employed: they can be hired on lower hourly rates and on worse terms and conditions, and do not have rights to benefits such as overtime and sickness pay. In January 2008, 58 per cent of Jobcentre Plus vacancies were for 'other business activities', largely comprising employment-agency vacancies (TUC Commission on Vulnerable Employment 2008: 29). In October 2008, the Department for Business Enterprise and Regulatory Reform estimated there were between 1.1 and 1.5 million agency workers (BERR 2008: iv). Numbers of both involuntary part-time and involuntary temporary workers are increasing, and in February 2012, the Trades Union Congress claimed that there were 1.3 million 'underemployed' adults, forced to take part-time work because there was no full-time work available. 'British jobs' therefore are not necessarily secure or well protected. Unsocial hours, low wages, temporariness, and lack of opportunities for promotion or personal development (Lindsay and McQuaid 2004; Belt and Richardson 2005; Devins and Hogarth 2005) can all prevent jobseekers from applying for particular positions. So too can the low status of many entry-level jobs. Jobs are not simply about earning money but have a social meaning.

It is this social meaning that is called upon so strongly in 'British Jobs for British Workers'. 'British Jobs for British Workers' is a claim for work on the basis of nationality above all. It is this that has primacy rather than efficiency or cost. Its unthinking nationalism may be deeply problematic, but it also contains a claim for decent, non-alienated, and secure work that is a far cry from the kinds of jobs that have proliferated in the UK over the past two decades. It is an assertion of the *social* relations of work, but these social relations are reduced to the national, encompassing both the national as a scale and as an idealized moral community. This means that what is important about the social relations of work and workers, the constraints on citizens, and the productive relations of immigration controls is missed. It also naturalizes and masks the social construction of competition between groups of workers. After all there are many groups of low-waged workers who could be imagined as in competition with the hard-working family man, and who have been so imagined in the past, most notably women, who are generally acknowledged today as being in the labour market alongside men rather than competing with them for jobs.

The logic of job competition that underpins labour migration policy should not be taken at face value. Indeed, there are some interesting exceptions to this logic that point to more creative ways of understanding the social relations of the labour market. For example, although asylum seekers are not allowed to work while their claims are being considered, and failed asylum seekers are not allowed any access at all to the labour market, detained (often failed) asylum seekers can be paid to work in the detention centre that is holding them. The jobs they perform are usually tasks like serving food, washing, painting rooms—that is, they are generally to do with the provision of services internal to the detention centre, most of which are managed by large corporations. Detainees are exempt from the minimum wage, and pay rates are either for routine work at £1.00 per hour, or specified projects at £1.25. Yet this is not treated as 'taking' jobs from British people who live near detention centres, and the minimum wage exemption is not regarded as undermining the local market. Similarly, according to a 2009 government statement, an annual 12 million hours is worked in prisons doing jobs like packing for large supermarket chains and putting together headphones for airline companies, as well as providing services within the prison itself (cited in: Investigating Prison Labour 2009). In the UK, minimum pay for prison labour is only £4 a week, yet despite the fact that this is labour that is paid substantially below the minimum wage, this is not constructed as having the potential to undermine the pay and conditions of 'more deserving' workers.

How is it that groups like detained asylum seekers, prisoners, but also interns and volunteers, fall outside the logic of competition? The answer seems to be that their work, although potentially paid, is nevertheless taken out of the labour market. This is similar to the situation regarding domestic labour. A housewife washing the windows in her family home may be working, but she is not a worker. Even though she is not paid, she is not cast as doing British window cleaners out of a job or undermining their labour market position, because she is not in the labour market. Her not being in the labour market is not simply because she is not paid. If she pays her child to perform the same task she will not be prosecuted for making use of child labour—that is, payment is not sufficient to turn the work into labour market activity. Noah Zatz argues that when the social relations of work are given primacy, when, as with detained asylum seekers, prisoners, or interns, work is imagined as 'for your own good' then it is non-market work (Zatz 2009). 'Detainees should be advised . . . that work opportunities are a privilege and a position of responsibility' (Detention Services Order 15/2008). It is not the nature of the task but the social relations that govern its performance that determine whether work is employment. Zatz describes these kinds of arrangements as 'paid non-market work'. Importantly these social relations are not independent of the law. The labour market is socially and legally constructed, and in the same way that immigration and citizenship law helps to 'produce' migrants, so employment law helps to 'produce' workers. In this way, whether or not particular types of work are considered as part of the labour market is fundamentally contested, and law does not simply regulate an already existing labour market, but helps to produce employment and labour markets as social fields: 'Law does more than give employment relationships a particular character. It produces employment as a relationship both coherent unto itself and distinct from others . . . In doing so, however, employment law draws on and rearticulates extant institutional forms and cultural categories' (Zatz 2009: 857). One of these extant institutions and cultural categories is the nation. The national labour market is not only about the territorial borders of the state, but also about social borders between the market and not market, between work and labour, set within a context that is strongly imagined as national but rarely interrogated.

4.3 Migrants at Work

Considering immigration and employment regimes in parallel, one cannot help but be struck by the extent to which they seem to be moving in opposite directions. Migration is increasingly onerously regulated and overseen at the same time as employment is de-regulated. At the same time as the public is urged to 'join the red tape challenge' and 'free up business and society from the burden of excessive regulation',[5] employers and public servants are required to monitor and regularly record the immigration status of workers and clients ever more closely. Immigration is to be excessively regulated, but working conditions, not. Compare the projected costs for the enforcement of the National Minimum Wage (NMW) in 2009/10 at £8.8 million, with the budget for the UK Border Agency (not including Customs Detection activity funding) for the same period at £248.6 million (UK Border Agency 2009a). The budget for in-country immigration control, (work permits, points-based system, removals, asylum processes) was £884.3 million (UK Border Agency 2009a: 56). The NMW had ninety-three compliance officers in 2009 and the Gangmasters Licensing Authority had twenty-five inspectors (personal communication from GLA policy officer July 2009). The proposed number

---

[5] See <http://www.redtapechallenge.cabinetoffice.gov.uk/about/> (accessed 21 June 2012).

of UK Border Agency Staff for Local Immigration Teams, the bodies tasked with bringing immigration controls to a local level, was 7,500.

This tension between immigration regulation and employment deregulation is ignored in the UKBA employment regime. Employment relations as imagined by UKBA—a single employer, prepared to guarantee work and take on responsibility for an employee for a set period of time, willing to take risks on their behalf and attest to their bona fides, seems quite atypical. As discussed in the previous chapter, the focus of immigration controls on excluding the global poor means that increasingly, only very limited numbers of those constructed as skilled and highly skilled are able to enter as workers—although these groups too can be severely constrained a result of the immigration regime (Anderson and Rogaly 2005; Bach 2008). Permits and sponsorship may bring advantages to employers in terms of retention, but they are not particularly flexible. Their acquisition requires employers to submit documentation within tight deadlines, to anticipate demand, and to take on employment responsibilities, in some instances even accommodation, for workers. This means employers risk tying themselves to obligations that are not necessarily profitable.

The kinds of jobs which are claimed by the hard-working family man, decent, secure, and honourable, are not the jobs that are often associated with migrant workers. The kinds of jobs that migrants are typically depicted as working in are characterized by low wages, insecurity, and obfuscated employment relations, in sectors such as hospitality, sex, agriculture, and private households (May et al. 2006; Shelley 2007; TUC Commission on Vulnerable Employment 2008). There are many qualitative studies detailing migrants' situations in what might be termed precarious employment in the UK (May Jon et al. 2006; Ahmad 2008; Pai 2008). Large-scale data are weak (House of Lords 2008) but Labour Force Survey (LFS) data suggest, for example, that recent migrants (defined in October 2008 as those who arrived between October 1997 and October 2007), are more than twice as likely as UK nationals to be in temporary work, and there are good reasons for believing that these data represent a significant underestimation (Jayaweera and Anderson 2008). Eleven per cent of recent migrants (12 per cent of EU8 nationals) who were employees responding to the LFS of 2007, said they were in work that was not permanent in some way. This compares with 6 per cent of the entire LFS sample. Whatever the scepticism about the extent of insecure work (Fevre 2007) recent arrivals are disproportionately concentrated in it.

This is not the work conjured by the 'British Jobs for British Workers' slogan, but is rather that more usually depicted as avoided by benefit scroungers. Migrants subject to sponsorship relations are not flexible and their employment relations are (usually) more transparent. For precarious work, employers must avoid being tied into sponsorship and other obligations, and turn to flexible labour already in the UK. Some of these migrants will be subject to immigration controls and to regulation through the immigration regime even though they have not entered as a worker; dependants and students, for example (King 2002). Others will be migrants not subject to immigration controls such as EU8 nationals. It is these groups, rather than those entering as migrant workers, who are most likely to be caught in poor employment conditions.

Low-waged migrants are increasingly inserted into more general debates about 'precarious workers' (Fantone 2007; Papadopoulos et al. 2008). This encompasses people working in temporary work, and with limited statutory entitlements including agency workers (Vosko et al. 2003). 'The concept of precariousness involves instability, lack of protection, insecurity and social or economic vulnerability... It is some combination of these factors which identifies precarious jobs, and the boundaries around the concept are inevitably to some extent arbitrary' (Rodgers and Rodgers 1989: 5). There have been refinements to the definitions involved in order to counter concerns about the fuzziness and the difficulty of turning this concept into workable instruments, as well as the variance of forms by sector and by country (Vosko et al. 2003; Dorre et al. 2006; Waite 2007). There is a danger that the term can become a catch-all, meaning everything and nothing at the same time, but unlike 'flexibility', it does capture notions of the flux and uncertainty for certain groups of workers (not only or even principally migrants) that are held by many to be an aspect of the 'new economy' (Herzenberg et al. 2000). Although the terms 'vulnerability' and 'vulnerable worker' are also used in the UK (Department of Trade and Industry 2006; TUC Commission on Vulnerable Employment 2008), the notion of precariousness captures both atypical and insecure employment and how this has implications beyond employment. An interest in precariousness has tended to go hand in hand with anxieties about the 'new age of insecurity' as depicted by theorists such as Beck (1992) and Sennett (1998). Chaotic and unpredictable working times can undermine other social identities. In this sense, precarious work results in *precarité*, a more general concern with precariousness of life which prevents people from anticipating the future (Barbier et al. 2002).

Precariousness brings to the fore these temporal aspects of work and its organization, and facilitates an analysis that is more sensitive to the temporalities of labour markets and of immigration and migratory processes and how these interact (Cwerner 2011; Fudge 2011). These temporal aspects are manifest both in migratory processes and in immigration controls. Together they have significant consequences for the nature and type of employment that migrants encounter. Certain stages of migration, when migration is viewed as a dynamic, temporal process, can be seen to mesh with the temporal requirements of certain types of labour markets (Anderson 2010a).

4.4 Precarious Work and Migratory Processes

Michael Piore (1979) argues that the imagined temporariness of new migrants' stay means that at the earlier stages of a migrant's immigration career, perhaps when he or she has lower subjective expectations, less language, and more limited understanding of the labour market, he or she is more likely to view work purely instrumentally. This perception of temporariness may be because the stay is envisaged as being for a limited period, but it may also be because people plan to move to better things, perhaps when their language skills have improved, and/or when they have better contacts or accommodation possibilities. Work which offers no opportunities for career progression may be perceived more opportunistically when the worker, whether student, migrant, or other, considers such work as a temporary position or an opportunity to get a foot on the ladder rather than a job for life (Curtis and Lucas 2001). Jobs that are not consistent with skills and experience, that offer little prospect of promotion, career development, or job satisfaction will be viewed very differently by those at a different life stage or who are subject to different constraints. Moreover, as mentioned in the previous section, jobs have a social meaning, and poor social status attached to particular types of jobs can be less of a disincentive for recent arrivals than it is for longer-term residents and citizens (Anderson et al. 2006). For recent migrants or those whose attachments are predominantly in the country of origin, low status can be compensated for by exchange rates, remittances, the status of working abroad, etc., or the person can simply lie about the kind of work that they do. Those on secondment from the local job centre are less likely to be excited and engaged with these sorts of opportunities than newly arrived migrants, and migrants consequently can be more attractive employees than the available British workforce (Anderson et al. 2006; Drinkwater 2007; Lucas and Mansfield 2008). For migrants, there may be additional non-pecuniary returns from work such as the possibility of learning English. There may also be more constraining reasons for taking up particular jobs: target earners may, for example, be concerned to repay debt incurred as a result of the migratory process. In this respect, precarious work may be work to which the temporary migrant as 'true economic man' (Piore 1979) is particularly suited.

EU8 nationals are a group where it is possible to examine migratory processes separately from immigration controls because, as EU nationals they are not subject to immigration controls. They are recognizably Piorean. They are nationals of eight of the ten new member states that joined the European Union in 2004. Eight of these were formerly part of the Eastern bloc (Hungary, Poland, Slovakia, Slovenia, Czech Republic, Estonia, Latvia, and Lithuania) and are collectively known in the migration literature as the

Accession 8 (A8), or more recently, the EU8.[6] The UK was one of only three states that permitted EU8 nationals access to the labour market with no transitional arrangements. It was anticipated that they would be a self-regulating flow of labour that would fill low-waged positions and return 'home' when no longer required, and Tier 3 of the PBS for low-skilled immigration was suspended from its inception on the basis that low-skilled vacancies could be filled by EU nationals (Home Office 2006b: para. 121). The only condition, imposed in 2004 and lifted in 2011, was that they register with the Workers Registration Scheme (WRS) for the first twelve months of their employment in the UK. However, while their relation to the labour market post-2004 was not structured through immigration arrangements, the fact that they were not UK citizens meant that their access to welfare benefits could be restricted. A new requirement of 'lawful residence' for access to welfare benefits was introduced specifically to prevent them from accessing social security for a period after entry (Currie 2008). Like the 'strangers' to the parish in the eighteenth and nineteenth centuries, they were able to move for work, but not to make a claim for support. Those unable to work, those who had not registered with the WRS or those who lost their job after less than a year, had no access to state support.[7]

Before 2004, there were already well-established communities of East and Central Europeans in the UK, particularly from Poland. Some of these were post-war EVWS migrants and their families, but others were more recent arrivals who had entered before 2004 to work in specific low-waged sectors, particularly the agricultural, construction, hotel, and au pair sectors. Their numbers significantly increased post-EU Enlargement, in part because this essentially served to regularalize the status of many who were residing in the UK illegally, but also because of large numbers of new arrivals. There were approximately 200,000 annual registrations with the WRS between 2004 and 2007, and those numbers exclude the self-employed, au pairs, and those who were required to register but did not (estimated to stand at between a quarter and a third of EU8 migrants). Numbers of arrivals began to decline with the recession, and stabilized in the range of 110–120,000 until 2010.

Labour migrants are usually in the prime of life, and WRS data suggests that the EU8 migration was no exception. It was overwhelmingly young: by 2009, 43 per cent of those who had registered with the WRS were aged eighteen to twenty-four years old, and 38 per cent were aged twenty-five to thirty-four (UK Border Agency 2009b: 10). Only 8 per cent had dependants living with them

---

[6] The other two states that joined the EU in 2004 were Cyprus and Malta, who did not have restrictions imposed on them. In 2007, Bulgaria and Romania also joined the EU, and they are known as the A/EU2. Their nationals are subject to transitional arrangements until 2014.

[7] In 2008, a survey conducted by the charity Homeless Link, found that approximately 25 per cent of rough sleepers in London were from East and Central Europe (Homeless Link 2008).

in the UK when they registered. There has been some debate about the proportion of EU8 nationals who came to settle rather than as temporary labour, and recent indications suggest that approximately half of those who entered the UK have since left (Pollard et al. 2008). WRS data, mostly gathered from relatively new arrivals, suggest that, whatever happened to their stay in practice, on arrival many were coming with a very temporary mindset (Jayaweera and Anderson 2008).

These Piorean workers, as well as being young were often well educated, and over-qualified for the jobs in which they worked, effectively 'high quality workers for low waged work' (Anderson et al. 2006). Of those registered between October 2006 and September 2007, 8.8 per cent were earning below the adult minimum wage of £5.35 an hour and 64.7 per cent were earning an hourly rate of between £5.35 and £5.99 (Jayaweera and Anderson, 2008).[8] The jobs they were working in were predominantly low skilled (UK Border Agency 2009b: 15), and 40 per cent of workers registered between January 2005 and March 2009 were working in the administration, business, and management sector, the majority of whom, as observed by the compilers in a footnote, 'work for recruitment agencies' (UK Border Agency 2009b: 12).

The effect of precarious work is, as it were, the flipside of the celebration of the 'work–life balance', when a person's economic productivity becomes the overwhelming priority. The consequences of precariousness and its implications for time use, the balancing between work, family (reproductive labour), and leisure, are gendered and experienced differently at different points in life. Migratory processes intertwine with the life course. Being young, EU8 migrants are rarely accompanied by dependants. For those with temporary mindsets, households can be simply temporary accommodation arrangements rather than social units, helping to explain their seeming greater tolerance of the unpredictable schedules that are characteristic of certain kinds of flexible working. They may be more geographically mobile which can in turn means greater availability for certain types of work. Doing precarious work, although associated with erratic or demanding time use, does not only have to be a consequence of circumscribed options, but may fit with the trajectory of the life course as a route away from an old past, or anticipating a different future. It may mark a specific life stage that is viewed as a discrete phase, and be viewed an apprenticeship to more a formalized labour market, as with student working.

Migratory processes help provide a source of labour (often over-qualified) that is prepared to tolerate low waged and insecure work, at least for a short

---

[8] These figures do not allow for the accommodation offset, an amount that can be taken off even the minimum wage if the worker's housing is provided by the employer, so they can serve as a benchmark only.

time. For certain jobs, this temporary but potentially intense commitment may be precisely what is required. Thus EU8 nationals often demonstrate 'non-enforced' temporariness: workers who, for a variety of reasons, are imagined as likely to be temporary, but without the possibility of this temporariness being enforced through immigration controls. This raises the question of what happens when the immediate apparent coincidence of interests between employer and worker dissolves (MacKenzie and Forde 2009). Appreciation of the impact of migratory processes should not result in an underestimation of the importance of discrimination, lack of recognition of qualifications and education, and other demand-side factors that can lead to many people being unable to move out of low-waged, low-status, and insecure jobs many years after they have obtained British citizenship (May et al. 2006).

The concentration of migrants (including legal residents who do not yet have permanent stay) in precarious work is in part an aspect of migratory processes, which are of course themselves functions of other kinds of processes, including employers' targeted recruitment. However, as people 'develop a more permanent attachment, their time horizon expands and in particular instability of employment is no longer a matter of indifference' (Piore 1979: 64). Employers can express this development in pseudo-cultural terms, claiming that as migrants stay longer in the UK, they become more 'British', more demanding and intractable (MacKenzie and Forde 2009). Employers who extol the virtues of migrants are thus often specifically thinking of recent arrivals (a nuance that is lost through the use of the definition 'foreign born'). Piore argues this development is related to the construction of and participation in community. However, it is also crucially related to legal status. European Union citizens comprise a Piorean case study, but importantly their temporariness is not state enforceable, and their time horizon may indeed expand. In contrast, the citizens of many non-EU member states are likely to find the development of 'permanent attachment' obstructed or downright prevented by immigration controls and citizenship legislation.

4.5 Immigration Controls as Legal and Social Constructs

Immigration controls reinforce some temporal aspects of migratory processes (the initial assumption of temporariness of some groups of migrants) and may undermine others (including a disposition to settlement). In most liberal democracies, length of stay has implications for rights-based claims (Cole 2000; Carens 2007), and certain groups can progress from temporary, to settled status, and thence to citizenship. Thus much of the international debate in recent times has focused on the possibility of reformulations of guest-worker schemes as states attempt to enforce temporariness and limit the length of stay of migrants in order to ensure that they do not develop the opportunity to make such claims (Ruhs and Martin 2008). These limitations do not only have consequences for citizenship. When migrant workers have a path to permanence, it is much easier to integrate them into labour law than when they viewed purely as temporary workers.[9] In this way, Piore's (1979) explanation of migrants' positions in secondary labour markets can be refined by relating differential labour market positions to the workings of immigration controls.

Immigration controls work with and against migratory processes to produce workers with particular types of relations to employers and to labour markets. The impact of illegality and its relation to 'exploitation' has received considerable attention (see Wright and McKay 2007 for a review), however illegality has tended to be theorized as *absence* of status (and therefore of limited access to state protection), rather than as immigration controls 'producing' illegality (De Genova 2002; Sciortino 2004). Such insights need to be developed into an examination of how immigration controls produce status more generally, in order to analyse the types of *legality* so produced, and the impact of these on migrants' positions in labour markets (Bauder 2006; Sharma 2006; Anderson and Ruhs 2010). The way in which immigration controls produce status can roughly be divided into three: the creation of categories of entrant, the influencing of employment relations, and the institutionalization of uncertainty.

4.5.1 *The Creation of Categories of Entrant*

Immigration controls are typically presented as a filter, allowing in the skilled, students, those with family ties, tourists, and other 'legitimate groups' like au pairs, while filtering out undesirables including criminals and those perceived to be without the skills to benefit the economy. In this rather narrow sense the role of immigration controls in constructing a labour force is broadly recognized. As discussed in Chapter 3, immigration laws and rules can require particular categories of entrant to have certain skills and experience and this is managed through the points based system. However, one does not have to be a Tier 1 or 2 applicant, or indeed to enter under the PBS at all, in order to participate legally in the labour market. Students, for instance, may work twenty hours in term time while some dependant visa holders have no restrictions on their labour market participation (often in contrast to the holder of the non-dependant visa). It is not only skills, earnings, and

---

[9] This point is not mine but came up in the course of a discussion at the conference Migrants at Work, Faculty of Law, University of Oxford, 22–23 June, 2012.

experience that shape categories of entrant however, but age, country of origin, and in some instances, marital status. An inherent bias against younger workers in a system that awards points on the basis of earnings and level of qualifications (both of which are likely to increase with age) is recognized for Tier 1 workers and those aged under twenty-eight are given twenty additional points.

Thus immigration controls are being used to shape and reinforce those aspects of migratory processes that mean that migrants are likely to have a younger age profile. They may also reinforce what Piore (1979) calls the 'plasticity' of the work force. Just because a visa category effectively 'permits' the applicant to be married or have children does not mean that the spouse or children are eligible to enter the UK, or to have recourse to public funds (including housing). This means that many migrants subject to immigration control may have dependants in their country of origin, but limited household commitments in the UK, making them more likely to work longer days and through weekends (Preibisch and Binford 2007). They can be imagined as 'free-floating labour', as fungible workers. The settlement process whereby migrants become embedded in social and other networks outside of work may further be artificially halted by immigration and citizenship requirements. Under the UK system, only Tiers 1 and some categories of Tier 2 can lead to permanent settlement.

4.5.2 The Moulding of Employment Relations

Immigration controls are not a neutral framework facilitating the sorting of individuals by intentions and identities into particular categories; rather, they *produce status,* and the type of visa obtained often has important and long-term effects on where migrants work in the labour market. Take, for example, the role of EU8 nationals in the construction industry. The importance of this group of migrants in this sector needs to be seen within the context of the prevalence of 'false self-employment' in construction. This status has resulted in widespread loss of employment rights, social rights, and has serious implications for health and safety in one of the country's most dangerous industries. It has also contributed to serious problems in the provision of training places by employers (Chan et al. 2010). However, it is not simply that migrants end up in construction because UK nationals avoid dangerous physical work. In the 1990s so-called Association Agreements allowed nationals from states that were going to join the EU to enter the UK as effectively 'own account self-employed' without the large capital sum required of other nationalities. Those who entered under such arrangements were not necessarily budding entrepreneurs—rather, self-employment was, for certain nationals, particularly men, one of the easiest ways to enter the UK and work legally. It is scarcely surprising that many of those holding self-employment visas gravitated to the construction sector, where this form of self-employment proliferated. Migration scholars such as Massey (1990) have demonstrated that networks of employment and immigration have their own dynamic over time, and once networks have become entrenched in particular sectors, they may continue to function even if the legislative framework shifts.

Immigration controls are not simply about conditions of entry across the border, but about conditions of stay. Once non-citizens have entered the UK (legally), they are subject to particular conditions depending on their visa status. Most non-citizens who are admitted to work have their access to the labour market limited in some way. Those entering as economic migrants can work for a recognized sponsor only, and must have a 'certificate of sponsorship' from their employer. An employer may withdraw the certificate of sponsorship at any time, and the Migrant will have to leave the UK within sixty days if they have not found another authorized sponsor (the certificate may be withdrawn immediately if the Home Office believes it was issued improperly).

Thus many workers subject to immigration control are effectively on fixed-term contracts that may be terminated at the employer's discretion, and the termination of these contracts has implications beyond the workplace. To this extent, migrants on work-related visas are dependent on the goodwill of their employer for their right to remain in the UK. In this respect, legal migrants subject to immigration control are also 'precarious workers'. The work permit/sponsorship system means that employers have powers of labour retention without jeopardizing their ability to fire (although hiring may indeed be more cumbersome). When asked why they employ migrants, employers have been found to frequently refer to *retention* as an advantage of migrant labour (Waldinger and Lichter 2003; Dench et al. 2006). Other perceived advantages, often racialized by employers, such as reliability, honesty, and work ethic must also be understood partly in terms of the level of dependence work permit holders have on their employers (Gordon and Lenhardt 2008). Moreover, while labour mobility tends to be thought of as a particular problem for the employers who require 'skilled' work, government restrictions on 'low-skilled' workers have received particular criticism because of their impact on retention. The National Farmers Union, for example, has been vocal in its opposition to the shrinking of the Seasonal Agricultural Workers Scheme (SAWS). Under this arrangement, visa holders can change employer, but only to another registered farm. Agricultural employers themselves acknowledge that there are practical difficulties with finding new employers in rural areas and often described SAWS workers as 'tied' by their permit.

> Migrant workers are an attractive source of labour to UK employers because of their work ethos, efficiency and dependency and because, particularly in the case of the SAWS, they provide a source of labour that is guaranteed to remain on farm during the crucial harvest period. (House of Lords 2008: 100)

Migrants who are not SAWS visa holders and citizens in contrast can 'easily move between jobs' or 'simply move on to other work' (Anderson et al. 2006).

Immigration controls produce a temporariness that, unlike the temporariness of EU nationals, can be enforced by the state through removal from UK territory. Not only do those subject to migration controls find their employment mobility limited by the state, but employers are handed additional means of control: should they have any reason to be displeased with the worker's performance, or indeed even have a personal grudge against them, not only the worker's job, but their residency, can be put in jeopardy. Compliant workers can feel unable to challenge employers, and in some instances, employers have taken advantage of immigration status as a means of exercising control over work permit holders including forbidding union membership. No claims can be made for the extent of such practices, but those on work permits may be conscious enough of this possibility to police themselves (Anderson and Rogaly 2005).

Immigration controls create dependence on employers, not just for work, but for continuing residence in the UK. The national framing of labour markets contributes to naturalizing these relations through reference to workers' alleged national predispositions, but also to making acceptable a relation that would not be acceptable for most citizens. Thus despite its importance, the social nature of the employment relation that is acknowledged in the prioritizing of nationals in the labour market, is in practice largely ignored.

4.5.3 *The Production of Institutionalized Uncertainty*

Immigration controls intervene in migratory processes and life stages to cut them into temporal chunks. This means that the process whereby migrants become embedded in social and other networks outside of work may be artificially slowed or halted by immigration and citizenship requirements. Immigration controls may be imagined as keeping migrants in an extended state of arrival, of waiting, thereby interrupting or suspending aspects of migratory processes whether of settlement, return, family reunion, or changing jobs. Enforced temporariness and uncertainty over visa renewals or family reunification, for example, can lead to a pressure to maximize the 'now'. Difficulty in planning the future fuels the urge to take advantage of earnings opportunities, however unappealing they may be. Without a time frame or anticipated future to work towards, people can struggle to cope, and find it difficult to make any progress or invest in themselves. Some migrants in precarious positions avoid serious relationships until their immigration status is secure, meaning that they remain unmarried far later than socially expected. In some cases this ambiguous position is described as not having become an adult, echoing studies that suggest that uncertainty postpones attainment of adulthood (Mills et al. 2005; Griffiths et al. 2012). Those who have overstayed or are otherwise 'illegal' are often at the far end of this spectrum (Ahmad 2008), but it is not confined to undocumented migrants, nor indeed to migrants. The idea of an overly powerful present and prolonged youth of young people with uncertain futures has been noted by others in non-migration contexts (Bindé 2000; Chowers 2002).

There are different ways in which immigration controls interact with migratory processes to create and extend precariousness. There has been considerable attention paid to the conditions of illegal workers, although little on how immigration controls produce illegality and less on how sponsorship arrangements and restrictions also create precariousness for those who are legally resident. Precariousness can be created by putting people in a position of temporariness and status anxiety that makes it difficult for them to plan ahead. Through immigration controls, the state plays a direct role in this uncertainty. This is both masked and exacerbated by bureaucratic viewpoints which tend to require black and white administrative categorization and evaluation of a person's immigration status at 'snapshot' moments in time, whilst also imagining the 'ideal' migrant to conform to a flowing sequence of events from arrival to settlement and naturalization as discussed in the next chapter.

In this way, workers who are subject to immigration controls may be more desirable to employers than those (migrants and citizens) who are not (Rosenhek 2003). Far from protecting the British labour force, it could be argued that under certain circumstances, immigration requirements actually create a set of employment relations that mean that migrant workers are preferable to British.

4.6 Conclusion

In general, migrants' concentration in poorly paid work is regarded as indicative of the desperation of migrants and their willingness to do jobs that British people turn down. Global inequalities, discrimination, poor language knowledge, illegality, and lack of recognition of qualifications all contribute to some migrants being prepared to take on jobs at wages and conditions that many UK nationals will not consider. This is the so-called 'three D's' argument, that migrants will do Dirty, Difficult, and Dangerous work that non-migrants will pass up. While sympathetic to migrants and often invoked by migrants' organizations and their supporters, it can come perilously close to endorsing employers' claims that British people have a poor 'work ethic' and chime with tabloid depictions of lazy welfare dependents. The person who turns down dirty, difficult, dangerous work is not the hard-working family man, striking outside the oil refinery, but the idle benefit scrounger who must be made to reject a culture of worklessness. There is a need to place the situation of migrants within a more nuanced analysis of the composition of the national labour market that acknowledges the constructive role of national policies, institutions, and regulatory structures and social processes (Ruhs and Anderson 2010a). This also requires an approach that thinks beyond immigration law and practice and integrates employment and welfare benefits into the analysis.

'British Jobs for British Workers' relies on an idea of the national labour market as having fixed characteristics with the possibility of returning to a former stability if only it were not for the disruption caused by migrant incomers. Yet the labour market is not static; labour supply, labour demand, employment type, employment relations, and indeed, what counts as work in the first place, are always changing. Labour markets continually adapt to and shape the demand and supply of labour (Bauder 2006; Anderson and Ruhs 2010). Migration is one among multiple factors that shape labour markets, and labour markets are one of multiple factors that contribute to shaping migration. The 'British labour market' is not a stable system, but constantly in flux, and segmented by gender, race, disability, and age, as well as by migration status.

What does this mean for the call of 'British Jobs for British Workers'? Firstly, it points to the impossibility of pinning down the undifferentiated British worker. As we have seen, many of those who are called 'migrant' in the public debate are British workers in law, even if not so regarded in practice. It also indicates the importance of defining 'migrant'. Definitions really do matter in understanding the role of migrants in segmented labour markets. Immigration controls are not neutral in these processes. In the same way as family law helps to produce family relations, rather than simply regulating pre-existing relationship forms, so immigration laws are not simply a neutral framework facilitating the sorting of individuals by intentions and identities into particular categories, but they are a means of *producing status*. When it comes to employment, immigration controls effectively subject workers to a high degree of regulation, giving employers mechanisms of control that they do not have over citizens. In practice, rather than a tap regulating the flow of workers to a state, immigration controls might be more usefully conceived of as a mould *constructing* certain types of workers through selection of legal entrants, and the requiring and enforcing of certain types of employment relations. Immigration law intersects with other legal regimes to produce certain types of legal subjects. Acknowledging the role of immigration controls in creating certain types of workers who may be more desirable to employers than national workers should facilitate a comparison with other categories of worker who are subject to specific controls such as those on welfare to work schemes or prison labour.

5

New Citizens: The Values of Belonging

Naturalization, or the processes of citizenship acquisition for non-citizens, makes visible the idealized intersection of migratory process and life course. Long-term migration to liberal democracies is typically imagined in policy and research as proceeding along a trajectory of entry, temporary stay, settlement, and citizenship. Naturalization is when migrants become citizens, the moment when the Migrant, no longer solely an 'economic migrant', an 'asylum seeker', a 'dependant', becomes integrated, a fully incorporated member of the national community. It is naturalization that enables what citizenship policy describes as 'full participation' through engagement in political, economic, and social relations. Thus citizenship is not simply a formal status, but it is typically presented as a good. It is membership and participation in a community of value. Naturalization procedures serve an important symbolic function both in delineating the boundaries of the national community, and in asserting that national community as a community of value. Migrants who are accepted as British citizens signify the kind of place that Britain is, and the fact that migrants are incorporated into the community is itself regarded as evidence of the country's value and values. In this way, naturalization reveals the permeability of the boundary between 'us' and 'them'. However, this inclusion is contingent, and formal citizenship does not neatly map on to membership in the community of value. In this way, naturalization also reveals the impermeability of the boundary between us and them, and the contingency of citizenship.

These are the tensions explored in this chapter which is concerned with the instability of citizenship, how it is related to the community of value, but also how it exists as a legal status that operates within a supranational system of states. It begins by considering the question of what citizenship is, briefly outlining some of its main characteristics in liberal theory, and the issues raised by migration. It then gives the context of British debates on citizenship from the 1990s to the present day, observing how immigration, settlement, and naturalization have moved from minor complications to a central focus of concern, and how this concern is mirrored in the developments of naturalization eligibility and requirements. I will argue that citizenship acquisition does not only actively promote a certain vision of Britain and Britishness as desirable, but it also has an important narrative arc, with citizenship as signifying stability and a state of undifferentiated equality. The chapter ends by discussing the importance of analysing citizenship as an integral part of the global state system, rather than solely focusing on individual relations to the states.

5.1 What is Citizenship?

Citizenship, subjecthood, and nationality overlap but need to be distinguished from one another. Importantly the particularities of histories of different states mean that the relation between citizenship, subjecthood, and nationality in legal and political practice varies by states, and 'citizenship' as a term has come to prominence relatively recently in the UK as compared to France, for example.

As discussed in Chapter 2, subjecthood designates allegiance, a personal link between a sovereign and a person. Nationality asserts belonging to a 'nation', an imagined community of people who are thought of as sharing a history, language, religion, 'culture', or some combination of these. This imagined community does not have to have a sovereign or a state. Subjects can swear fealty to the same sovereign, but they can identify as different nations. The English, Welsh, Scots, and Irish 'nations' were all British subjects before British subjecthood was (more or less) abolished, and people born in all these are (confusingly) considered British nationals. In fact, although in many states 'nationality' is more akin to ethnicity, while citizenship is the legal status of membership, unusually in the case of the UK 'British national' is interchangeable with 'British citizen'.

Citizenship designates a legal relation between an individual and a state: a person must be granted entry to the territory of the state of which he is a citizen and he cannot be deported from that state. Citizenship also indicates a political relation: a citizen is a stakeholder, or has a membership in the political community delineated by the (nation) state. In this way citizenship fuses the legal and the political. In Hobbes' classic formulation of the exchange of obedience for protection, a citizen submits to the rule of the state, and in so doing is guaranteed freedom from internal and external threats. But citizenship can also designate a relation between citizens that works *against* subordination to a sovereign or 'subjecthood'. Thus, 'The most revolutionary transformation of the French Revolution—indeed, of any revolution—was that from subject to citizen' (McPhee 2006: 26). The question of whether citizenship is about protection from the state or about obtaining the state's protection is theoretically resolved within a liberal polity by citizens being cast as both subject to the law and sovereign over it. Citizenship indicates the nature of relations between the individual and the collective, and between belonging and political community.

The liberal individual at the heart of liberal citizenship, although abstracted, has certain characteristics. He is a property owner and most fundamentally, he owns himself, his body, his person, and his labour. Laura Brace has argued that ideas of self-ownership are central to the property relation, and that 'Property as a moral space tied to integrity and self-government generates duties for others and connects the individual and the collective' (Brace 2004: 10). Property and citizenship are both forms of relations between individual selves. Like the property relationship, the citizenship relation is often imagined as a contract, a legal and moral relation, bound up with freedom and belonging, and when necessary enforced by the state through the rule of law. 'Belonging' is a property relationship, and both property and citizenship take self-ownership as a starting point and it is in this way that the liberal individual relates to others.

This starting point of self-ownership has different implications for women than for men. The disembodied self is removed from 'nature', but women 'cannot escape their bodies or leave them behind to enter the world of the industrious and the rational; they are not understood as independent beings in the sense of being able to control and govern themselves' (Brace 2004: 188). This does not mean that women are straightforwardly excluded from subjecthood or indeed from citizenship. Women may be subordinate but they are indispensable. They and their bodies are critical to the creating and the imagining of nations and communities. Nations need mothers, and citizens need wives. It is important too that these are the right kind of mothers and the right kind of wives, as it is in the home that the community of value is nurtured and reproduced.

Women's subordination was assumed and later codified in nationality laws. The 1870 Naturalisation Act was concerned to enable the renunciation of subjecthood and the abolition of indelible allegiance because 'it conflicted with liberalism and individualism, the freedom of action which is now recognised as the most conducive to the general good as well as individual happiness and prosperity' (Report by the Royal Commission on the Laws of Naturalisation and Allegiance 1868, cited in Dummett and Nicol 1990: 89). This marked a shift whereby allegiance was no longer perpetual and only decided by birth. However, the principles of liberalism and individualism were to be applied only to men and only men were given control over their allegiance. After the 1870 Act, a woman who married an alien automatically lost her British nationality, and if she married a British man who renounced his nationality, she had no option to retain hers. While wives were given the right to own and sell property separately from their husbands by the 1882 Married Women's Property Act, they were not to be able to retain British nationality independently of their husbands until 1948.

Citizenship generally continues to be imagined and represented as a good, but aside from this and the centrality of the individual, there is no single liberal citizenship tradition. The emphasis that is given to individualism, the polity, and the social varies, and while some liberals regard active citizenship as central to the good life, others regard it as instrumental for the realization of certain individual and collective goods. Liberal individualists focus on the political community as a means of maximizing individual welfare, with the state mediating between individual conflicts of interest and the collective good. All persons are free to pursue their definition of the good, and the state must intervene minimally, but is needed to protect property and individual rights. In contrast, communitarianism emphasizes the collective 'community' as constitutive of what it is to be a human being. The community is not only constituted by law and can be imagined as pre-dating the political. This shared community relation and common history confers identity on atomized individuals and authority on the state and forms the basis of citizenship. Republican models also seek to encompass the collective, but have given more emphasis to civic engagement, arguing that political participation and deliberative democracy as well as the rule of law are necessary to preserve liberty. There is a need for protection from the state, but also from unadulterated individualism and from domination by special interests (Pattie et al. 2004: 11).

Through rationality, self-mastery, and the virtues of property owning industry, the Citizen, is civilized, to be distinguished from those lacking the resources to be responsible citizens. The liberal individual is reasonable and capable of perceiving his own self-interest and of respecting the rights of others—that is, he has a certain moral disposition and is thereby able to enter into relations of equality with other self-owning liberal selves. However, the centrality of self-ownership to citizenship has meant that those legally or socially constructed as vulnerable or dependent often could not be citizens. At various times and places certain types of people such as racialized others, women, slaves, children, beggars, those who were not able bodied or of 'unsound mind', were not legally recognized as having a right to their own person. Those who were not recognized as self-owners were often held to be *naturally* unfit for citizenship. They could not (and some cannot) contract, inherit, choose or not to labour (Welke 2010). Such people were subject to a differentiated inclusion, a partial and often mediated membership, through husbands, fathers, and masters. The relation between liberal citizens and those not suitable for citizenship were relations of domination and subordination, and these relations were highly varied. At certain times and under certain regimes, both master's wife and slave were not legally recognized as full persons, yet a wife was not the same as a slave (see Chapter 8). The law lends weight to certain characteristics, giving them significance and consequence and thereby helping to create identity (Welke 2010: 8).

The development of citizenship in liberal democracies has generally been viewed in a cumulative and linear way as a history of the expansion of rights and membership to previously excluded groups. T.H. Marshall famously traced the development of citizenship in Britain as moving from the establishment of civil rights, to political rights, to social rights. These rights were gradually extended to non-property owning men, to women, and in limited way, to children. The Marshallian tale of progress, where, through citizenship, recognition and equality are gradually expanded to incorporate new social groups, has now, it seems, reached its end. The unfolding of citizens' rights cannot be extended beyond nation state boundaries, and the contemporary challenge is generally seen as not about increasing the purview of citizenship, but enriching it—how to deepen rather than widen citizenship.

The relations of universalism and equality that are held to characterize contemporary citizenship in liberal democracies are typically imagined as enacted within bounded national societies (Bosniak 2006). Indeed, citizenship rights and boundedness are inextricably bound up together. The lengthy presence of non-citizens on state territory has become recognized as a challenge to states and citizenship in law theory and practice (Carens 2002), and it raises the question of how the claims of citizenship as signifying equality and resistance to subordination can be reconciled with its designation of 'outsiders'. Non-citizens are subject to the law, but they are typically not sovereign over it (Cole 2010), and in this way they bear comparison to past groups who were not granted rights of legal personhood. While a core value of citizenship is the moral equality of citizens, liberalism espouses recognition of equality of rights of *persons*. What happens to political theories of rights when faced with people who do not all stay in their states claiming their citizens' rights, or participating as active citizens? What happens in particular to people who must struggle to have their personhood recognized in the first place, who do not, as Charles Mills puts it, start from the Cartesian *cogito ergo sum,* which is the luxury of abstraction, but who are all too aware that they exist because their existence is manifest in their subordination to others (Mills 1998)? This is particularly pertinent given that this reality is linked to differences in the content of the relation between state and citizens across the world: citizens of some states have access to far greater protections and welfare than citizens of others, and as discussed in Chapter 2 this is not just a question of bad luck, but frequently related to economic and political inequalities between different states that have particular historical roots. Migrants draw attention to exclusion and boundaries and when it comes to immigration, 'citizenship stands not for universalism but for closure' (Bosniak 2006: 31).

The position of the Migrant also exposes the distinction between formal citizenship, that is, citizenship as legal status, and 'substantive citizenship' or the rich content of citizenship, its sets of duties, rights, and activities. Formal citizenship, like subjecthood and like nationality is mainly allocated through 'accident of birth' (Shachar 2009; Stevens 2011). This may be constituted by birth on the territory, *ius soli*, or by birth to a national, *ius sanguinis*. *Ius soli* does not eliminate inconsistencies. There is the matter of what constitutes territory for the purpose of subjecthood, which became a challenge for Britain as an imperial power, particularly as not all who were born on 'British' territory were suitable subjects (Dummett and Nicol 1990). For the purposes of *ius sanguinis* the relationship between nationality, in the sense of ethnicity, and formal citizenship becomes critical, as does whether citizenship passes through a mother or father and the nature of the relation between the parents. *Ius sanguinis* foregrounds the membership of women, which as has for centuries been more contingent than the membership of men.[1] Migrants too provide evidence for this lack of fixity. In some states people can only become fully privileged members through birth, but in most liberal democracies it is possible for some to 'naturalize' and acquire membership of the national political community. Naturalization is the process through which individuals can become citizens, given the same status as those who are 'natural-born' citizens (or subjects), hence the term. In this way a key characteristic of citizenship is that it is a unitary status with no distinction between the natural-born and the naturalized.

It is also possible in many states to acquire some kind of status between citizenship and non-citizenship; what has in the past been termed 'denizenship'. People with settlement status might be considered the contemporary equivalent of denizens. In the UK, currently those with this status are not subject to immigration control, are legally protected from discrimination, and have equal access to welfare and employment rights, but they do not have 'right of abode', and it is possible for them to be deported. This kind of status complicates the Citizen/non-citizen binary as many of the advantages that are often associated with citizenship, such as equal access to welfare benefits and the possibility of sponsoring family members, are also available to those with settled status. Sawyer (2010) argues that the possibilities of settlement as well as citizenship indicate that there has in the past been

---

[1] This has not always been so, and under common law there seems to have been no separate provision for married women to change their allegiance in line with their husbands. For women the trajectory of subjecthood, and from subjecthood to citizenship, has not necessarily been progressive.

space for 'good enough belonging' outside formal citizenship. Considerable ambiguity about the nature of Britishness, what it is, and its relation to nationality and subjecthood, in the past left some space for informal inclusivity on the grounds that 'it has not been necessary to formally be part of the fabric of society for practical day-to-day purposes, since that depended mostly on actual, rather than even explicitly lawful residence' (Sawyer 2010: 7).

Unpacking the requirements placed on those who want to naturalize indicates the delineations of the community of value, for the Migrant is expected to be a good citizen and comply with the idealized citizen. It has been argued that formal and substantive citizenship should be kept apart for analytical purposes, and that the issues raised by citizenship acquisition are purely legal. Phillip Cole among others has argued in contrast that 'the question of the legal acquisition of citizenship is a central and theoretically complex area for political theory' (Cole 2010: 3). Ways in which non-citizens can become citizens, or acquire citizenship are not simply legal details and technicalities, but indicate and shape the foundations of how membership is imagined (Honig 2003; Cole 2010). The ways in which individuals become citizens, and who is able to become a citizen, reveal ideals of citizenship, membership and statehood in specific states, and how the nation/state community is imagined. In this way, formal and substantive citizenship are inextricably linked and we can see citizenship's moral space, a space that extends beyond the Migrant to encompass migrant and citizen alike.

5.2 British Citizenship: The Context of Debates

The relation of England to the territories now known as Scotland, Wales, and Ireland, and what this meant for the allegiance of people to the English Crown has been much the subject of considerable struggle, and has not reached a stable resolution. In Chapter 2, I discussed the relation between Empire and British subjecthood, and how and why naturalization was of particular concern to the dominions. The standardization of imperial naturalization had been the subject of an imperial conference in 1911, but the 1914 British Nationality and Status of Aliens Act did not succeed in standardizing naturalization. It did however establish basic requirements for naturalization: a person had to be of 'sound mind', 'good character', to have an 'adequate' knowledge of the English language, and be subject to a residential qualifying requirement.

After the 1948 British Nationality Bill, a person was no longer naturalized into the status of subjecthood but citizenship of the UK and colonies. This was a response to Canada, and, it was anticipated, other dominions creating their own citizenship which signalled the need for a framework under which dominions could legislate for their own citizenships as the primary status. Their citizens would not lose the status of British subjecthood, and as UKCCs, British colonies would share the status of citizenship of the United Kingdom and colonies with the United Kingdom as 'Commonwealth Citizens'. There was some dispute about the term 'citizenship', but 'The dominions are insisting that we shall not be in a different position from them. They create their citizens' (Lord Chancellor, Parliamentary Debates House of Lords Vol. 155. Cols. 784–5, cited in Dummett and Nicol 1990: 138). In contrast to France, this new status of citizen did not mark the overthrowing of subjecthood in favour of the democratic self-government of the citizenry. In the UK, subjecthood was and is regarded as perfectly compatible with citizenship: 'There is no contradiction in promoting citizenship so that people uphold common values and understand how they can play their part in our society while upholding our status as subjects of HM The Queen' (Home Office 2002b: para. 2.1). From the outset, citizenship has been a contested term in the UK, where public debate is far more comfortable with and focused on 'Britishness'.

Current policy on naturalization must be situated within the context of more than a decade of policies and reviews on citizenship more generally. Although this was a feature of New Labour governance, concern about the state of British citizenship pre-dates this. In 1990, under a Conservative administration, the Commission on Citizenship published *Encouraging Citizenship*, to define, review, and develop 'active citizenship', and the report's recommendations included the granting of 'civics training' in schools (Murdoch 1991). The phrase has however been strongly associated with the incoming New Labour government in 1997 which emphasized 'active citizenship', an attempt to transform citizens from what was perceived as 'passive recipients of public services' to actively engaged participants in public life (Mayo and Rooke 2006). Citizenship was increasingly cast as about rights *and* responsibilities. The virtues of responsibility, self-sufficiency, and independence, and the role of work in achieving self-realization were emphasized in multiple policies but most clearly in increasing welfare conditionality. This was presented within a framework of social justice: work was the solution to poverty. The Citizen's duty to work arose out of concern both for her own good and for the good of the community.

In 1997, then Secretary of State for Education, David Blunkett, set up the Advisory Group on Citizenship to examine education in citizenship and democracy in schools under the chairmanship of Sir Bernard Crick. In 1998, it published a policy review of citizenship education in England, and in September 2002, following its recommendation, citizenship education was introduced as a statutory subject in English secondary schools. Citizenship may be acquired by birth but it is also a faculty to be learned.

Citizenship in both the 1990 Commission and the Crick Report had strong elements of communitarianism. It was argued that although formal citizenship had been extended to a wide range of social groups in Britain this did not mean that they were participating in public life—that is, formal citizenship was not congruent with 'full participation', or good citizenship. This fracture, between formal citizenship and good citizenship, is precisely what naturalization processes seek to bridge, not least through the good character requirement of contemporary procedures. Yet the interest in the symbolic role of naturalization seems to be relatively recent and neither the Commission on Citizenship nor the Crick Report engaged with naturalization or immigration (Murdoch 1991: 440).

In June 2001, David Blunkett moved from the Department of Education and became the Home Secretary. Less than a month later there were a series of disturbances in towns in northern England. These became known as the Bradford 'riots' and were presented as having markedly racial dimensions. In response, Blunkett set up the Community Cohesion Review Team to identify views and practices to promote social cohesion and draw lessons for national policy and practice. Its report, under the chairmanship of Ted Cantle, found a lack of shared values and a: 'Depth of polarization in our towns and cities ... Separate educational arrangements, community and voluntary bodies, employment, places of worship, language, social and cultural networks, mean that many communities operate on the basis of a series of parallel lives' (Cantle 2001: para. 2.1).

The Cantle Report urged the promotion of 'a greater sense of citizenship'. This call had been a feature of the political landscape for some years, but the perceived racial dimension to the riots, and in particular the findings of so-called parallel lives among 'second-generation' Asian communities led to a concern with long-term migrant 'integration'. This was highly racialized—there was no mention of whether or not the white participants in the disturbances were second-generation children of white migrants. 'Second-generation migrants' exemplified the gap between membership and engagement in public life that had been indicated in the Crick Report. They were an instance of a group that might have formal citizenship, but was marginalized and not integrated. Yet, as Back et al. wrote, 'The young men of Burnley, Bradford and Oldham who took to the streets in the summer of 2001 had grievances that had nothing to do with "assimilation". Indeed, they are all too well assimilated into a society divided by racism and discrimination' (Back et al. 2002: para. 5.4).

The combination of New Labour communitarianism (with its bent towards the pre-political community and nationalism), and anxiety about race resulted in a new focus on naturalization procedures to 'rebuild a sense of common citizenship, which embraces the different and diverse experiences of today's Britain' (Home Office 2002b: 12). As well as several recommendations regarding the integration of second-generation migrants, the report recommended the promotion of English-language acquisition and an oath of national allegiance from naturalizing citizens. In this way, naturalization procedures, social cohesion, and more general concern with active citizenship and citizenship education were brought together and became ever more tightly linked, particularly following the London bombings in July 2005. In 2006, the Prime Minister declared a duty to integrate on the part of 'all our citizens'. The use of the possessive 'our' here is interesting, suggesting a self-conscious emphasis on the inclusivity of British citizenship at the same time as indicating that some people are failing to measure up: 'integrating at the point of shared common unifying values . . . isn't about what defines us as people, but as citizens, the rights and duties that go with being a member of our society' (Blair, 8 December 2006, quoted in Zedner 2010: 383).

In 2007, then-Prime Minister Gordon Brown requested a review of British citizenship to clarify the legal rights and responsibilities of different categories of citizenship and nationality, and the incentives for residents to become citizens. The *Lord Goldsmith Citizenship Review* was also requested to 'explore the role of citizens and residents in civic society, including voting, jury service and other forms of civil participation'. The report's recommendations included the introduction of primary civic education, as first suggested in 1990, and the proposal for a national day to celebrate Britishness. However, in contrast to the Commission on Citizenship report of 1990, it emphasized naturalization and formal legal status. No longer were 'migrants' confined to an appendix, but they had moved to centre stage in debates about what it meant to be British.

In sum, changes to naturalization eligibility and procedures took place within a broader debate about political engagement, Britishness, and national identity. The debate instigated by New Labour suggested that citizens were not participating in society, and that formal citizenship had become leached of substance. This was reflected in naturalization procedures which had been reduced to a box-ticking, bureaucratic exercise. It was in this context that citizenship acquisition was seen as needing a wholly new approach.

5.3 British Citizenship and Naturalization

For more than two decades, British citizenship and associated naturalization procedures were based on the 1981 British Nationality Act. This Act had marked the downgrading of relations with former colonies (former 'British subjects'), and the abandonment of *ius soli*. There were elements of continuity in naturalization processes: naturalization was not a right and continued to be at the discretion of the Secretary of State, and there was no right of appeal against refusal. Requirements to be of sound mind and good character (that is, to be rational and to have the right moral purpose), were carried over into the 1981 Act, as were the language and the residential requirements. The precise length of stay required varied according to immigration status, but it generally included being free from immigration restrictions for twelve months. The Act also formally separated naturalization from immigration controls.

The residential requirement apparently relates the formalities of naturalization to the informal relations of belonging and could be read as an attempt to accommodate the moral equality of persons within a citizenship model. As with any legal process there is an inevitable arbitrariness over the length of time that constitutes sufficient legal residence. The residential requirement is what links immigration to citizenship, and it is this that enables immigration controls to do the dirty work of citizenship. The separation of immigration from citizenship legislation has obscured the ways in which immigration controls have always acted as a constraint on naturalization through their control of temporality. Whether or not a visa is renewable, the length of time that a migrant is legally permitted to stay, and whether it is possible to switch status, determine if a non-citizen is able to stay for long enough to fulfil the residential requirement. In this way 'low-skilled' workers, divorcees, and others not suitable for the community of value can be excluded on apparently technical grounds that are ostensibly not to do with citizenship and naturalization but immigration matters. Those so excluded were and continue to be generally people whose labour was considered unskilled, or not labour at all. Certain categories of temporary visitor and worker, and the grey area between the two, au pairs, working holidaymaker, volunteer, etc., were thereby excluded from citizenship by default.

Citizenship under the 1981 Act was not as stable as it seemed, but changes in access were generally subsumed under immigration rather than nationality matters. This was to change in the early 2000s as the government introduced significant changes to the processes of citizenship and settlement. There was a move to incorporate aspects of subjective identity and social relations into the process of attaining the legal status of citizenship, emphasizing the *becoming* a citizen over the *acquiring* of citizenship. The shift began in 2002 with the publication of the white paper *Secure Borders, Safe Haven*. Although this is a White Paper explicitly concerned with immigration and naturalization, interestingly, produced after Crick and Cantle published their reviews, it makes mention of the white working class, who are incorporated with the inclusive 'our' and compared with racialized minorities:

> Too many of our citizens are excluded from meaningful participation in society. This is true of those in white working class communities whose alienation from

the political process, along with their physical living conditions and standards of living, leaves them feeling excluded from the increased wealth and improved quality of life which they see around them. In the same way, those who have entered this country and joined friends, family or ethnic groupings may find themselves experiencing relative economic disadvantage and sometimes overt racism. (Home Office 2002b: 10)

The document included a chapter on citizenship and nationality which asserted the need to move beyond citizenship indicating only 'the convenience of obtaining a British passport' (Home Office 2002b: para. 2.12). Citizenship is described as being about upholding 'common values' and playing a part in society, and 'should bring with it a heightened commitment to full participation in British society and a recognition of the part which new citizens can play in contributing to social cohesion' (Home Office 2002b: para. 2.6). This lay behind the moves to incorporate ideas of identity and belonging into the legal processes of naturalization. Demonstrating 'belonging' was no longer largely a matter of the length of time a person had (legally) been resident in the UK. Naturalization procedures became the grounds for asking and answering the questions like, what is Britishness and what are British values? Unlike the straightforward question, 'how long have you legally resided in the UK?' these sorts of value-laden questions do not have settled answers and this allows for new spaces of contestation to open up. The subheading of *Secure Borders, Safe Haven*, '*Integration with Diversity in Modern Britain*' indicates the intention to answer these within a multicultural framework:

> The government welcomes the richness of the cultural diversity which immigrants have brought to the UK – our society is multi-cultural, and is shaped by its diverse peoples. We want British citizenship positively to embrace the diversity of background, culture and faiths that is one of the hallmarks of Britain in the 21st Century. (Home Office 2002b: para. 2.2)

As noted above, the 1914 requirement that applicants have an adequate knowledge of English had been carried over into the 1981 Act, but this had not been particularly strictly enforced, and if the form was filled in correctly this was deemed to demonstrate 'adequate knowledge'. The new proposals were to introduce a test for language and the understanding of British society. The change from a bureaucratic tick-box approach was also to be marked by the introduction of a citizenship ceremony including a citizenship pledge of allegiance to the monarch. Alongside this were changes to the procedures of citizenship deprivation—seen as a corollary of attaching renewed importance to citizenship acquisition.

In 2002, the Nationality, Immigration and Asylum Act followed through on these proposals and introduced the requirement that citizenship applicants had 'sufficient knowledge of life in the UK'. It also strengthened the language requirement for naturalization (Ryan 2010). A language test in English, Welsh, or Scottish Gaelic, was to be introduced. The inclusion of Welsh and Gaelic is arguably principally symbolic, important in the light of the emphasis given to the multinational nature of the UK in citizenship education material. As of 2010, nobody had applied to take the tests in Welsh or Scottish Gaelic (Ryan 2010). Notably, the 2002 White Paper referred to the importance of 'the ability to speak our common language', presumably referring to English rather than the other two languages. The use of a test is in itself also a symbolic requirement. A test is its own language, not only does it require literacy, but a submission to abstraction, measurement, and uniformity, in short, the language of reason, universality, and measurement. Those who have less education, and come from poorer, non-English speaking countries, are likely to find the test more challenging than those who are well-educated and wealthy.

The Life in the United Kingdom Advisory Group, chaired by Sir Bernard Crick, was appointed to advise on suitable standards of language and knowledge of British society, and it explicitly situated its work within a much broader policy remit, including 'a wider citizenship agenda', community cohesion, and raising the status of British citizenship (Home Office 2003). Their specific recommendations, that applicants either pass a 'citizenship test' or complete an English language with citizenship course, were implemented in 2005. In 2004, the Advisory Board on Naturalisation and Integration (ABNI) was established, again chaired by Crick, to provide independent advice on citizenship and integration and more particularly, to develop proposals for language and citizenship courses and tests for applicants to British citizenship. These requirements have been gradually extended. Since 2006, language requirements have been applied to people who are seeking to enter the UK under certain immigration categories (workers and, in 2010, partners). From 2007, settlement applicants also had to pass a language and test of their knowledge of life in the UK (Ryan 2010).

Legislation passed in 2009 introduced further fundamental changes to obtaining citizenship. In particular it broke the link between length of residence and right to settlement and naturalization, and a new status of 'probationary citizen' was introduced. This was not a secure residence status, and although using the terminology of 'citizenship', it brought no citizenship rights. However, a change in government meant a pause in implementing most of these changes and the elimination of the previous government's proposal to encourage migrant volunteering or 'active citizenship'. These were deemed 'too complicated, bureaucratic, and in the end ineffective' (May 2010). This retreat from one of the more communitarian aspects of the previous government's proposals suggests that the relation between naturalization and the encouragement of good citizenship of those who are citizens at birth is less prominent under the current administration. The coalition Government continues to highlight problems of participation, but the concept of the 'Big Society' is more focused on the incorporation of the 'Broken Britain' white underclass than new immigrants.

Both the Labour and coalition administrations have been increasingly preoccupied by settlement. As we have seen, settlement and citizenship are related in that one must have settlement (be free from immigration restrictions) in order to be eligible for citizenship, and changes in the rules for settlement therefore have consequences for naturalization. Restrictions on settlement had already been tightened by extending the period of temporary residence necessary before economic migrants could apply for settlement from four to five years in 2006 (the requirements are three years for a spouse or civil partner), but nevertheless, Conservative Home Secretary Teresa May stated that it is 'too easy at the moment to move from temporary residence to permanent settlement' (May 2010). In 2011, a consultation was launched having as one of its themes 'allowing only the brightest and the best to stay permanently' (Home Office 2011a: 12). Those people with upwards of £2 million to invest in the United Kingdom were to have their paths to settlement shortened by limiting their required period of temporary residence to two and three years. The very small numbers whose settlement was facilitated in this way were more than outnumbered by those affected by a more general removal of settlement rights, a move which turned the vast majority of non-family migrants into temporary migrants. This has a direct policy benefit for a government concerned to limit net migration, as in theory at least it means increasing the numbers of temporary residents and increasing the pressure on those non-EEA nationals who enter to also leave. It makes it far more difficult to turn informal belonging into formal membership. This means that the space for 'good enough' belonging without formal citizenship is increasingly narrowed and that the difference in rights between citizens and non-citizens is widened.

5.4 British Values

Citizenship acquisition, as Honig discusses, demonstrates the 'choiceworthiness' (her term) of citizenship and the ideals of citizenship (Honig 2003). 'British values' are reified through naturalization processes and the rhetoric associated with them, but what are they? And what is 'life in the UK' from the Shetland Isles to Salford? Or shared between the mansions of Holland Park and the council estates of neighbouring Shepherd's Bush? What, precisely, is meant by the formal requirements of good character and knowledge of life in the UK?

There is no definition of 'good character' in nationality law, and interpretation of this requirement became increasingly harsh as the rhetoric about British values became more strident. A good character is required of all those aged over ten-years-old, and if an applicant is the parent of a child who was convicted of an offence or subject to an Anti-Social Behaviour Order (ASBO), this might justify refusal on the grounds that the applicant was 'negligent in ensuring their good behaviour' (Home Office 2010b: 9). The 'good character' requirement accounts for an increasing number of rejections of naturalization applications, accounting for 28.5 per cent of all refusals in 2010, and showing a steady increase, from 11.5 per cent in 2002 (Home Office 2011e: table cz.09). In contrast, the refusal on the basis of delay in replying to enquiries was 18.3 per cent in 2002, and 10 per cent in 2010, again the change being steady (Home Office 2011e: table cz.09). The good character requirement is described as demonstrating 'respect for rights and freedoms of the UK, [having] observed its laws and fulfilled your duties and obligations as a resident' (Home Office 2010a: 15). To fulfil this requirement, citizenship applicants are expected to not have any unspent criminal convictions, and to not have served a prison sentence of more than thirty months; they must not be an undischarged bankrupt; and they must have paid tax and national insurance contributions if they have been employed or self-employed. These run alongside the requirements not to be involved in terrorism, crimes against humanity, war crimes, or genocide. Thus the genocidal dictator and the person who has made an error in their tax form, may both fail on grounds of good character.

Adequate knowledge of life in the UK is assessed on the basis of knowledge of the Home Office produced handbook *Life in the United Kingdom: a journey to citizenship* (Home Office 2006a). This was originally prepared for information purposes, but when test requirements were introduced and the 2002 legislation was implemented the test came to be based exclusively on the handbook (Ryan 2010). It comprises nine short chapters, the first historical, followed by three chapters on the nature of the UK ('A changing society', a profile of the population, and how the UK is governed), four on more practical information ('Everyday needs', 'Employment', 'Knowing the Law', and 'Sources of help and information') and the last, arguably aspirational, 'Building Better Communities', outlining cohesive communities, good citizens, and the responsibilities of British citizenship. The handbook purports to describe what it is that non-citizens need to know about the UK in order to attain British citizenship, and in this respect may be seen as at least a partial description of what constitutes the Britishness to which naturalized citizens are being admitted.

When specified, it seems that British values are surprisingly universal, or at least might reasonably be held by liberals regardless of nationality. In the section headed 'The rights and duties of a citizen', for example, readers are informed, 'All good citizens are expected to help the police prevent and detect crimes whenever they can' (Home Office 2006a: 88). Freedom of speech, respect for the rule of law and democracy, and particularly the Universal Declaration of Human Rights are the main requirements. However, one element that is particularly emphasized in the rhetoric about citizenship and Britishness is diversity and multiculturalism (Rattansi 2002). As the *Life in the United Kingdom* booklet puts it: 'The UK has been a multi-national and multi-cultural society for a long time, without this being a threat to its British identity, or its English, Scottish, Welsh or Irish cultural and national identities' (Home Office 2006a: 25). The history of England's accommodation of Scottish, Welsh, and Irish claims within the polity has had a profound impact on the ways in which pluralism has developed as a means of shoring up power within the establishment and within different 'communities', however defined (Feldman 2011). As we have seen in the 2002 White Paper, for all the mentions of the Celtic fringe, this diversity is contemporaneously principally associated with migration. Its ahistorical, empire-free presentation means that as well as indicating diversity, migration also stands as proof positive of the 'choiceworthiness' of the United Kingdom as a place to live. It demonstrates that Britain is a 'stable and attractive place in which to settle' (Home Office 2002b: 4).

Migration is typically presented as both a threat to and constitutive of British citizenship, and citizenship policy allows for the assertion of British values simultaneously as stable, and as under threat. As discussed in Chapter 2, it has often been argued, by government and others, that far from immigration controls serving to institutionalize racism, they are in fact necessary to avert racism. David Blunkett's foreword to *Secure Borders, Safe Haven* asserted the need to control the movement of foreigners in order to limit 'hate, intolerance and prejudice' (Home Office 2002b: 3). This is echoed in multiple Home Office forewords and introductions to immigration and citizenship White Papers and legislation. The watchword is 'tolerance': 'we' are proud to be a 'tolerant' society. Tolerance is, as Wendy Brown has discussed, a civilizational discourse and is associated with western liberalism, posing as universal, but in fact designating the difference between the civilized and the barbaric (Brown 2006). Tolerance plays two roles here: the incorporation of migrants, particularly those from a 'different culture', into British citizenship is held up as proof that Britain is tolerant. But tolerance is also demanded of migrants and especially of naturalizing citizens. Tolerance is simultaneously a requirement for inclusion and grounds for exclusion; it is both a self-conscious welcome and a veiled threat.

The presentation of tolerance as a distinctively British value is important in squaring the circle of how to inculcate common values while continuing to assert respect for diversity and to encourage individualism and self-sufficiency. Tolerance is a mark of self-mastery. The Citizen chooses what she thinks and exercises rationality over emotion, tolerating even what she finds deeply distasteful. The exercise of tolerance indicates reason, and the power to abstract from one's own 'culture'. Tolerance is the virtue held by rational self-owners, and working-class people and other people who are 'degenerately white' are often represented as not as tolerant as the middle classes. What is not tolerable is racism and sexism ('it will sometimes be necessary to confront some cultural practices which conflict with these basic values—such as those which deny women the right to participate as equal citizens' (Home Office 2002b: para. 2.3). While tolerance is part of the British identity, it is unstable, easily undermined, and under threat because of global conditions. As migrants move to citizenship and embrace tolerance and are tolerated, they have an investment in the control of immigration, which facilitates their tolerated status. As well as being tolerant, naturalizing citizens are also encouraged to 'participate' in society. It is in participation as well as shared values that the Migrant comes together with the Citizen. What constitutes participation is typically exemplified by voting and joining political parties (although presumably not those political parties that advocate 'intolerance'), working in schools and jury service and volunteering.

Britain is not solely populated by tolerant volunteers, well acquainted with life in the UK. The first edition of the handbook *Life in the United Kingdom*, although prepared by well-educated and informed citizens, made the mistaken assertion that 'usually, "Britain" refers to the mainland and "Great Britain" includes Northern Ireland' (Stationary Office 2004: 17, cited in Ryan 2010: 20).[2] In order to acquire the rights of formal citizens, those who want to naturalize have to demonstrate 'super citizenship' in a way that citizens by birth do not because naturalization is about the idealization of national citizenship. It is in this sense aspirational, indicative of the Good Citizen rather than the typical citizen, and migrants must gain entry to the community of value and not simply the state. In the debate around the 2009 citizenship proposals, then-Immigration minister Phil Woolas was clear about this. When questioned about the proposal to reject naturalization applicants who demonstrated 'an active disregard for British values', he had refused to rule out the possibility that protesting about British intervention in Afghanistan and Iraq might be treated as such a disregard: 'As a point of principle...if you don't break the law and you are a citizen, that's fine. But if someone is applying to be a citizen to our country we do think that you should not only obey the law but show you are committed to our country' (Travis 2009).

---

[2] 'Great Britain' comprises England, Scotland, and Wales. The United Kingdom comprises Great Britain plus Northern Ireland (but not the Isle of Man and the Channel Islands).

5.5 Citizenship and Equality

One of the values that all prospective citizens must lay claim to is equality of the citizenry, and the 2002 White Paper was clear about 'our commitment to the equal worth and dignity of all our citizens' (Home Office 2002b: para. 2.3). The *Life in the United Kingdom* handbook recognizes that there continues to be discrimination between citizens, but this is very much presented as an unfortunate anachronism. Yet there is a growing inequality in addition to the acknowledged stratifications of gender, class, race, sexuality, disability, etc. Citizenship is increasingly stratified according to those who have attained it by birth, and those who have attained it by naturalization. Citizenship as formal legal status is premised on equality before the law, but as we have seen, formal membership of the state does not equate to membership in the community of value. This is not an unfortunate consequence of some of 'our' citizens not being sufficiently tolerant but is assumed in policy and in political contributions to debates. Previous chapters have observed the ways in which data and public debate equate the Migrant with the foreign born, thereby lending no weight to citizenship. This stands in contrast to the rhetorical value attached to citizenship and its acquisition. The distinction, not valid in law, between naturalized citizens and those who have natural-born citizenship is increasingly creeping into the rhetoric of policy as discussed in earlier chapters (see, for example, Migration Advisory Committee 2012). The implication is that 'citizenship', a term Britons have never been at ease with, is technical, a legal formality, and self-consciously inclusive. It is not the same as 'Britishness'.

The rhetoric around family migration is a good example of how naturalized citizens are distinguished from other citizens. Ninety per cent of grants of settlement to family members go to dependents of UK citizens (Blinder 2012: 2), but there is clearly a strong policy assumption that many of the British citizens supporting the applications of dependents and spouses are 'born abroad'. For example, in the 2011 Family Consultation there was a suggestion that a person should have had a certain period of legal residence in the UK in order to be able to sponsor a marriage visa (Home Office 2011b: paras 2.14 and 2.15). There was also a proposal that marriage applicants should be able to demonstrate a *combined* 'attachment' not just to each other, but to the UK. In the research paper written to accompany the 2011 Family Migration Consultation, the Home Office included a table on 'sponsor history' that distinguished between those sponsors who were British citizens from birth and those who were not. Those who had acquired British citizenship were included with sponsors who were settled non-citizens (Home Office 2011c).

The distinction between foreign born and foreign national and more particularly between the British citizen born abroad and the British citizen born in the UK has, as we have seen, long lurked in the data and debate on economic migration. This differentiation emerges rather differently when it comes of family migration, and is encapsulated in a distinction between the 'citizen' and the 'taxpayer':

> Families are the bedrock of society... It is obvious that British citizens and those settled here should be able to marry or enter into a civil partnership with whomever they choose. But if they want to establish their family life in the UK, rather than overseas, then their spouse or partner must have a genuine attachment to the UK, be able to speak English, and integrate into our society, and they must not be a burden on the taxpayer. Families should be able to manage their own lives. If a British citizen or a person settled here cannot support their foreign spouse or partner, then they cannot expect the taxpayer to do it for them. (Home Office 2011b: 3)

But just as the formalities of having citizenship are not sufficient to gain entry to the community of value, neither in practice it seems, is paying taxes. This was apparent with the publication of an article jointly authored by the immigration and employment ministers, about research on migrants and welfare benefits in January 2012. Headlined as '370,000 migrants on the dole', the research as usual included the foreign born as 'migrant' (Winnett 2012). The figure of the taxpayer was once again invoked in contrast to the Citizen:

> The integrity of our benefits system is crucial to the reputation of our welfare state—to whether taxpayers feel they are getting a fair deal. There's a natural instinct that says that no one from other countries should receive benefits at all. But if someone works and pays taxes here, it is not unreasonable that we should help out if they fall on hard times (Grayling and Green 2012).

Migrants and welfare benefits are once again linked together, and migrants (including citizens) not only threaten the integrity of the immigration system, but potentially the integrity of the welfare state itself. The language of fairness and integrity that has been so fundamental to immigration and asylum policy is mirrored in the language of welfare benefits.[3] The authors make a claim to the 'naturalness' of belonging and claims making that seems to derive from being 'from' the country or at least, not from another country. But as liberals are able to assert reason over instinct in a somewhat hedged way ('it is not unreasonable'). Even then, this reason does not allow that welfare benefit is a right for those who have paid taxes, who do not seem to be the same as the

---

[3] In the spring of 1998, President Clinton denounced fraud and abuse perpetrated against 'working families' who 'play by the rules' because prisoners or their households continue to get public payments due to lax bureaucratic enforcement.

taxpayer who must get a fair deal. Rather, for those not born in the UK, this is 'helping out', a mark of the tolerance and compassion of the UK authorities rather than any entitlement on their part. Thus is it through the taxpayer that the property ownership of the true citizen stakeholder is made manifest. Like the Good Citizen, the taxpayer not only excludes migrants (whether or not they have paid their taxes), but also the benefit claimant and the dependent spouse.

5.6 Citizenship as a Global System

Masked by the rhetoric of citizenship as natural belonging or as an idealized trajectory, are the instrumental reasons for acquiring particular citizenships that often figure large in people's explanations of why they decide to naturalize. While these are principally seen in terms of protection against expulsion, citizenship also facilitates mobility. As much as it is associated with belonging and stasis, citizenship is also about being mobile. Citizenship is not, as is often assumed by social contract theorists, constituted simply internally, but it is part of a global state system. There are global hierarchies of citizenship, both in terms of the claims that can be made of the state of citizenship, but also in the ease with which a person can travel. A person who has a US or EU passport, that is, from a wealthy country, is likely to find it much easier to travel to a wide range of countries than a person from a lower-income country, for example, from Nigeria. In the UK it is people who are nationals of lower-income countries, that is, those who tend to be more conventionally thought of as 'migrants', who are more likely to take up citizenship than nationals of the EEA and other higher-income countries. This is despite the high costs of application (settlement, £937–£1350 for an adult worker; *Life in the UK Test* £50; citizenship fee £836 for a single adult; none of it refundable if an application is rejected). There was a marked decline in applications for British citizenship from the 2004 EU Accession states after EU Enlargement, despite an increase in the numbers of migrants from those states and state investment in citizenship rhetoric discussed above. Rutter et al. conclude that this is 'because this group has the fewest restrictions in the UK on their rights of movement and abode and on their social rights, thus the least "need" to apply for citizenship' (Rutter et al. 2008). Treating citizenship as a means to an end runs counter to the original policy intention to raise the status of citizenship and makes its acquisition more than a box-ticking, bureaucratic exercise.

It is the global and systemic nature of citizenship that lies behind the irrevocability of citizenship for the majority. A person with dual citizenship can revoke one of their citizenships, but they cannot revoke the status per se. While ardent citizenship admirers, liberals and republicans alike, might feel that the intolerant ASBO-child-breeding criminal does not deserve citizenship, formal citizenship cannot be stripped from them. They may be denied the privileges of citizenship in various ways, imprisoned, subject to forced labour, they may even be executed by the state, but they are still formal citizens, whether or not they deserve this precious attribute. In this respect, while naturalization demonstrates citizenship as the gift of the bestowing state, citizenship is also required by the global state system which is a 'supranational regime'. Hindess points out that the globalism of the state system significantly limits the role of citizens in the government of contemporary states, but it is often overlooked in the discussions of national citizenship (Hindess 2000). Thus descriptions of the journey to citizenship depict a non-citizen moving through various stages to full citizenship, when in fact the non-citizen is rarely stateless or without any citizenship status whatsoever anywhere, but rather, the Citizen of a different state to the one in which they are currently residing. Indeed, effective statelessness may be preferable to citizenship and some migrants have a strategy of destroying their documents on arrival in a new state in order to avoid removal. States do not offer blanket protection for their citizens from deportation. It is only that they cannot be deported from their state of citizenship. Most (but not all) states will generally facilitate the deportation of their citizens from states in which they are resident. The consular passes produced to enable deportations indicate that the relation of state to citizen is not reducible to protection from the encroachment of another state. Thus while non-deportability is cast as a right, what it means in practice is that states cannot refuse to accept their citizens when they are ejected from another state's territory. As Clara Lecadet, writing about the Expelled Migrants Malian Association puts it: 'They felt abandoned by the country that expelled them because they were non-citizens, but also by their homeland, which didn't prevent the process and didn't support them after their return. The expulsion is thus experienced as a double rejection' (Lecadet forthcoming). That is, citizenship is part of a global state system which requires mutual recognition by states and, with the exception of asylum, acknowledgement of their responsibility to admit and govern their own citizens.

5.7 Conclusion

Naturalization processes, as well as being used to promote ideas of British values and lifestyle, manifest an important teleology. Migrants are imagined as coming for a short time at first, then settling, and finally attaining citizenship. This teleology itself has its symbolism: citizenship is an arrival point and an intention to continue to live in the UK is an often unremarked requirement of naturalization. The language of journey is often used—the booklet, *Life in the United Kingdom* is subtitled: *A Journey to Citizenship*. This is a progressive liberal narrative, the move from a negatively charged exterior to inclusion and equality. It is also a narrative that enhances the stability of citizenship. It may be a struggle to arrive, but it is secure, and having arrived, a citizen is British, one of 'our' citizens, in possession of a unified and honourable status. In practice the law is often more complicated and citizenship is neither secure nor necessarily unified. The narrative arc is one of the achievement of justified self-mastery, freed from excessive dependence on others for status, able to work where one wants, to leave one's spouse without losing residency rights, etc. It serves as a reminder not just of British values, but of the value of citizenship that cannot be taken for granted. The person who has entered the UK as a partial and separated self, that is as a worker, as a spouse, or as an asylum-seeker, becomes, through citizenship, a fully recognized person, a person who is active in the spheres of the social, the economic, and the political.

This teleology indicates confusion at the heart of the citizenship agenda and across administrations about the ultimate aim of citizenship policy. Is citizenship, as the teleology suggests, an end point, a *reward* for being 'integrated', in effect a personal benefit that enables an individual to claim a variety of rights? Or is it part of a process, a social good that *facilitates* cohesion? Is citizenship an end in itself, or is it a means to a cohesive society? The answers yield very different policy implications. If citizenship is primarily a reward that gives access to resources, its restriction is part of what gives it value, while if it is primarily a social good, that suggests that there is a benefit in facilitating the broadest possible access to it. This tension is manifest in the implementation of policy options. These can be prefaced as means of facilitating cohesion as a social good but end up as a means of restricting individual's access to citizenship. For example, proficiency in English was justified as helping 'to ensure migrants play a full part in British life outside the workforce', or, in the case of spouses 'improve employment chances', yet as tests are imposed and standards raised these increasingly look like obstacles to naturalization, mirroring the obstacles to immigration so politely instigated in Natal discussed in Chapter 2. While the current citizenship debate had its basis in concerns about cohesion, the tests and other restrictions have in practice often become obstacles to achieving the legal status, rather than enablers of integration. Although the naturalized citizen is required to be the embodiment of the 'Good Citizen', the guardian of citizenship, serving as proof of the state's commitment to rights, in practice she will be constantly reminded of her tolerated status.

6

Uncivilized Others: Enforcement and Forced Exit

Previous chapters have demonstrated how difficult it is to define and instrumentalize the term 'migrant', even before introducing the refinement of legal status. Arguments about who is and is not illegal are part of the active contestation and constitution of borders. Legislation, however well drawn and sophisticated, can never cover all permutations and eventualities. Huge numbers of court judgments, lawyers, and advice sessions indicate that, whatever the claims of politicians and the media, deciding who is illegal and who is not, is not straightforward. Moreover, although it tends to be thought of as a one-way process, with migrants moving from legality into overstaying, it is possible to move in and out of a range of legal statuses: a person can enter a country illegally, but then seek to make their status legal by applying for asylum or entering a programme that will help them to attain legal status, or indeed they might, as with EU8 nationals in 2004, find their status is made legal because of changes at a supranational level.

Immigration controls may be seen as necessary to maintain order and protect scarce resources, but there can be a deep discomfort about the enforcement of these controls and its compatibility with the values of bodily integrity and respect for rights.[1] Groups that take a rights-based approach often portray the state as terrifyingly punitive and arbitrary, violating the human rights of migrants on a regular basis, detaining and returning asylum seekers in fear of their lives, splitting up families and raiding workplaces. In contrast, tabloid media and opposition politicians (of every party) depict borders as left open to 'illegal immigrants' with little chance of deportation, who work, claim benefits, and have access to other rights that should be the preserve of citizens. The following two chapters will explore this apparent contradiction.

---

[1] As indicated by migrants themselves: 'investigations into . . . complaints have invariably found that detainees confuse the lawful use of force with being assaulted' (Home Office 2010c).

This chapter begins by examining terminology of deportation and illegality with reference to the relation between the legal and the political. It then considers the increase in deportation from the UK, and the shift from border enforcement to in-country removals. This raises the question of how people become illegal, and how they move in and out of legal status. There is not a straightforward legal/illegal binary opposition, and migrants often become 'semi-compliant', residing legally but in breach of conditions. These processes and the impact of deportation and deportability on migrants' lives will be examined. The chapter then turns to the impact of enforcement and deportation on citizens, not only as a result of the relationships they have with non-citizens who are deportable, but also through the increased visibility of enforcement and the application of checks to all residents and not just migrants, and through the engagement of citizens with anti-deportation campaigns.

6.1 Terminology: Deportation and Illegality

The contested nature of terminology in this area is an indication of the intensely politicized nature of claims to knowledge and analysis. As with 'migrant', particular terms may be used with a view to their legal definition, or more rhetorically, to indicate a political or normative position. In legal terms, deportation is what happens to people whose removal is deemed 'conducive to the public good' by the Secretary of State, and to those expelled after serving a prison term. Deportation is therefore strongly associated with criminality and it continues to have legal effect until revoked, usually affecting a prohibition on entry to the UK for a certain number of years. It has a (very limited) right of appeal. In contrast, removal is an administrative procedure with no right of appeal and no legal consequences after enforcement—that is, it is legally possible to return immediately to the UK. Removal is applied to people who have entered illegally, overstayed, or violated the conditions of their visa. It is also applied to people who have been refused permission to enter on arrival, and subsequently removed. A sub-category of removals, 'voluntary departures', is constituted by those who leave after they have been served with a removal notice. Since 2005, all enforcement data include in the category of 'unnotified voluntary departures' (UVDs) those served with removal notices and who leave the country without telling the authorities.

The terms 'deportation' and 'removal' are used interchangeably in this chapter despite these legal differences. The difference between deportation and removal has become blurred over the years with the increasing criminalization of immigration law breaches, and, post-April 2008, with the introduction of mandatory re-entry bans for those breaching immigration laws. Both removal and deportation refer to the non-arbitrary and lawful removal of individual non-citizens from state territory (Anderson et al. 2011). Although difference in terms of appeal rights and right to return can be important to some individuals, in practice for most there are multiple difficulties with exercising these rights. 'Deportation' captures the spectacular manifestation of state power on the body more effectively than the bureaucratic-sounding 'removal'. It can therefore be an uncomfortable term.

> Other forms of expulsion lurk in its shadows; their invocation always threatens to destabilize its legitimacy...Doesn't a plane full of deportees resemble transportation? Don't the shackling and chemical pacification of deportees invoke the galley slaves...Perhaps the contemporary deportation of aliens is invested with former practices and historical memories in such a way that it can never be merely the deportation of aliens. (Walters 2010: 82–3)

These associations with past practices now deemed illiberal can also be illuminating, reminders not only of the legacies of a discredited past, but rendering contemporary deportation's structures and patterns and the negatively racialized bodies they are wrought upon disturbingly familiar.

There is a multiplicity of adjectives attached to migrants who are the subject of enforcement—undocumented, irregular, clandestine, trafficked, *sans papières*, etc. Terminological usage suggests a political position. States, populist media, and the general public, tend to use 'illegal', thereby presenting illegal immigration as a problem associated with crime, to be solved through borders and enforcement. Civil society groups and migrants' organizations often prefer 'undocumented', concurring with states that not having the right documents constitutes a problem, but situating its roots in vulnerability and lack of protection and access to rights (Migrants Rights Network 2008; TUC Commission on Vulnerable Employment 2008). Both terms are not without their difficulties. Civil society groups are uncomfortable with 'illegal' because it associates migrants with criminality. On the other hand, as advice agencies can attest, many 'undocumented' migrants are in fact holding large numbers of documents, the problem being that none of them are considered to be the right ones. Moreover, the term suggests that the solution to people's difficulties is documentation, when it could be argued that it is requirement for immigration documentation that is part of the source of the problem in the first place. The same could be said about the terms 'irregular' or 'unauthorized', often used by academics in an attempt to remain independent from particular positions.

For the purposes of this chapter I have chosen to use the term 'illegal'. This is partly shorthand for 'making illegal', drawing our attention to the state-constructed nature of the category of illegal immigrant. Illegality is not an aberration, nor is it a lack, but it is an inevitable consequence of nation state-organized citizenship and immigration controls. Illegality is a normative as well as descriptive term (as we have seen in Chapter 2, so too is (im)migrant), and this is in part what gives rise to NGO concerns about criminalization. The Illegal Immigrant is constructed as such by law, and whether he is morally deviant (whatever that may mean) is a different matter. Law is not to be confused with morality. The claim that immigrants are not illegal on the grounds that they are not criminals carries with it normative assumptions about both immigrants ('good guys') and criminals ('bad guys'). It implicitly claims that the Migrant belongs in the community of value, in contrast to the Criminal, who does not. The Criminal, no more than the Migrant, is not necessarily morally aberrant. Equally, the illegal migrant can also be a criminal, and the simple possession of a false identity document, for instance, is a criminal offence, as is the failure to have an asylum document at an asylum interview. This arguably says more about the law than it does about the Migrant who has committed the offence, but simply stating that the Migrant is not a criminal allows the process of criminalization to not be critiqued. This is particularly important to foreground in the context of the 'overcriminalization' that features in many capitalist democracies, the use of criminal law for regulatory purposes and the positing of criminal justice solutions to complex social and economic problems (Husak 2008). The huge expansion in the catalogue of immigration crime in Europe and the US, as well as the UK (Story 2005; Bosworth and Guild 2008; Webber 2008; Fernandez et al. 2009; Commissioner for Human Rights 2010; Bosworth 2011b), has taken place in the context of the proliferation of criminal prohibitions more generally. This has led to ordinary people committing 'crimes' on an increasingly regular basis, oftentimes without even knowing it, only protected from punishment by official discretion (Husak 2008). Thus the Illegal Immigrant's conviction that he is not 'really' a law breaker is shared by citizens who, even if they know they are in technical breach, would not consider themselves law breakers, or even if they know they are breaking a law, would not consider themselves 'criminals'. Moreover, in eschewing 'illegality' completely we can overlook connections between mobility and criminality that, as we have seen in previous chapters, have a long history and that have resonance for deportation practices as mentioned above. I have therefore chosen to use the term illegal, and will leave the reader to imagine the quotation marks over 'illegal' which serve to differentiate the descriptive from the normative.

6.2 The UK and Deportation

The main agency concerned with policing borders and enforcing controls is the UK Border Agency (UKBA) whose core objective is to secure the border and reduce migration. In 2008 this was established as an executive agency of the Home Office, but unlike many other executive agencies it retained policy-making power and continued to be responsible for proposing legislation and guiding it through Parliament. It was also responsible for delivering services and had specific targets and a business plan (UK Border Agency 2011). There are dangers associated with reducing a complex political task to a target-driven mass-production model (Heyman 1999), and one of the challenges facing UKBA was to manage the competing demands of facilitating efficient flows with 'security' (Salter 2007). This is particularly difficult because security concerns in this context are not limited to protection from potential international terrorists, but including those who 'undermine British values' (UK Border Agency 2011). Businessmen and citizens as well as 'migrants' can be consigned to long queues and lengthy waits. In 2011–12 these contradictions exploded in a political row between the civil service head of UKBA and the Home Office minister. This led to the civil servant leaving his job and to the announcement that operational management was to be separated from policy matters. From March 2012 enforcement was designated the responsibility of the UK Border Force which was split from UKBA and answerable directly to ministers. UKBA continues to have responsibility for in-country enforcement and has oversight of detention. There has been increasing outsourcing of immigration management to private companies, most obviously through the private running of detention centres and removal escort services to companies like Group 4 Securicor and GEO. These are significant contracts with the average estimated cost of holding a person in detention for one week being £1,230 per head in 2006 (Hansard 2006).

People can be deported from the UK at the borders ('at port') or after they have entered the country ('in country'). Total numbers of removals from the UK in 1998, including those removed at port were 34,920 (Home Office 2007a: 83). By 2008 this had risen to 67,980 (Home Office 2009: 27). The data must be treated with care, not least because, as noted above, in 2005 data began to attempt to include 'unnotified voluntary departures' (UVDs)—that is, people informed of the Home Office's intention to deport them who leave without notifying UKBA. Thus people who had previously not been counted in the figures at all are now included.

Despite these technical problems, data excluding UVDs and removals from the port do seem to indicate a steady increase in the late 1990s through to the mid-2000s, and there was a marked political enthusiasm for deportation at this time. Deportation was one element of a threefold strategy to reduce the numbers of asylum seekers (Spencer 2011) and it moved from being an unfortunate necessity to a policy tool. In 2004, Prime Minister Tony Blair announced targets on deportations of asylum seekers. Presaging net migration, he announced that the number of monthly removals was to exceed the number of 'unfounded applications'. In 2008, UK immigration minister, Liam Byrne, boasted, 'We now remove an immigration offender every eight minutes, but my target is to remove them more and remove them faster' (WiredGov 2008). The 2009 UKBA Christmas card depicted a blue background and a white Christmas tree made out of a series of statements ending with an innocuous 'Seasons Greetings and a Happy 2010' in red forming the trunk. The branches were formed by seasonal celebratory claims including: 'we have a tougher enforcement regime within the UK deporting a record number of foreign national prisoners', 'we are getting stricter on those who don't play by the rules', and 'we are enforcing tough penalties'.

Asylum seekers represent a relatively small proportion of entrants to the UK, but they are disproportionately represented in the removal figures. Of the 6,210 people who were removed in-country in 1992, 390 or 6.3 per cent were asylum seekers, but this proportion had risen to 47 per cent in 1998 (Home Office 2002a: 91). This was even before Tony Blair announced in 2003 that he was taking 'personal control' of asylum policy and one of his main priorities would be swifter and more efficient removals of asylum seekers (Gibney 2008: 157). The numbers of asylum seekers deported as a proportion of asylum applications rose significantly after Blair's announcement. In 2002, 15.5 per cent of asylum applicants were deported, but in 2007, despite a 72 per cent drop in asylum applications, 57 per cent of applicants were deported (Wistrich et al. 2008: 56).

For the purposes of analysis it is helpful to distinguish between two types of enforcement: the prevention of entry and enforcement on the territory. The prevention of entry is concerned with the policing of the territorial border (which can extend beyond that border to visa control processes in embassies, the checking of documents by transportation companies and authorities, etc.). The Home Office data on enforcement include as removals 'port refusals', as well as those deported having entered UK territory. One of the most striking aspects of the rising numbers of deportations is the increase in the proportion of those removed 'in-country'. In 1998, 21 per cent of removals were following enforcement action, but in 2008 this had risen to between 33 per cent and 52 per cent (Home Office 2007a: 91; Home Office 2009: 68). Data collection issues mean that these figures can't be directly compared, but it does indicate a significant change in emphasis. Between 2008 and 2010, when data are comparable, deportations overall declined, but the numbers of people deported in-country rose. When excluding port removals, the total number of people deported during 2010 was 41,968,10 per cent higher than during 2009 (38,052) and the highest figure since 2006 (Home Office 2012b: table rv.01).

This shift in enforcement from the territorial border to 'in country' has been marked by the tightening of requirements on employers regarding the employment of illegal workers and the significant increase in workplace raids and penalization of employers. Employers have been required to check the employees' right to work since 1997, when it became a criminal offence to take on someone who did not have permission to work. They were able to provide a statutory defence against the £5,000 fine if they had taken copies of specified documents, and in practice, enforcement against employers who employed migrants illegally was very low. Between 2001 and 2006, only fifty employers were proceeded against for illegally employing migrants, of whom twenty-eight were found guilty. This began to change in 2004 when the documents to be checked by employers were refined and a National Insurance number alone was no longer regarded as sufficient evidence of the right to work. The Immigration, Asylum and Nationality Act of 2006, which came into force in 2008, raised the penalty for employers who fail to check their workers' entitlement to work in the UK to a maximum of £10,000. Employers became required to re-check the documents of those who have a temporary right to work every twelve months to ensure eligibility for employment. Employers who knowingly employ a worker with no permission to work could be found guilty of a criminal offence and incur an unlimited fine and a two-year prison sentence. In the three years between September 2008 to September 2011, 5,730 businesses were served with civil penalty notices (Hansard 2011). In 2009/10, UKBA conducted over 5,500 illegal working enforcement operations (Home Office 2010d: 4).

6.3 Illegality: Entry and Overstaying

But how does a migrant become illegal? This is most straightforwardly done through the clandestine crossing of borders, or their crossing using fake documents. Both these forms of entry are, in theory, possible to detect with sufficient resources, although in practice the resources required are massive and potentially require substantial infringements of rights of citizens that would go beyond the lengths of queues in Heathrow Airport. However, there are also other forms of illegal entry that are far more nebulous and not possible to detect through physical monitoring of territory and papers alone. People can claim to fulfil entry requirements when they do not—if their visa requires them to be single with no dependents but they are married or have children, for instance. As seen in Chapter 3, migrants must categorize themselves as primarily economic, social, or political beings for the purposes of control, and this rarely fits the circumstances of people's lives. This can be interpreted, rightly or wrongly, as misleading about intentions; for example, a person can enter on a student visa but their primary motivation may be to spend time with a romantic partner rather than studying. When entering illegally is a question of motivation, intention, and desire, it is far harder to police, but attempts are made to do so. This means there is a significant reliance on immigration officers' personal judgement and intuition that takes its place alongside biometrics and hard science in the policing of borders. When passengers seem confident and affluent this may make them less likely to be stopped. 'Passengers with very cheap worn clothing, who look "very impoverished", may be asked how much money they have brought with them' (Woodfield et al. 2007). As with criminalization, a vicious circle can be established: the poor are more heavily policed and so more likely to be found in breach and so more likely to be policed.

There are many ways in which a non-citizen can become an illegal migrant. Illegal entrance is probably a relatively unusual means of becoming an illegal immigrant in the UK. Far more typical is entering legally on a visitor or student visa, for example, and staying longer than one has permission for ('overstaying'). One pathway into illegality that is often overlooked is through birth. Children who are born in the UK to people without legal status may be born into illegality without ever having crossed an international border. The numbers of people born into this situation are not inconsiderable. Sigona and Hughes estimated in 2010 that there were 155,000 under-nineteens illegally resident in the UK at the end of 2007, of whom 85,000 were UK-born (Sigona and Hughes 2010: 29). Thus, as Etienne Balibar puts it, borders exist not only 'at the edge of the territory, marking the point where it ends' but 'have been transported into the middle of political space' (Balibar 2004: 109).

As with past attempts to control vagrancy and to implement transportation, sheer numbers militate against effective enforcement of internal controls. Given the best estimates of numbers of illegal residents in the UK were between 417,000 and 863,000 (Gordon et al. 2009), and the cost of removal of asylum seekers[2] was estimated in 2005 to be £11,000 per person (National Audit Office 2005), immediate deportation of all illegal residents would cost more than the entire annual Home Office budget. It is simply not possible to deport everyone immediately and some prioritization is inevitable. Deportation is constrained by practical considerations, not least cost, meaning that who is subject to deportation is subject to a considerable degree of discretion.

---

[2] This comprised £2800 for detection and arrest, £5800 for detention, £1500 for obtaining travel documents and legal costs, and £900 for removal. Deporting non-asylum seekers may be cheaper as they are less likely to be detained. Foreign national prisoners, in contrast, might be more expensive to deport as they tend to be detained, and detained for longer. The figures are indicative only.

From such choices, one can discern implicit rankings of who should and should not be allowed to remain in the state, as well as who should proceed to citizenship. All non-citizens are deportable, but some are more deportable than others (Kanstroom 2010; Anderson et al. 2011). In the UK, EU citizens have greater protections against expulsion than other non-UK nationals, and conviction of a serious crime is, unlike other non-citizens, not sufficient to enforce a deportation order against an individual. The individual must be shown to present a continuing threat to the society in question.

Prioritization of removal has to be undertaken with some caution, as prioritization of one group implies that another is not a priority. In a public debate which is generally negative to migrants, and unremittingly hostile to illegal immigrants, having a group of illegals that is not a priority for enforcement begins to sound like being a 'soft touch'. The importance of prioritization was highlighted in the 2007 five-year enforcement plan, which set its priorities in terms of harm, and distinguished between those whose breaches caused the greatest harm (traffickers and terrorists), through the intermediate, to those who caused the least harm, which was defined as 'undermining the integrity of the system' (Home Office 2007b: 6). The priority targets were set in alarming terms that nevertheless allowed discretion—who actually is the trafficker and terrorist can prove hard to pin down. 'Undermining the integrity of the system' is also vague, indeed, as with welfare benefits, it can be regarded both as posing a fundamental threat, and interpreted as merely bending the rules. For example, although US and Australian nationals were thought to comprise a significant proportion of visa over-stayers, these were not deemed an enforcement priority in practice:

> From our analysis of detected overstayers, some may be doing so inadvertently, of whom many are thought to be young and from countries with reasonably high GDP per capita and perhaps with high levels of education. Anecdotal evidence suggests that these groups do not intend to stay long term in the UK and require low levels of encouragement to return home. Some groups overstay deliberately as a way of evading immigration controls and some of these may then go on to make an unfounded asylum claim. (Home Office 2007b: 10)

As previously noted, it is the immigration of the poor that controls are generally designed to prevent, and 'poor countries' and countries whose citizenry are black are very likely to coincide. There are also some groups that are more likely to be targeted in practice. Enforcement data suggest that there are certain sectors that are particularly likely to be the subjects of successful workplace raids, and particular countries of origin that are subject to removal. Certain individuals and groups are constructed as more suitable for expulsion than others, with criminality, race, and gender being key (Bosworth 2008; Weber and Bowling 2008; De Genova and Peutz 2010).

6.4 Illegality and Semi-compliance

Borders are then inevitably inscribed 'inside' as well as 'outside' of any given national state. Non-citizens who are granted legal entry to a state are faced with a barrage of restrictions on their behaviour that go way beyond simply obeying the law. Some are forbidden access to the labour market, or can only work in certain sectors, for certain employers, or for certain hours. Some are not allowed to claim benefits or health care. Some are not allowed to marry in the country. The complex web of borders created by the many different types of restrictions that vary by immigration status means that a non-citizen can be residing legally within a state, but render himself liable to removal on the grounds that he has broken often very complex conditions of entry—a situation that Martin Ruhs and I have described as 'semi-compliant' (Ruhs and Anderson 2010b). We focus on semi-compliance with reference to breaking employment conditions, but there are many other ways in which a migrant can be legally resident (that is, having entered on a valid visa, in their own identity, and not overstayed) but violate the restrictions attached to their status, including leaving a spouse or claiming benefits to which they are not entitled. Semi-compliance is contrasted with 'non-compliance', which is when people are residing illegally as well as breaking conditions, and both can be distinguished from compliance, when migrants are legally resident and in full compliance with the restrictions attached to their immigration status. Unlike the strictly defined situations of compliance and non-compliance, the category of semi-compliance is extremely broad and captures a range of violations of conditions particularly when applied to employment (Ruhs and Anderson 2010b).

Numbers of semi-compliant migrants are likely to be significant. In research conducted in 2004, we found (for a non-representative sample) that some types of visas were correlated very highly with semi-compliance. By far the majority of au pair visa holders for example were semi-compliant, as were student visa holders. Not all knew that they were breaking their conditions of entry, and when they did, visa holders often differentiated between types of illegality. We found that illegal entry, overstaying, and working on false documents or on a visitor's visa were generally perceived to be unambiguously illegal, including by those who were themselves in this situation, but working in breach of certain conditions was typically not considered 'really' illegal. Active attempts were made to be in a position that migrants interpreted as bending rather than breaking the immigration rules. They switched and re-entered to move from one type of semi-compliance (working on a visitor's visa, for instance) to another (working full-time on a student visa) (Ruhs and Anderson 2010b). It was not only migrants making this kind of distinction.

For example, au pair host families almost without exception encouraged their au pair to take on bar work and informal cleaning jobs. Their use of social connections to find their au pair temporary work was not imagined by them as facilitating illegal employment even though in fact this is what they were doing. Rather, they felt that they were giving their au pair a chance to earn a little extra money on the side (Anderson 2007).

The concept of semi-compliance exposes non-territorial borders, and the fact that there is not a straightforward legal/illegal binary opposition. Spaces of semi-compliance are created by law and practice and leave considerable room for personal judgment, not just for migrants and employers (who may have their own reasons for interpreting how and why certain rules could be considered bent rather than broken), but also for individual enforcement officers, who are thereby given a considerable degree of unregulated power. Whose semi-compliance counts as illegality, and whose as bending the rules is subject to discretion. The grey area and possibilities of discrimination indicate a potential relationship between the ways in which illegality is imagined and consequences for particular groups of migrants. Semi-compliance is an area which certain groups can inhabit more comfortably than others. Those who, because of nationality, gender, race, occupation, etc., are more easily imagined as (illegal) migrants may find themselves more likely to be reported as suspicious, their status more likely to be checked and, if semi-compliant, more likely to be subject to the discretion of immigration enforcement officers. As much for research as for enforcement agencies and the tabloid press, the wealthy and the white rarely figure as migrants, let alone illegal migrants.

These kinds of issues were summed up in a communication from the personnel department of Oxford University in late 2011. Staff were informed that the practice of inviting speakers who were passing through to give one-off seminars was now subject to regulation. While they might not be residing illegally, the UKBA would treat such an individual as an illegal migrant if 'found on University property' without 'an appropriate visa'. Some dons reacted with derision to 'this interference with our academic affairs' (Boyd 2011). Indeed, many academics have given papers in states where they are not citizens, and put down that they are 'tourists' on their visa forms. 'Illegal immigrants' are 'Othered', and underpinned by ideas about class as well as race. It is this that makes applying the term 'illegal immigrant' to people engaged in academic presentations rather than fixing the plumbing or pulling the carrots seem so inappropriate that the response can be not to take it seriously.

This also demonstrates the lack of fit between immigration rules and regulations and the kind of economic and social relations that characterize contemporary working lives. Not only are populations imagined as homogenous, static, and quantifiable, but work is firmly contractual, conducted within formal employment relations and within a public rather than a private sphere. There are many types of employment that do not fit this model and groups such as artists and entertainers have been particularly hard hit, with reports of non-EU musicians, artists, and actors finding it increasingly difficult to enter, even if they are not intending to work. One artist described how she was only permitted to enter the UK with a severe warning, as she had a visitor visa but was carrying watercolour paints in her bag, and might, therefore, be thinking of 'working'.[3] Even those who are not working in the creative or knowledge industries are often not in conventional employment relations as discussed in Chapter 4. The kind of work that non-citizens do is often precarious, insecure, and marginalized. The world of work as imagined by immigration controls is a world that is often very different from the world of work as it is experienced, and this is an important way in which semi-compliance is produced. The regulation of forms of semi-compliance can require heavy-handed monitoring and enforcement, but nevertheless there have been increasing attempts to do so, and a move away from the view that certain types of semi-compliance are relatively unharmful (Ruhs and Anderson 2010b: 206).

6.5 Deportability and the Community of Value

Those who are in breach of immigration conditions, who overstay, or who enter illegally are, to use de Genova's term, 'deportable'. When examining the impacts of illegality, deportability is critical. For every single person that is actually deported, the consequences are magnified by the feelings of deportability that are induced (De Genova 2002). It is not simply deportation itself, but anxiety about deportation that has a significant effect on the quality of life of migrants, on their perceived universe of constraints and opportunities, and on the practical likelihood of their claiming the most basic of rights (Krause 2008; Talavera et al. 2010). Anxiety about deportation is clearly partly related to personality, but also to consequences of deportation: an asylum seeker from Congo or a single mother with dependent children is likely to be more concerned about deportation than an Australian gap-year backpacker, for instance. The perceived probability of deportation is also likely to be a factor in people's experiences of deportability, and although perception matters, there are, as noted above, some groups who are more likely to be deported than others. Considering deportability rather than 'illegality' allows for the subjectivity of the various actors, and suggests a range of answers rather than a straight yes or no.

---

[3] See <http://www.manifestoclub.com/artist-testimonies> (accessed 23 November 2011).

The lens of deportability rather than the legal/illegal binary opposition also links the situations of legal and illegal migrants who find that they are constrained because of immigration status. As discussed in Chapter 4, migrants on temporary visas are likely to be more compliant and less challenging to their employers because they are dependent on them for visa renewal and for their residence in the UK, and are held in states of protracted temporariness through the operation of immigration and citizenship procedures. Deportability captures the anxieties that attach to the insecurity of migrants' status and its consequent unpredictability. It makes the non-citizen and not only the Illegal Immigrant an 'eternal guest' (Kanstroom 2010). Deportability, like overstaying, draws attention to temporalities of immigration, which often go unnoticed or are subsumed into discussions of integration, settlement, and citizenship acquisition.

Unpredictability can have profound consequences that are difficult to name but very recognizable. Human subjectivities are not confined to the present but are future-orientated, concerned with potential, with where one is going as well as where one is. We are all temporal beings with plans and expectations, and an imagined future is an important aspect of human agency (Emirbayer and Mische 1998). The impact of being embroiled in bureaucratic procedures or enforcement proceedings which leave migrants territorially present and acknowledged but temporally suspended, is considerable. In 2010, an asylum seeker, Osman Rasul, killed himself in Nottingham following nine years of limbo in the asylum system. As one friend of his put it: 'His life was governed by an interminable waiting: for meetings with solicitors, for correspondence from the Home Office, above all for an end to the paralysing uncertainty in which he had lived for the best part of a decade' (Faife 2010). Migrants caught in extended temporariness may not be able to work legally or claim benefits for many years. The 2010 Parliamentary Ombudsman Report on the UKBA, for instance, found that as a result of a shift in priorities, including dealing with the removal of foreign national prisoners, 'for years on end thousands of applicants had been left in limbo, unable to obtain any indication from the Agency of when they might be given a decision on their status' (Parliamentary Ombudsman 2010: 11). The situation for immigration detainees, who can be held in detention indefinitely, captures this suspension:

> I don't know when I'm going to get back to my life. Could be any time, could be five years, could be five days. We don't know, you know, that's what's killing us here . . . They are too slow, they are too slow . . . who gives this power to them to keep these people here for years and years and years, to make them mental and crazy? (Ahmad Javani, quoted in Phelps 2010: 6).

Non-citizens' residence, even when settled, is also contingent on them not being found guilty of a crime. After the so-called Foreign National Prisoner (FNP) scandal of 2006, the government introduced 'automatic deportation'— that is, deportation without discretion for non-EU foreign nationals who were guilty of a 'serious criminal offence' or sentenced for a period of at least twelve months. The FNP, 'discovered' in 2006, serves as a justification of detention and deportation as moral practices. Numbers of deportations of FNPs are noted separately in the data,[4] and their deportation is prioritized. The case of FNPs reveals that deportation is not only a tool of border control, but perhaps the most visceral way in which state officials signal who belongs (Cohen 1994; Anderson, et al. 2011). It is a means of affirming the political community's view of what membership is. In this way deportation is constitutive of citizenship, making clear the normative qualities of membership and the nation as a community of value (De Genova and Peutz 2010; Walters 2010). It indicates that the nation is both protected and worth of protection. Criminals, foreign or not, do not belong to the community of value, but the citizen criminal cannot be deported. In contrast, the non-citizen criminal must be excluded because he (the FNP is gendered as male) can be.

Who is (not) fit to belong is far more complex and internally contradictory than seems at first sight. It changes over time, and is constrained by legal, political, and moral considerations which may draw on rival accounts of membership. For this reason the identification of FNPs, particularly those who are convicted of sexual, drug-related, or violent crimes, as uncontentiously deportable, serves as an important ideological marker, suggesting that it is possible to come to some popular consensus over the desirability of deportation. In contrast, the response to the detention and deportation of children, particularly those who have been resident for some time or born in a state, suggests that this consensus can be somewhat shaky. In practice, even FNPs are not without their supporters. The media and public debate can characterize their deportation as unproblematic, but interestingly those tasked with detaining them are often particularly ambivalent about their removal—far more so than they are about asylum seekers, for instance. FNPs have often lived for many years in the UK. They may have regional accents, British-based family, and watch the same television programmes as many of the detaining officers (Bosworth 2011a). They do not fit the 'good migrant' model of victims or social contributors, but they can translate their status into overtly political terms: 'We don't have a law. Terrorists they got 42 days. They are protected. They are arguing about twenty days or forty days, I see it on the telly. They are arguing about terrorists and we are decent people' ('Daniel', quoted in Phelps 2009: 13).

---

[4] In 2007, 4,200 FNPs were deported, and in 2010, 5,235 (Vine 2011: 11).

Notably 'Daniel' is claiming access to the community of value of 'decent people' because while he may be a 'criminal', he is not a terrorist.

6.6 Citizens and Deportation

Citizens are definable by their exemption from expulsion. A citizen who has been criminalized may be denied the right to vote, to freedom of movement or association, or to welfare support, they may even be executed or abandoned to die, but they may not be deported from their state of citizenship (Wacquant 2007; Gibney 2011).[5] They can be stripped of their citizenship in order to be deported, providing this does not leave them stateless, but qua citizens, they cannot be expelled or detained. In the UK, the only exception is the case of UK-national children who are detained and removed from the UK with a parent, and anecdotally, a figure of 300–400 annual expulsions of UK national children was suggested in the mid-1990s (Sawyer 2006). Such children cannot independently exercise a right to family life, and if their UK-national parent does not exercise their parental right to be with them, they will be deported. In the case of a UK-national husband and a third-country-national wife, the right to family life means that the spousal relationship can enable the wife to remain in the UK, but having a parental relationship to a UK-national child would not be sufficient to enable her to remain. It is not possible to obtain figures on citizens who are under eighteen and subject to enforcement actions since this is not accommodated within the law, and for the same reason there is no mechanism for them to appeal against such actions (Sawyer 2006). Then Home Office minster, Liam Byrne, when asked about the detention of British national children, replied that 'The child's status in the removal centre would effectively be that of a guest'. Sawyer explores the implications of this practice:

> Any child with a foreign parent is at risk, since their British parent may die or decide that he no longer wants them. The Government policy that says that 'Every Child Matters' needs a proviso: 'Except Those With A Foreign Parent'. Such children are tolerated by, rather than under the protection of, the UK, notwithstanding their citizenship. (Sawyer 2006: 165)

While adult citizens are not deportable, this does not mean that they cannot be expelled or detained by mistake. Notably, the guidance to immigration officers on enforcement is prefaced by the statement, 'in particular the detention of persons who are not immigration offenders must be avoided'! Jacqueline Stevens, drawing on empirical research with legal representatives, court papers,

---

[5] Those with criminal convictions are routinely refused entry by many states where they do not have citizenship.

and judicial decisions, and a range of enforcement staff, estimates that in the USA Immigration and Customs Enforcement (ICE) has detained or deported 4,000 US citizens in 2010 alone (Stevens 2011). No such research has been conducted in the UK, but there have undoubtedly been cases. Take the thirty-year-old Tulah Miah, for example, a British national of Bangladeshi origin. Like several of the cases examined by Stevens, he was mentally ill, and he was falsely identified as a failed asylum seeker and deported to Pakistan (Dyer 2008).

Citizens are not deportable but their states of citizenship can facilitate removal from their territory under certain circumstances; most commonly, when they are accused of a crime. Extradition is hedged about with greater legal protections than deportation, but it indicates that states are prepared to remove their own citizens. Citizens are also affected by the deportation of friends, colleagues, and family. They can also be charged with civil and criminal offences related to the illegal immigration of a non-citizen. There have long been versions of 'carrier sanctions' penalizing those bringing in undesirable aliens. In 1793, the Registration of Aliens Act obliged captains to report numbers, names, and occupations of foreigners and introduced a £10 fine for every passenger not reported, rising to £20 in 1836. In 1987, the Carriers' Liability Act raised this to £1,000 per non-admitted foreigner. This was doubled in 1991 and extended to transit passengers in 1993. The UKBA publicizes data about employers who are served with penalty notices, their business, how many illegal migrants they employed, and what the fine issued is (although they have been criticized for not including in their estimates of fine income, fines that have been reduced or dismissed on appeal). It is striking that of the approximate 300–400 individuals and businesses named monthly, almost without exception their names suggest that they are of non-European background, and that they are running small catering businesses, or sometimes car-valeting services. These are the businesses that are the easy wins: small (without large personnel or legal departments), visible (on the high street), and high employers of migrant labour (because of the economics, employment relations, and labour processes of their sector and their personal networks). The employers are tolerated citizens rather than the Good Citizens.

Citizens are also affected by increasing enforcement more generally. It is not legal to request a passport *only* from a person whom a prospective employer thinks might be a migrant, and consequently increasingly passport checks are enforced on all new job holders. The UK's deportation turn has been accompanied by an increased visibility of enforcement. When the UK Border Agency was reformed in 2008, much was made of its new uniform as 'increasing the visibility of immigration staff' (Home Office 2007b: 25). The Home Office signed an 'advertiser-funded' deal with Sky TV enabling it to contribute to the costs of developing and making a fly-on-the-wall documentary series called *'Border Force'*, promoting the work of immigration enforcement officers, following them on workplace raids, interrogating suspects, stopping people on entry, and as they deport people from removal centres.[6]

The everyday awareness of immigration enforcement is not restricted to its entertainment value. Ordinary citizens are increasingly involved in the policing and monitoring of borders, and there has been a decentralization and localization of enforcement. Public-sector workers including health workers, doctors, teachers, university lecturers, social workers, youth workers, as well as employees of carriers (airline officials, lorry drivers, etc.) have obligations to report any evidence of infractions of control. In a bid to bring immigration staff and officers 'closer to the communities they serve' (Home Office 2008: 3), some seventy Local Immigration Teams (LITs) staffed by 7,500 officers were established to liaise with 'local communities' and immigration-crime partnerships. Enforcement is not an optional extra for citizens, but is increasingly the duty of the Good Citizen.

Efforts to control certain non-deportable groups have given rise to novel forms of state practice and legal status. Practical and legal constraints mean that there are non-citizens who do not have a straightforward right to reside, yet whom the state cannot remove, and state controls over them mean that these practices can extend beyond non-citizens to everyone present in the state. The figure of the terrorist plays an important role in this, eliding the foreigner, the Criminal, and the Citizen. Human rights constraints meant that some foreign national terrorist suspects could not be deported because they might face torture or death. This motivated an attempt to detain them indefinitely without trial on the grounds that a trial would put secret intelligence at risk. The House of Lords found this to be incompatible with the Human Rights Act, ruling that it discriminated on the grounds of nationality or immigration status. In response, the government introduced control orders, designed to restrict the movement of foreign nationals and British citizens when ministers say that a trial is not possible. The substitution of *removal from* the state with restrictions *within* the state has important implications for citizens. Unlike deportation, they can be imposed on the general population. Measures originally designed to secure citizens, whether anti-terrorist legislation or employment protection, can potentially over time serve to undermine some of citizenship's basic protections.

6.7 Anti-deportation Campaigns

Increasing enforcement and political concern with 'public trust' in immigration systems should not lead to the conclusion that the public in liberal states

---

[6] See: <http://sky1.sky.com/show/uk-border-force> (accessed 22 September 2011).

is unambiguously behind the recent deportation turn or in favour of harsh measures to deal with asylum seekers or illegal migrants. It is true that in the UK, public-opinion polls have consistently demonstrated in recent years a preference for tougher restrictions on entry and reflected the view that there are too many immigrants in the UK. However, remarkably few people claim that their own neighbourhood has problems attributable to migrants. The Citizenship Survey found that approximately 84 per cent of respondents report that in their local area, people get along well (Communities and Local Government 2010: 5). Apparently, much of the opposition to migration comes from general concerns about Britain as a nation rather than from direct, negative experiences in one's 'own' community (Blinder 2011b). Such a tension has been examined by Antje Ellermann who has noted that public attitudes to deportation vary greatly across the public-policy cycle. While 'at the stage of agenda-setting and policy formulation, the benefits of regulation —restoring the integrity of the immigration system, public safety, fiscal savings . . .—dominate . . . Once implementation gets under way the public comes face to face with the costs of deportation' (Ellermann 2006: 296). Confronted with the human face of deportation, public attitudes towards removal are less affected by attempts to 'demonize' and make scapegoats of migrants, and can become more sensitive to the claims of those the state is attempting to expel.

Deportation may often be 'a radically individualizing and thus also atomizing and isolating event' (De Genova and Peutz 2010: 23), but it does not always go uncontested (Burridge 2009; Varela 2009; Talavera et al. 2010). Anti-deportation campaigns in support of particular individuals and families are a feature of many liberal democracies. These campaigns are often mobilized around neighbourhoods, schools, and churches, and typically use the media and local politicians to try to prevent deportations (Freedman 2011). While they sometimes draw upon a language of human rights to contest deportation, more often they draw on ideas of good citizenship by stressing an individual or family's tangible contribution to the community. Those in danger of deportation are presented as hardworking students, devoted church congregants, conscientious colleagues, and/or valuable local volunteers. To take an example from the National Coalition of Anti-Deportation Campaigns website: 'O. is a much loved and valued member of the community and has worked hard as a volunteer . . . She is a member of St Mary's Church . . . She regularly attends English classes and would like to train as a hairdresser since she did some voluntary work'.[7]

---

[7] See <http://www.ncadc.org.uk> (accessed 29 March 2011).

These campaigns typically call for the person facing deportation to be granted a right to lawful settlement in the state rather than a right to citizenship per se. Nonetheless, they appeal to a very similar ideal of membership in the 'community of value'. Indeed, such a normative account of membership is often directly contrasted by campaigning groups with what are perceived to the bureaucratic processes of decision-making and removal of state officials. State decision-making is characterized as heavily rule-bound rather than concerned with inner disposition: 'solicitor applied using incorrect paperwork'; 'refused because he did not have enough evidence'; 'The Home Office do not believe that he is gay, because he did not reveal all of the traumatic details of his story straight away'; etc. The subjects of anti-deportation campaigns, by contrast, are typically presented as people who are prepared to, to quote again the Home Secretary's introduction to the UKBA enforcement strategy, 'work hard, play by the rules, speak English and get on through merit' (Home Office 2007b: 2). Moreover, they are residing within communities that comprise self-consciously active citizens, who evince pride in and commitment to their local community.

Anti-deportation campaigns present a local neighbourhood or city as a community that welcomes individuals whom the state is attempting to deport. They assert a local identity depicting 'local communities' as composed of caring and responsible citizens, set in contrast to the state or, more particularly, the Home Office, which is a faceless bureaucracy not sympathetic to the plight of individuals. This privileging of the 'the local community' and conformity with community values, not only asserts the primacy of a normative conception of citizenship over what is presented to be a legalistic and bureaucratic one, it also challenges who has the *right to judge* who is a member. There is an implicit (or explicit) claim that citizens have some authority to determine the boundaries of membership, an authority that is seen as stemming from their real world experience and knowledge of their community. This challenge can slide into an active questioning of *which community* is the appropriate one for determining whether someone is a member. The City of Sanctuary movement, for example, which has recently been imported from the USA, states, 'Our goal is to create a network of towns and cities throughout the country which are proud to be places of safety and welcome for people whose lives are in danger in their own countries'.[8] It specifically aims to engender sanctuary 'as part of the city's identity', and emphasizes the importance of building relationships between asylum seekers and 'local people as neighbours, friends and colleagues'.

---

[8] See <http://www.cityofsanctuary.org/> (accessed 29 March 2011).

To be sure, campaigns against deportation are typically on behalf of asylum seekers and on this basis, they also make human rights claims on behalf of the potential deportees. To this end, they often refer back to conditions in the countries from which they have come. But the extent to which such campaigns characterize potential deportees as members of the state's community of value is striking. In official government discourse, these communities of value are equated with citizenship, but in anti-deportation campaigns, they are typically expressed as 'belonging': the 'Lydia and Bernard Belong to Manchester' campaign, 'Selamawit Belongs in Salford', 'Jhoselyn and Justina Belong in London', amd 'Florence and Precious Belong to Glasgow' were all listed on the website of the National Coalition of Anti-Deportation Campaigns in March 2011.[9] These responses to deportation, which is used to trace formal membership, assert belonging in the face of legal rejection from the polity, and thereby indicate the space between citizenship and belonging.

If such local campaigns demonstrate tension between state attempts at deportation and local attempts at inclusion, challenges to state judgments over who can and who cannot be deported are not necessarily supportive of migrants in general, or evidence of a progressive local people versus an oppressive state. There is little evidence that seeing the realities of immigration enforcement up close necessarily changes people's attitudes to deportation in more general policy terms. On the contrary, the language used by various anti-deportation campaigns in support of particular individuals suggests only a replacement of grounds for determining who should stay and who should not, and not a challenge to the idea of deportation as such. Rather than a 'faceless bureaucracy' determining who should be deported on the basis of formal legal criteria, the claim is that a richer, communitarian standard of who belongs (often assessed by local communities themselves) should prevail. Yet this raises the question of whether a more subjective account of who belongs is necessarily preferable to one based on formal legal status. The former subjective account seems to leave vulnerable those individuals who do not elicit the sympathy of the local community, perhaps because they are from an unfavoured ethnic or racial group (for example, the Roma) or are single, unsociable, or lacking in the requisite community spirit. They may also be foreign national prisoners:

> The FNP is incompatible with this narrative of good migrants. Some NGOs sought to distance themselves from these embarrassing service users: a demand grew for detainees who are 'just' asylum-seekers to be kept separate from FNPs, who (in the words of one NGO in a policy submission) had 'by their actions demonstrated their contempt for the laws of the UK'. (Phelps 2011)

---

[9] See <http://www.ncadc.org.uk/> (accessed 29 March 2011).

Clearly, a more communitarian and local account of who is a member may generate forms of exclusion that conflict with the rights-based commitments of the liberal state. This explains why it is not uncommon for local communities and civil society groups to campaign *against* the constraints on expulsion imposed on governments by international human rights law and regional treaties and agreements like the European Convention on Human Rights and European Union directives. The recent outcry over the failure of UK courts to order the deportation back to Iraq of a non-citizen with a British-based family convicted of killing a young girl in a hit-and-run accident is a powerful case in point (Guardian 2010). Support for expelling (or preventing residence by) unfavoured individuals and groups can even impact upon the residence status of British citizens. When it was reported that the convicted child molester and former rock star Gary Glitter was house-hunting in the city of Oldham in the north of England, a local protest group of several hundred people formed to protest and to put pressure on local estate agents not to sell him a property. Interestingly, this campaign followed the organization of a Facebook page set up to protest Glitter's return to the UK from Cambodia on the grounds that he was a danger to British children (Anderson et al. 2011).

The normative criteria drawn on by anti-deportation campaigns to determine membership is two-edged with respect to deportation in general. On the one hand, the criteria may, as we have seen, expand the boundaries of community—who is considered one of 'us'—by including some who do not have legal residence in the category of those protected from deportation. On the other hand, by privileging subjective identification over human rights considerations, the criteria may be insensitive to the costs of deportation for those who are deemed unworthy of membership. The violation of the norms and values of the community can come to justify ignoring any other claims the non-citizen may have for not being deported.

6.8 Conclusion

As enforcement has moved inside UK territory, so UK nationals as well as migrants are increasingly aware of immigration controls. British citizens witness checks as well as being themselves subject to them, and are also required to enforce restrictions. The proliferation of enforcement practices means that illegality is made more visible. In a vicious circle, legally uncertain areas are subject to a complex and punitive regulatory regime thereby forcing more people into illegality. This risks undermining the credibility of enforcement. Were the University of Oxford to be raided and dozens of illegal seminar speakers discovered and arrested, this would not be simply be regarded as a job well done, but serve to raise questions about the potential for there to be hundreds or thousands of undiscovered illegal seminar speakers roaming around other universities. The danger with tough enforcement is that it can never be tough enough. The tougher the enforcement, the bigger the 'problem' it uncovers. But at the same time, tough enforcement can give rise to disquiet, particularly around its compatibility with human rights and citizens' protection from arbitrary state interference. Immigration enforcement leaves its marks not just on individual non-citizens, but on communities and citizens more generally, through requirements to police and be policed by immigration control mechanisms, but also through the spotlight it throws on the normative values of citizenship. Yet the normative values aspired to through liberal citizenship generate particular concern with the spectacular display of state power on individual bodies, and it is this that will be explored in the following chapter.

7

Uncivilized Others: Rescuing Victims

Citizens may be broadly in agreement with government immigration policy and acknowledge the consequent logic of illegality and deportation, but its actual practice can be deeply unsettling. The lack of access to rights of undocumented migrants, detention, and deportation (particularly of children) are often seen as violating their human rights. One of the ways of managing the discomfort of immigration enforcement is to invert these kinds of arguments and posit immigration controls and enforcement as a response to human rights violations. In the same way as asylum processes supported human rights, so too it is claimed can immigration controls. This is the language of trafficking which is now firmly on the political agenda. Thousands of individuals, hundreds of groups, and dozens of newspapers are determined that it should end, and it is to be stamped out by the identification and rescue of victims and imprisonment of perpetrators. Ending trafficking reconciles immigration enforcement with human rights and trafficking seems to be a rare patch of common ground between NGOs, activists, and states.

Migrant and labour-rights activists have appealed to state commitments to fight trafficking as a means of advancing the rights of migrants, particularly undocumented migrants. This chapter will unpack some of the implications of this move and will consider how the role of the state in creating vulnerability is overlooked by an emphasis on individual morality rather than by studying institutional structures. Responses to 'trafficking' present the UK as a site of free labour and space of equality that is free from 'slavery', but they also reveal anxieties about the nature of the market, its relation to society, and more particularly, its compatibility with ideas of the nation. The chapter begins by tracing the development of anti- trafficking policy in the UK, setting it in its international context. It argues that the presentation of the Victim of Trafficking (VoT) as embedded in social relations of power and control contrasts with the more general portrayal of the economic migrant as a self-interested rational actor. I will go on to examine who counts as a VoT and demonstrate that, as with the question of who counts as a migrant, the VoT differs in law, in data, and in public debate. While the apparent depoliticiza-tion of migration comes about by the emphasis on 'facts' and data, the depoliticization of trafficking comes about through the focus on values, which places the plight of the victim of trafficking beyond politics. The chapter concentrates on the case of trafficking as 'modern-day slavery' to examine the implications of the usage of the language of slavery, and the ways in which it can limit responses to very real challenges. 'Trafficking' is not only increasingly presented as a human-rights focused response to difficulties of enforcement, but has introduced the language of harm prevention into the heart of immigration control. In this way, the 'humanitarian border' (Walters 2011) has moved into political space.

7.1 Development of Anti-trafficking Policy

The struggle against trafficking brings together coalitions of groups that are often opposed to each other on other issues: radical feminists in a struggle to overturn patriarchy; evangelical Christians who are concerned to shore up patriarchy; migrants' support groups fighting for the rights of non-citizens; state politicians and civil servants whose principle concern is stopping irregu-lar migration. There is considerable media coverage of the issue, tending to concentrate on salaciously presented cases of 'sex slaves', but also dealing with forced labour and illegal immigration. This concern is not restricted to the UK, but is very much presented as an international struggle and for this reason, I will begin by setting the legislative and political developments around trafficking within their international context.

Between 1904 and 1933 there were four international instruments suppress-ing 'the White Slave Traffic', the procurement by force or deceit of a white girl or woman for 'immoral purposes'. The initial trigger for this anxiety and seemingly protective response was growing female migration from Europe and Russia to the Americas and parts of the British Empire (Doezema 2000). There was also anxiety in the USA about the trafficking of white women within the United States, stemming from their perceived vulnerability to the depredations of free black men (Holden-Smith 1996). In 1949, the newly created United Nations adopted the Convention for the Suppression of the Traffic in Persons and of the Exploitation of the Prostitution of Others, a legally binding instrument that punished persons who 'to gratify the passions of another procures or exploits the prostitution of a person...even with the consent of that person' (United Nations 1949: Art. 1). This was not ratified by many states, and for over four decades following 1950, there was little inter-national engagement with questions of trafficking.

This changed in the late 1990s, with debates around the UN Convention Against Transnational Organised Crime, adopted by the UN General Assembly in 2000. The Convention was supplemented by three additional protocols dealing with Smuggling of Migrants, Trafficking in Persons—especially women and children, and Trafficking in Firearms. Anne Gallagher traces the origin of the Trafficking Protocol to a proposal from Argentina for a new convention against trafficking in minors which came at the same time as European institutions were beginning to develop detailed policies on trafficking and the United States had issued a memorandum on measures to be taken to combat violence against women and trafficking (Gallagher 2001; Chuang 2010). This was also a period of increased intra-European migration following the fall of the Berlin Wall. Emigrants from former Communist states had previously been limited to small numbers of political refugees, recognized by the Geneva Convention, which, as discussed in Chapter 3, had been designed for their protection. These same states were now seeing significant emigration of people, many of them women, who were constructed not as 'political refugees' but as economic migrants. Improved and lower-cost international transport, and increasing global integration, were all also resulting in larger movements of people internationally, and women were becoming increasingly visible as migrants (the so-called 'feminization of migration'). Anti-trafficking lobbying, policy, and practices reflect and reinforce, firstly, deeply held concerns with prostitution/sex work, and, secondly, concerns about international migration.

The Protocol on Trafficking in Persons was hailed for giving the first international recognized definition of trafficking:

'Trafficking in persons' shall mean the recruitment, transportation, transfer, harbouring or receipt of persons, by means of the threat or use of force or other forms of coercion, of abduction, of fraud, of deception, of the abuse of power or of a position of vulnerability or of the giving or receiving of payments or benefits to achieve the consent of a person having control over another person, for the purpose of exploitation. Exploitation shall include, at a minimum, the exploitation of the prostitution of others or other forms of sexual exploitation, forced labour or services, slavery or practices similar to slavery, servitude or the removal of organs. (United Nations 2000: Art. 3(a))

Notably, the definition is not restricted to prostitution, it does not require the crossing of international borders, and neither does it mention immigration status. A study of the Trafficking and the Smuggling Protocols reveals that key distinctions between trafficking and smuggling are, firstly, that trafficking can take place within national boundaries, and, secondly, that entry into a state can be legal or illegal in the case of trafficking, but not smuggling.

The Palermo Protocol, as it is often called,[1] is on one level hugely successful. As of October 2011, it had 117 signatories. Compare this to the thirty-two signatories to the UN Convention on the Protection of the Rights of All Migrant Workers and their Families, approved by the UN ten years earlier in 1990. However, the Palermo Protocol is *not a human rights instrument*. It is an instrument designed to facilitate cooperation between states to combat organized crime, not an instrument designed to protect or give restitution to the victims of crime. The emphasis is on intercepting traffickers and smugglers and on punishing and prosecuting them. States are to strengthen border controls to prevent both trafficking and smuggling. Border controls, not human rights protection, lie at the heart of the trafficking as well as the smuggling protocol. While states are encouraged to offer protection to trafficked persons, in particular to consider providing victims of trafficking the possibility of remaining, temporarily or permanently, on their territory, actual obligations are minimal and the protection provisions are weak (Gallagher 2001).

The UK government was an early signatory to the Trafficking Protocol, but at the time signalled that trafficking was not a big problem in the UK: 'available evidence points to the majority of illegal immigrants to the UK being here by their consent and that the number of trafficked people is small by comparison' (Home Office 2002b). It claimed that victims were mainly prostitutes and that trafficking usually involved a breach of immigration law. In recognition of this, the 2002 Nationality, Immigration and Asylum Act introduced a new set of offences of 'traffic in prostitution'. This new offence was introduced in the context of the promotion of managed migration and the circumscription of the rights of asylum seekers as discussed in Chapter 3, and the significant increases in deportation of asylum seekers laid out in Chapter 6. As we have seen, after the end of the Cold War, the political refugee (white man who enshrined the practice of democratic politics) morphed into the bogus asylum seeker whose rights claims were far more contested. The extension of protection to refugees was no longer straightforwardly the hallmark of liberal democracies' freedom and respect for rights for non-citizens. It is precisely at this moment that the victim of trafficking materializes.

While in the 2002 White Paper, *Secure Borders, Safe Haven* (Home Office 2002b), the government signalled a recognition of the expanded definition of trafficking to include non-sexual labour, early legislation cast trafficking as having only to do with prostitution, and the 2002 immigration offence was consolidated in the Sexual Offences Act 2003 into broader offences of 'trafficking for sexual exploitation'. This emphasis on trafficking for the purpose of

---

[1] Not quite correctly in fact, as technically the three are known collectively as the Three Palermo Protocols.

prostitution changed with the Asylum and Immigration Act of 2004, which introduced a new offence of 'trafficking people for exploitation', defined as contravention of Article 4 of the Council of Europe's Convention for the Protection of Human Rights and Fundamental Freedoms, which prohibits slavery and forced labour. It also prohibited the use of people for the acquisition of benefits. In 2006 the government issued a consultation and in March 2007, an Action Plan on combating trafficking. Trafficking, including trafficking for forced labour, was now firmly on the UK policy agenda.

By 2007, the terms of the debate had shifted significantly, and trafficking had come to be perceived as a major immigration issue, partly because of the new emphasis on trafficking for forced labour. It was no longer a 'small' problem. Home Secretary John Reid, in his foreword to the 2007 Home Office strategy *Enforcing the Rules*, claimed that 'Failure to take on the people traffickers who are behind *three quarters of illegal migration* to this country leaves vulnerable and often desperate people at the mercy of organised criminals' (Home Office 2007b: 2). The image of the VoT thereby invoked large numbers, echoing fears of 'floods' and 'hordes' of ('illegal') migrants, but the dominant emotion evoked was pity rather than fear. Again this needs to be seen within the more general shift in policy outlined in previous chapters, which saw the demonization of asylum seekers, and an anxiety about numbers of new entrants to the UK following EU Enlargement.

There are striking contrasts in UK policy documents between the portrayal of the Migrant as an economic actor and the Migrant as a victim of trafficking. Two months after the trafficking consultation, in May 2006, the government issued its document outlining the points-based system (Home Office 2006b). In this, the economic migrant is portrayed as motivated by self-interest, self-assessing online, identifying the appropriate rational (sensible) course of action. In contrast, the victim of trafficking has 'been made vulnerable through economic, political or social dislocation' (Home Office 2006c: 15). Potential trafficking victims are depicted as experiencing unemployment, poverty, and gender inequality. They may be constrained through poverty, lack of education, misinformation, and family circumstance. Unlike economic/labour migrants, victims of trafficking are not disembodied individuals—indeed, they are typically defined by their bodies: prostituted, violated, beaten, dead (O'Connell Davidson 2006; Andrijasevic 2007). They are embedded in backward social relations of gender, tribe, and caste. The labour migrant (and the smuggled migrant) is stereotypically male, which is not to say that labour migrants cannot be female but rather that this is a deviation from the imagined norm. In contrast, the victim of trafficking, embedded in social relations, embodied, is typically female.

7.2 Who Counts as a Victim of Trafficking?

There has been considerable legislative and criminal justice activity around trafficking in recent years in the UK and in 2010/11, the Crown Prosecution Service recorded 103 prosecutions for human trafficking (surprisingly few if the Home Secretary's 2007 assertions are taken at face value) (CPS 2011: 42). But what trafficking exactly is, and who counts as a victim of trafficking, continue to be opaque. This is true at both national and international level, as David Feingold puts it:

> Over the years, what we have found in the trafficking field could be called numerical certainty and statistical doubt. That is, bold statements are made with great force: 'There are 1.2 million children in sexual slavery' (UNICEF); '5,000 girls are trafficked each year between Nepal and India' (numerous sources); '600,000 to 800,000 people are trafficked worldwide each year' (U.S. government). However there is almost never any indication as to either the provenance or the basis for the figures. (Feingold 2010)

There are significant discrepancies in international estimates, with regularly cited estimates of numbers ranging from 2.5 million (International Labour Office 2008), to 12.3 million (Hansard 2010). There seems to be general agreement that numbers are 'increasing' but when scientifically interrogated, the numbers tend to reduce significantly. Thomas Steinfatt (2003), for example, considered the claim beginning in the late 1990s that there were 80,000–100,000 trafficked women and children in Cambodia, noting the equation of sex workers with sex slaves. Empirical research conducted suggested the number of sex workers was closer to 20,000, of whom approximately 2,000 were indentured (Steinfatt 2003). The difficulty in ascertaining precise numbers is by no means restricted to Cambodia. Even in the USA, where it would be reasonable to expect that there are more resources to devote to data gathering than there are in Cambodia, only a total of 1,326 victims of trafficking were identified between 2000 and 2007 in contrast to the 50,000 annual incomers estimated by the government (although for no apparent reason these estimates were revised down dramatically to between 14,500 and 17,500 in 2004). This was not for want of resources: in 2006 £28.5 million was set aside to fight human trafficking in the UK (Markon 2007). Challenges in data gathering at a national level are multiplied as they are gathered internationally. The US Government Accountability Office, for example, found that the US State Department estimate was 'questionable':

> The accuracy of the estimates is in doubt because of methodological weaknesses, gaps in data, and numerical discrepancies. For example, the U.S. government's estimate was developed by one person who did not document all of his work, so the estimate may not be replicable, casting doubt on its reliability. Moreover, the

quality of existing country level data varies due to limited availability, reliability, and comparability. (United States Government Accountability Office 2006: 51)

The report contrasts the large numbers of victims claimed with the considerably smaller numbers of victims given official assistance, and the discrepancy between those who present at agencies as victims of trafficking, and those who are legally recognized as victims.

Assumptions about prostitution, sloppy thinking, typographical errors, and what constitute good media stories all contribute to the inflation of trafficking numbers internationally, as do the interests of NGOs—often underfunded, particularly if they are dealing with matters around undocumented migration—and governments, keen to demonstrate that they are on the side of the good guys.

These kinds of issues are reflected in UK debates. In 2008, Dennis MacShane MP claimed in a House of Commons Debate that there were over 25,000 sex slaves in the UK (Hansard 2007). When challenged, he said that the number came from an article in the tabloid newspaper, the *Daily Mirror*, and that he used to be a *Daily Mirror* reporter and so trusted the article. As Professor Julia O'Connell Davidson pointed out in a 2009 radio programme, the same report said that many of the women were forced to have sex with up to 30 men a day—that is, up to 750,000 men every day were exploiting sex slaves (O'Connell Davidson 2009). In 2006 and 2007, the police conducted two major operations into trafficking and prostitution, called Pentameter 1 and Pentameter 2. These operations uncovered nothing like the numbers of victims or perpetrators that might have been anticipated given the large numbers of sex slaves that have been estimated. Pentameter 1 raided 515 establishments, led to 232 arrests, and 88 women and girls 'rescued', Pentameter 2 raided 833 premises and identified 164 victims of trafficking (Joint Committee on Human Rights 2006; United Kingdom Human Trafficking Centre 2009). A *Guardian* newspaper investigation by Nick Davies discovered that following Pentameter 2, only fifteen people were convicted (Davies 2009). Moreover, ten of these were jailed under the 2003 Sexual Offences Act, which makes it an offence to transport a person into prostitution even if they are willing participants. Only five people were found guilty of forcing women to work as prostitutes, and they in fact were not picked up through the Pentameter 2 operation (Davies 2009).

It is not only a question of numbers. Those who are identified as victims of trafficking are often quite different from the VoT as depicted in the media. While the victim of trafficking tends to be imagined and depicted as a migrant, and more particularly, a young woman forced into prostitution, those recognized through the National Referral Mechanism (NRM) as victims of trafficking do not necessarily fit this stereotype. The UK introduced the NRM in 2009 as part of improving procedures for the identification of VoT. It specifies 'First Responders' that is, NGOs and statutory bodies who are formally able to refer people whom they think are VoT to 'Competent Authorities'. Competent Authorities are authorized to determine whether a presumed person is in fact a VoT, and the UK Competent Authorities are the UKBA and the UK Human Trafficking Centre (UKHTC). Non-EU citizens are dealt with by UKBA, while those whose situations do not raise immigration questions are dealt with by UKHTC. In 2009 in the UK, a total of 527 people were referred to the NRM, and 74 per cent of them were women (Anti-Trafficking Monitoring Group 2010: 8). Forty-five per cent of referrals were for sexual exploitation. Of the 477 people referred to the NRM between April and November 2009, 371 were from non-EU states (Nigeria, China, and Vietnam being the most important countries of origin), 72 from EU states (not including the UK), and 34 were UK nationals (Anti-Trafficking Monitoring Group 2010: 33). The 'positive identification' rate of cases as a whole was 19 per cent, that of UK nationals was 76 per cent, EU nationals 29.2 per cent, and nationals of non-EU states 11.9 per cent (Anti-Trafficking Monitoring Group 2010: 9). So in practice, UK nationals are far *more* likely to be found to be victims of trafficking than are non-EU nationals. Interestingly, in the light of the posited shift from asylum to trafficking in terms of symbolic human rights protections, it is not unusual for non-EU women who are referred as victims of trafficking to also be claiming asylum. According to the Poppy Project, a designated first responder, of 181 women who were able to provide information about their immigration status, 168 were or had been in the asylum system (Stepnitz 2012). The same UKBA caseworker is charged with making both asylum and trafficking evaluations.

In previous chapters we have seen the difficulties of who counts as a migrant, and the significant discrepancies between the Migrant in law, in data, and in rhetoric/public debate, and these are also manifest in the differences between the VoT in law, in data, and in public debate. Take the tragedy in Dover in 2000, when fifty-eight Chinese people died in the back of a truck having paid £15,000 each to the group that organized their illegal entry to the UK. This was widely publicized as an instance of 'deadly traffic in humans' (Buerkle 2000). However, given that they had entered voluntarily into the contract and were entering the UK illegally, it is doubtful that they would have been designated 'trafficked' had they been found alive. Like many illegal entrants discovered in extremely dangerous and difficult conditions, the likelihood is that they would have been classed as smuggled and in all probability returned to China. Once dead, it is possible to agree on male (illegal) migrants being victims of trafficking, but while alive, it is likely that they are participants in smuggling, having 'consented' to come to the UK for work.

One obvious response is that these statistical questions do not matter, what matters is doing something, or put another way, it is: 'not about the numbers. It's really about the crime and how horrific it is' (Tony Fratto, Deputy White House press secretary, quoted in Markon 2007). However many people are suffering, it is still too many, and we all tend to agree that trafficking is abominable. Who can object to anti-trafficking? 'This is not a party-political issue but an issue of moral imperative' (Hansard 2010). However, as Wendy Brown puts it, 'a sure sign of a depoliticising trope or discourse is the easy and politically cross cutting embrace of a political project bearing its name' (Brown 2006: 16). Trafficking is not beyond politics, but it is depoliticized. While I have argued in Chapter 3 that questions about migration are depoliticized by 'facts', by the idea that one simply has to feed in the right numbers and the correct policy comes out, questions about trafficking are in contrast depoliticized by 'value', by being beyond politics.

7.3 The Politics of Trafficking

While at least there can be recourse to matters of 'fact', like formal citizenship or country of birth for definitions of migrant, when it comes to VoT, activists, immigration authorities, police, and policymakers, must instrumentalize concepts like 'exploitation', 'coercion', and 'consent'. Moreover, they are doing so in a context which acknowledges the embeddedness of social relations. In situations which are framed as those of 'poverty, war, crisis and ignorance' (Home Office 2011d: 6), how is 'consent' to be understood? The identification of trafficking victims is not simply a matter of ticking boxes, or indeed of listening to stories of abuse and exploitation and judging them true or false; it is inevitably about making political judgements. Where do tolerable forms of labour migration end, and trafficking begin? When do social relations mean that a contract is not a recognition of equality? When is it simply entrepreneurial to be 'primarily driven by profit' (Home Office 2011d: 6), and when is this the mark of a trafficker? These kinds of questions reveal the deep liberal tensions that underpin the question who counts as a victim of trafficking, but which are differently weighted, depending on whether the focus is sex trafficking or trafficking as modern-day slavery.

7.3.1 Sex Trafficking

The victim of trafficking is first and foremost imagined as a migrant woman or girl forced into prostitution. Internationally, the policy discussions and research on trafficking have been very much focused on prostitution, and the 2000 Trafficking Protocol makes particular and special reference to sexual exploitation and exploitation of the prostitution of others. The debates that preceded the Protocol were highly polarized between those who might be termed 'feminist abolitionists', and those people arguing for a 'sex workers' rights' perspective. Abolitionists argue that prostitution reduces women to the status of bought objects, and is always and necessarily degrading and damaging to women. Thus they recognize no distinction between 'forced' and 'free choice' prostitution, and hold that in tolerating, regulating, or legalizing prostitution, states permit the repeated violation of human rights to dignity and sexual autonomy. Prostitution is a 'gender crime', part of patriarchal domination over female sexuality, and its existence affects all women negatively by consolidating men's rights of access to women's bodies. All prostitution is a form of sexual slavery, and trafficking is intrinsically connected to prostitution. From this vantage point, measures to eradicate the market for commercial sex are simultaneously anti-trafficking measures, and vice versa (Anderson and Andrijasevic 2008).

Feminists who adopt what might be termed a 'sex-workers' rights' perspective reject the idea that all prostitution is forced and is intrinsically degrading. Since sex-workers' rights' feminists view sex work as a service-sector job, they see state actions which criminalize or otherwise penalize those adults who make an individual choice to enter prostitution as a denial of human rights to self-determination. They also strongly challenge feminist abolitionists' simple equation of the demand for trafficking and the demand for prostitution. From this standpoint, it is the lack of protection for workers in the sex industry, rather than the existence of a market for commercial sex in itself, that leaves room for extremes of exploitation, including trafficking. The solution to the problem thus lies in bringing the sex sector above ground, and regulating it in the same way that other employment sectors are regulated (Anderson and O'Connell Davidson 2003).

This emphasis on prostitution/sex work has exemplified important tensions in liberal thought but has tended to generate more heat than light. It has paradoxically both emphasized and obfuscated some of the key issues that are a feature of trafficking debates through what is taken for granted. Firstly, as Julia O'Connell Davidson (2006, 2011) points out, a crucial challenge of prostitution for liberals is that 'it can't be reconciled with the fictions of disembodiment that are so central to liberal understandings of contract and political subjectivity'. Not any body (with the requisite skills and experience) will do. As discussed in Chapter 3, this is in contrast to low-skilled work in general, which is imagined as fungible and easily replaceable labour. Prostitution raises urgent and persistent questions about what labour power is, how we can imagine it as separated from the person of the worker, and what are the consequences of so imagining it for human well-being, but these are not only questions for prostitution (O'Connell Davidson 2011). The imagining of women's relations to their persons and their bodies has always been more fraught than it has been for men (which is not to say that men's, particularly black men's, relationship to their bodies and personhood is straightforward; Mills 1997). For centuries in England, wives had no legal rights over their children, or over property brought to a marriage, and they did not have property in their personhood (Pateman 1988). By emphasizing the horrendous abuses endured by so-called sex slaves rather than examining the more mundane nature of the economic and social exchanges of the sex sector, trafficking foregrounds embodiment but makes it peculiar, and isolates it from a challenge to the fiction of disembodiment and property in the person more generally.

Secondly, taking prostitution as the starting point emphasizes relations of (gender) domination. For abolitionist feminists, these relations are systemic and spring from patriarchy, but others less critical of patriarchy such as evangelical Christians, can regard these as individualized abuses of power, or proceeding from cultural backwardness of 'traditional' societies (O'Connell Davidson 2005). This confuses questions about the nature of 'consent', 'choice', and 'exploitation'. Abolitionist assumptions tend to pervade popular debate which take for granted that it is not possible for women to choose to work in commercial sex, and those who do so are almost always victims of violence or personal pathologies. And since this position also insists that prostitution is not and can never be work, the question of what does and does not constitute an exploitative working relationship also does not arise; the problem is perceived as about domination rather than exploitation.

7.3.2 Trafficking and Modern-day Slavery

Both of these have important implications when it comes to trafficking for the purposes of forced labour, or 'modern-day slavery', as it is known (Bales 2005). The principal focus of concern of anti-trafficking activists was originally sex trafficking, and it has only been as a result of concerted efforts by campaigners and activists that trafficking for the purposes of forced labour has been acknowledged as an issue. This means that the debate is framed in a way which foregrounds the body and physical integrity, without challenging the liberal fiction of disembodiment, and emphasizes slavery as domination, rather than as a mode of organizing labour.

Liberalism has long attempted to draw a 'bright line' between free and forced labour, turning them into binary polar opposites; work that is undertaken freely, and work that is performed involuntarily (Brace 2004). However, while freedom is a core value of liberalism which demands that restrictions on liberty must be justified, the question of what *liberty is*, is deeply contested. Is it 'negative liberty' or the absence of coercion (Berlin 1969); is it 'positive liberty' or autonomy and self-direction (Mill 1948; Dworkin 2011); or is it a more republican liberty, the absence of domination (Pettit 1997)? More particularly, what is the relation between freedom and labour? Are VoTs unfree because they are subject to coercion, because they lack autonomy, because they are dominated, or all of these? And how can one distinguish between the coercion of much economic migration ('the dull compulsion of economic relations') and that of trafficking? What is 'free labour'?

From the mid-nineteenth century onwards, a contract is imagined as an agreement between juridical equals that acknowledges self-ownership, with one person selling their labour power to another for a particular term or purpose, with no consequences for the legal or political status of either party. However, this is 'an invention of the nineteenth century' (Steinfeld 1991). In the past, indentured servitude was viewed as perfectly compatible with ideas of 'free labour': servants could be physically beaten, forbidden from marriage, runaways could be captured and compelled to work additional terms in punishment, but they would still be 'free' (Steinfeld 1991). This has changed, and the powers that masters previously exercised over servants are no longer legally compatible with what we would now call free labour. Thus the very idea of free labour is socially embedded and historically particular, and attempts to distinguish between free and forced labour in practice reveal 'a moral/political judgment about the kinds of pressures to enter and remain at work that are considered legitimate and those that are not' (Steinfeld 2008). Workers cannot be divided into two entirely separate and distinct groups— those who are working involuntarily into the misery of slavery-like conditions in an illegal or unregulated economic sector, and those who trip voluntarily and happily to work in a well-regulated and protected job they choose to do for the sheer pleasure of it.

While inability to leave a labour relation is mitigated, consent to enter is regarded as crucial to legitimate labour relations. Yet, as John Dawson wrote 'the instances of more extreme pressure were precisely those in which the consent expressed was more real; the more unpleasant the alternative, the more real the consent to a course which would avoid it' (Dawson 1947, cited in Steinfeld 2008: 14). The fewer one's alternatives, the more likely one is to enthusiastically consent to a situation, which can be labelled 'unfree' (see Anderson and Hancilova 2011 for some examples). This is particularly tricky given the variation between countries and economic sectors in terms of what is socially and legally constructed as acceptable employment practice, and indeed in terms of what is considered an employment practice at all. These problems of definition are in the end political problems: what is the nature of property in the person? When is commodification no longer acceptable? When does exploitation become unacceptable, and why? In terms of trafficking, these problems are transformed into problems of identification and provoke very different kinds of questions: How can one correctly identify a victim of trafficking? How does one know when a person has not 'freely' consented, or has been subjected to unacceptable exploitation?

7.3.3 *Trafficking and Immigration*

Given that movement across international borders is not a requirement for trafficking to take place, what is the distinction between trafficked migrants and imprisoned workers, or between foreign sex slaves and British sex slaves? For feminists, labour, and migrant rights' activists, why is being forced into prostitution or to labour at the barrel of a gun when you are in your home town, less heinous than being forced into prostitution or work elsewhere? What is the relation between trafficking and immigration?

The association of the slave with the foreigner and the non-citizen draws on a long tradition (Patterson 1982; Lape 2010). Like citizenship, it suggests a teleology: slavery is an antiquated form of human relations that is out of place in the modern world. In medieval times, serfs were tied to their masters; in the Atlantic slave trade, slaves were owned by their masters—that is, they did not own themselves. Slavery and trafficking continues to link foreignness with backwardness, often with foreigners importing 'traditional' employment relations, or gender and other status-dominated relations, in the same way that they are said to import 'traditional' marriage practices. Thus contemporaneously it is not only the slave who is the foreigner, but also the slave holder, the sex trafficker, and the master. Slavery is the mark of barbarism. The victim hails from a traditional pre-capitalist world and is typically subject to 'foreign men' who are uncivilized and do not respect her rights. While embedded in social relations, she is remarkably recognizable wherever she comes from, and wherever she is abused. Indeed, for all the invocation of the history of anti-slavery, there is a reticence about Britain's history of empire and colonialism and descriptions of modern-day slavery can be remarkably ahistorical. Slavery as a mode of organizing labour, as Julia O'Connell Davidson has pointed out (O'Connell Davidson 2008; O'Connell Davidson 2010), is no longer a legally endorsed *system* in any modern state,[2] and overt racial domination is not acceptable within liberal democracies (Goldberg 2002). In contrast to the Cold-War refugee, and akin to the 'third-world refugee' in a refugee camp,

---

[2] While not promoting a slave system of production per se, it is worth noting that the Thirteenth Amendment to the US constitution explicitly authorizes slavery and involuntary servitude for those convicted of a crime: 'Neither slavery nor involuntary servitude, *except as a punishment for crime whereof the party shall have been duly convicted,* shall exist within the United States, or any place subject to their jurisdiction'. Kamil Ghali has argued that 'sexual slavery is a daily phenomenon for some prisoners. There is ample evidence establishing the existence of sexual predators that prey on weaker and smaller inmates. These smaller inmates are sold to other inmates for further exploitation' (Ghali 2008).

the VoT is an 'ahistorical humanitarian subject' (Malkki 1996). She is peculiarly suspended between the particular details of her own pathological history and categorical victimhood. She is a category of person within the international order, which is what renders her so recognizable. Like the third-world refugee (the asylum seeker), the VoT must be pitied, but at the same time kept out.

Yet focusing on the foreigner raises some very real contradictions for states. Firstly, low-waged migrants can come from states where the options are considerably poorer than those available in the UK—they have different frames of reference, and potentially different forces acting to determine the legitimacy or otherwise of their consent to enter and to remain in particular employment conditions. It is the recognition of the potency of the force of the 'dull compulsion of economic relations' that underlies fears of migrants' undercutting the wages of the national labour force. As the UK government action plan put it: 'One of the difficulties we will face in investigating trafficking for forced labour is distinguishing between poor working conditions and situations involving forced labour' (Home Office 2007c: 40). Moreover, the set of alternatives available to a migrant are different from those available to a citizen, even leaving aside the consequences for residence, because they often do not have access to the welfare system.

Secondly, while the right to leave an employer and to work for whom one wishes is regarded as a defining element of what constitutes 'free' labour (Steinfeld 1991; Steinfeld 2001), this is not a right that non-citizens necessarily have. Those who are on particular visas can find that they are very constrained in whom they can work for or the terms of their employment, as discussed in Chapter 4. The employment contract dramatically affects the legal and political status of the worker, and has consequences, most obviously for the right to reside, that are way beyond the employment relationship. The migrant worker in this way is not the juridical equal of the employer. In this way immigration and citizenship laws mean that non-citizens are in relations of domination and subordination to citizens through the creation of dependency, and this dependence is systemic rather than a consequence of individual abuse. While extreme abuse of this system is presented as slavery, the system itself might more fruitfully be analysed as related to indenture.

There are very real ways in which migrant labour is constrained to such an extent that, were migrant workers Good Citizens, their freedom would be in doubt. But importantly, migrants are not the only group who must work within such constraints and it is not only migrants who are subject to peculiar force. Those on welfare benefits, for example, face losing benefits for up to three years if they turn down community work or the offer of a job in order to send 'a clear signal to those who are going through this process that if you co-operate, if you work with us, you will go through this quite happily and nothing will happen to you' (Watt and Wintour 2010). Under the Incentives and Earned Privileges Scheme, convicted prisoners can face a system of sanctions should they refuse work or not do it to the required standard. This is not forced labour since prisoners have been 'convicted in a court of law' (International Labour Office 1930: Art. 2).

Robert Miles (1987) famously argued that the limitations on migrants' entitlement to commodify their labour power that result from state-imposed restrictions (as with sponsorship) generate a form of unfree labour. Yet this crucial insight has been overlooked in the plethora of studies on migrant labour and 'trafficking' (O'Connell Davidson 2010), which have focused on 'evil employers' and traffickers. The personalized dependencies generated under such circumstances are typically imagined as a result of 'illegality', which is regarded as a key explanatory variable for understanding migrants' vulnerability to abusive practices both in the workplace and in their daily lives. This approach means the root of the difficulties faced by undocumented migrants becomes morally reprehensible individuals who take advantage of migrants' illegal status to exploit them in the workplace, extract extortionate rents for poor properties, demand sexual services, etc. The language of trafficking extols free labour while leaving these systems intact. It marks the United Kingdom as a site of free labour and equality. It draws attention to the backward employment and social relations of the Migrant, in contrast to those of the Citizen, yet it also overlooks the key point of difference between the Migrant and the Citizen, which is that the Migrant is subject to immigration controls.

7.4 The Moral Economy of the UK

Trafficking and slavery serve as a tremendous reminder of the formal freedoms of liberal democracies such as Britain. As mentioned above, this celebration should be seen within the context of a series of considerable practical constraints, but rhetorically the UK is quite simply imagined as a site of free labour and equality. Britain has overcome both slavery and serfdom, and in the forewords to both the trafficking consultation and the trafficking action plan, anti-trafficking is located firmly in the 'tradition' set by the 1807 Slave Trade Act, which abolished the slave trade in the British Empire:

> While we are preparing to mark this historic event we must recognise that there is another challenge facing us in today's modern world. Thousands of people are still forced to live in slavery type conditions around the world, including in the UK, as a result of the modern criminal practice of trafficking in persons. (Foreword by

Home Office Parliamentary Under Secretary of State Paul Goggins MP and Scottish Executive Minister for Justice Cathy Jamieson MSP, Home Office 2006c)

In fact, while presenting itself as the archetypal site of free labour, the UK had no offence criminalizing forced labour, other than that incorporated in the 2004 Immigration Act. Effectively, this meant that forced labour for non-citizens could be prosecuted, but not for citizens. This changed when the 2009 Section 71 of the Coroners and Justice Act made slavery, servitude, and forced or compulsory labour a specific criminal offence, so 'trafficking' finally came home, and forced labour was made illegal for British as well as foreign nationals.

Trafficking enables 'us' to congratulate ourselves on the freedom and rights within the British economy, and to respond morally and emotionally to the gap between us and them, between privilege and suffering. In the first case, trafficking and slavery are tremendous reminders of formal freedoms. By situating trafficking for forced labour within the context of the transatlantic slave trade, those who combat modern-day slavery firmly identify freedom with the ability to sell one's labour in the marketplace, the opportunity offered by capitalism. Yet importantly, this marketplace is not morally neutral, but a place of values as well as value, where worth can be incommensurable. Rather than assessing the Migrant's value through the language of points and of economic costs and benefits, what matters when it comes to human trafficking is the rhetorically priceless 'value of life': 'Human trafficking is a crime that demeans the value of human life and is a form of modern day slavery' (Home Office 2007c: 34). In contrast to the tables, regressions, and economic analyses of impacts that inform policymaking around economic migration,[3] the *Action Plan Against Human Trafficking* is peppered with qualitative accounts, the words of migrants themselves. In contrast to the 'economic migrant', the VoT regularly speaks (or 'testifies') at an international level. Her account is heard, selected, and promulgated by a range of anti-trafficking activists, including state agencies.

Although heard, the VoT is usually heard only under very specific conditions and the only option for her is to be rescued; any suggestion of agency undermines victim status and leads to 'moral equivocation' (Brown 2006). The victim cannot be angry, or take action, for in this case she is not deserving of help. She can only be rescued. This is not to say that trafficking policies cannot be used in some circumstances, for individuals to improve their lives. They are.

---

[3] The Home Office did commission an attempt to quantify and put a monetary figure on the amount of physical and sexual abuse of people trafficked for sexual exploitation, which came up with an approximate estimate of £1 billion (this relied on estimates such as a rape representing an emotional cost of £61,440 and a cost to the health service of £2,082). (Home Office 2005: 37; Dubourg et al. 2007)

But enforced passivity of the VoT can mitigate against this, and as Sealing Cheng puts it: 'What status quo are we buttressing when we reduce the lives and aspirations of the disenfranchised into uncomplicated stories of poverty and abuse by traffickers?' (Cheng 2010: 216).

Trafficking is a rare site of consensus in immigration politics, when the Home Office and migrants' organizations can find themselves both denouncing exploitation and abuse of migrants, both recognizing the peculiar vulnerability of undocumented migrants. However, this is not a consensus about immigration. It is a consensus that acknowledges that there have to be limits to the market, that there are social norms and obligations. While migrants and labour organizations tend to flag their concerns in terms of the human rights or the labour rights of migrants, for states this is placed within the context of the national moral economy. Yet at the same time, the market, through contract and employment, is presented as the solution to the problem of trafficking, seen as traditional, status-weighted, and oppressive relations. The market brings with it freedom, and choice, and property rights, including property in the person, are bound up with liberty. The language of trafficking represents this freedom not simply as a freedom to make rational, cost-benefit analyses and act accordingly, but as indicating a moral good. Yet at the same time it proscribes limits to the market. 'Neoliberalization has undoubtedly rolled back the bounds of commodification and greatly extended the reach of legal contracts' (Harvey 2005: 166), and there is anxiety about the limits of contract, particularly when it comes to do with matters of embodiment and personhood—most obviously about sex and prostitution, but also domestic services, care work, adoption, body organs, and so on. The question of the relation between labour power and personhood is also particularly apparent when it comes to labour migration—economic migrants are presented as of value insofar as they contribute to the economy, 'making migration work for Britain'. The commitment to combat trafficking demonstrates that non-citizens are not regarded purely as commodities, moved about for maximizing profit. Through anti-trafficking, it is apparent that the state and, importantly, the nation, acknowledge that there are human beings who cannot be simply traded as factors of production. In this sense, a commitment to anti-trafficking rescues the national labour market.

In this way, trafficking is connected to the moral economy. It flags the social norms and obligations and the extent of tolerable inequalities: 'we're not saying that migrant workers should be given cushy jobs, but they are entitled to the minimum', as a prosecutor on one UK trafficking court case put it (The Independent 2010). There is a relation between the economic and the social, and what is efficient is not the only guide to what is good. As discussed with reference to the call 'British Jobs for British workers'—British employers have a duty to employ British people even if it undermines short-term profits—when it comes to our relation with others, there are also moral and political norms and sentiments that influence behaviour. Trafficking outlines the borders of the British moral economy and affirms that Britain has certain values, reflected in its employment norms.

'Trafficking' turns 'us' into moral actors, able to respond to the inequalities that are in our midst as well as far removed. We are moved by the plight of forced labourers and slaves, and are thereby enabled to access the moral high ground. The *Not For Sale* campaign (see <http://www.notforsalecampaign.org/news/2010/11/17/free2work-app-launch/>) offers an iPhone app to enable consumers to know 'the story behind the products' and reduce their 'slavery footprint' by making appropriate 'consumption decisions'. These sorts of campaigns and products appeal to modern-day abolitionists seeking to stop slavery through responsible consumerism. However, as Laura Brace has argued, the politics of these kinds of movement are incredibly limited:

> If we label people as slaves, not only do we place them within our own liberal economy of guilt and render them hopelessly vulnerable, but we also do not have to face thinking of them as servants, and so recognising our own demand for their services...In thinking of her as a slave we attribute the same 'strange power' to ourselves as the eighteenth-century consumers did, and substitute that for the complicated, social, global relations of labour. These are some of the power relations of domination and servitude that are left intact when we choose only to know about slavery. (Brace 2010)

In short, while trafficking indicates relations of domination, it does not deal with the elephant in the room of immigration and citizenship controls, which are the principle mechanism of domination for non-citizens. We can condemn employers' threats to reveal undocumented migrants to the authorities in order to ensure their obedience, yet not question the mechanism of control itself. Indeed, immigration controls and enforcement are transformed to become means of protecting migrants from traffickers. Concern with trafficking focuses on borders and immigration controls while missing the crucial point that immigration controls produce relations of domination and subordination, thereby leaving state responsibility for the consequences of this completely out of the picture.

7.5 Putting the State Back In

Britain's enforcement policy and practice is always contextualised within commitment to the community of value that is, immigration enforcement does not ignore liberal values but directly invokes them. Take the Home

Secretary's foreword to *Enforcing the Rules*, an outline of the five-year enforcement strategy:

> Britain is a country where people work hard, play by the rules, speak English, and get on through merit. It has a proud, centuries-old record of integrating immigrants from around the world and, many times down the years, it has become home to communities fleeing persecution. That is why I am keen now to press on and sign the Council of Europe Convention on Action against Trafficking in Human Beings. Failure to take on the people traffickers, who are behind three-quarters of illegal immigration to this country, leaves vulnerable and often desperate people at the mercy of organised criminals. (Home Office 2007b: 2)[4]

Here we have immigration enforcement set within the context of the UK as a place of liberal freedoms and 'fairness', ruled by the social contract, concerned to foster tolerance and stamp out racism and exploitation. As the foreword suggests and in public discourse at least, an ethical approach has tended to be associated with asylum and those 'fleeing persecution'. However, as we have seen, by the 1990s, the extension of protection to refugees was no longer straightforwardly the hallmark of liberal democracies' freedom and respect for rights for non-citizens.

It was the arrival on the scene of the VoT that marked the emergence of the prevention of 'harm' as a concern of immigration policy. Harm is associated with the body, with shared human physical (and related mental) fragility, with suffering bodies, and in policy terms, with public health, drugs, commercial sex, and other activities that are deemed risky. The VoT is particularly associated with prostitution, that is with a 'harmful' activity, and there is a long history of using the language of 'harm' to describe the range of physical and mental consequences of prostitution for women (Weitzer 2010). Radical feminists such as Janice Raymond (1999), Patricia Hynes (Hynes and Raymond 2002), and Melissa Farley (2003), have raised concerns that originate in Victorian responses to the Contagious Diseases Act to apply to so-called 'prostituted women' today (Agustín 2007; Doezma 2010). There has been a particular and growing concern with migrant women whose involvement in the sex industry as 'victims of trafficking' has made them vulnerable to 'trafficking harms'. In *Secure Borders, Safe Haven* (Home Office 2002b), 'harm'

---

[4] The foreword continues:

> But, equally importantly, the fact that many immigrants, at the end of their journey, end up in shadowy jobs in the grey economy undermines the terms and working conditions of British workers. That's not fair. It chips away at the social contract and fabric of our country. Resentment of it breeds discontent and racism. This is especially keenly felt among those who believe they are not getting the economic or social opportunities they should because others, who have flouted the rules and often the law, seem to be getting on ahead of them. That's not fair either. (Home Office 2007b: 2)

is mentioned only twice but both times it is with reference to trafficking. Notably in that document, trafficking was felt to be an issue for 'particularly those working as prostitutes' (Home Office 2002b: para. 5.31). The elision between trafficking and illegality is what, in 2007, enabled the movement of the language of 'harm' into the mainstream of immigration management and enforcement. *Enforcing the Rules* comprises some thirty-six pages, and the word 'harm' or 'harmful' occurs no less than sixty-two times (Home Office 2007b). The prevention of harm is now a central plank of enforcement policy not just anti-trafficking policy, and in February 2010 the UKBA published *'Protecting our Border, Protecting the Public'*, a document setting out how the UKBA will protect the public from the 'untold harm' which derives from crime, terrorism, and illegal immigration (Home Office 2010e).

The language of harm that has slipped into immigration enforcement is extremely powerful. While the scope of positive duties may be controversial, the prevention of harm is something that can be easily agreed upon by people with a wide diversity of overall conceptions of the good. Moreover, in a liberal society it is harm that justifies compulsion, as John Stuart Mill writes, 'the only purpose for which power can be rightfully exercised over any member of a civilised community, against his will, is to prevent harm to others' (Mill 1948: 73). It is difficult for a liberal to argue that harm should not be prevented, even if it requires force.

There are problems in practice with this argument when it comes to enforcement and more specifically, there are three obfuscations that using the terminology of 'harm' brings about. Firstly, there is the question of what, in the case of immigration enforcement, is meant by 'harm'? In *Enforcing the Rules*, 'harm' is defined as 'all the potential negative consequences of illegal migration' (Home Office 2007b: para. 12). This is clearly tautological, and moreover assumes that the 'potential negative consequences of illegal migration' are not deeply contested. There is also a lack of clarity about the relation between 'harm' and migration: how is the harmful outcome related to the migratory process? Are migrants more vulnerable to harm because they do not speak the language, do not know their rights and do not have contacts in receiving states, for example (which is the argument of many NGOs); or is it because organized crime is involved in facilitating their movement and employment (the argument often put forward by state agencies)? With regard to immigration and enforcement, the range of 'harms' is presented as varying in seriousness from undermining public confidence in the immigration system, to terrorism and security threats. This illegal immigration, it seems, harms a wide variety of types of actors: it causes harm to businesses, citizens, and to the community. It also causes harm to the state by 'undermining confidence in the system'. Everyone, it seems, is harmed somehow by illegal immigration, and it is in everyones' interests to stop it. There is a wide variety of potential victims, each with different interests and agendas: the unemployed citizen struggling to get a job, the hard-pressed business playing by the rules, and migrants themselves. These latter are particularly vulnerable to harm, as victims of exploitative employers, as victims of traffickers, and (when legally resident and working) as victims of other migrants who take opportunities that are rightfully theirs. Immigration controls protect migrants as much as citizens.

The problem with this argument is that for many migrants, it is their immigration/citizenship status that makes them vulnerable. The determining of status and its policing and enforcement, that is a key component of their vulnerability, is the responsibility of the state. Thus the same body that is charged with protecting migrants from harm is also charged with creating and policing the boundaries between citizens and non-citizens, and with deporting them if they are found to be in breach of the law. The issues this raises can be seen from this practical example from the *Oxford Times* headline on 22 November 2010. It purports to be about twenty-three 'missing persons', eighteen of them asylum seekers. A police spokesperson explained:

> What happens with some people is they come into the country illegally and then they can be taken into criminal gangs and kept against their will and used in unlawful businesses. Whether they're victims of crime or simply illegal immigrants, we want to trace them. Primarily it's to make sure they're okay and not being abused in any way. Secondly if they are here illegally they need to be dealt with by immigration services... There's no specific suggestion of trafficking, but we investigate every possibility. (Allen 2010)

So, readers were urged to use the photographs to identify the people concerned because they might be at risk of harm. All of the missing asylum seekers were minors approaching eighteen or aged just over eighteen; many of them had been in local authority care. Given the policy of removing unaccompanied asylum-seeking young people when they reach the age of majority, it is not unrealistic to expect that they might have a reason for disappearing from the authorities at this particular stage in their lives. This is not to deny that they might be vulnerable to being exploited by unlawful businesses; indeed, they might join that group of 'vulnerable and often desperate people' whose plight was highlighted by John Reid in the ministerial foreword (quoted in Home Office 2007b: 2); migrants who are working illegally and who are grossly exploited. But their 'deportability' is the key factor in making them vulnerable to exploitation and abuse. At the same time as allowing that 'threats of deportation through reporting status to the authorities' may constitute evidence of trafficking, the state will also enforce these deportations in order not to attract abusive claims. In the language of 'harm prevention' the role of the state in producing vulnerability is made invisible in favour of its role as a protector.

7.6 Conclusion

The ethics of migration management, who is allowed entry and who is not, may seem important, but rather removed from the daily lives of citizens, but the ethical questions raised by enforcement are both different and more clearly related to their relationships and concerns. Relations of dependency and power are infiltrating everyday practice as the UK government seeks to decentralize and localize enforcement. Anti-trafficking responses do little to destabilize these relations, but rather clothe them in the language of helping and harm prevention. But the prevention of harm to migrants is a poor basis on which to try to develop ethically comfortable enforcement mechanisms: it relies on an idea of harm that is so vague as to be platitudinous, it equates compulsion for the good of others with compulsion for your own good, and it ignores the role of the state and immigration and citizenship legislation and practice in reinforcing dependencies and vulnerabilities.

The rhetoric, policies, and practices of anti-trafficking reveal deep political tensions within liberalism, yet place anti-trafficking beyond politics. The argument that immigration enforcement can be a means of harm prevention and protection for migrants as well as citizens was promoted by the previous Labour government and it seems set to continue. The re-inscription of the state as the legitimate protector of migrants' rights that is facilitated through anti-trafficking concerns is deeply problematic. The language of harm and of trafficking suggests that migrants are a special case whose vulnerabilities are different from those of citizens. But one of the key sources of increased vulnerability for migrants lies in their subjection to immigration controls. There is ample empirical evidence that certain groups of migrants fear state intrusion and offers of protection because of their immigration status—even when they are not resident illegally. To suggest that further immigration controls and policing is the solution is missing the point that this is a mechanism of production of vulnerability.

8

Immigration and Domestic Work: Between a Rock and a Hard Place

In December 2008, a Chinese woman, Mrs Wang, was deported. She had been staying in Oxfordshire having entered on a visitor's visa to spend time with her sister, brother-in-law, and two-and-a-half-year-old niece. She had told officials that she was looking after the toddler, and in the eyes of the immigration officer charged with her case, this meant that she was working as an unpaid nanny and therefore in breach of the conditions of her stay. Her sister saw it differently: 'When you come to see your family, you're not just sitting there doing nothing. You help out, but she's not an unpaid nanny. She told the border officials that she was looking after her niece, because in my culture the most important thing is the children, but she was here to see all of us.' (Bardsley 2008). Whether care in private households is work varies according to who does it. Would a wealthy white American aunt have counted as an unpaid nanny? What of British citizens caring for children who, if they are claiming benefits, can be often hustled out of the home and into the marketplace as soon as possible? Domestic and caring labour reveal the contingent, gendered, and racialized nature of what counts as work and the contradictions that emerge when it intersects with immigration controls. Notably for Mrs Wang, the fact that she was 'working' did not give her rights, but, the *Oxford Times* reported, only served as grounds for a deportation order that meant that she would not be able to return to the UK to see her family for at least ten years.

This chapter will consider the case of domestic and caring work as a site where the social construction of labour is revealed and contested, and examine the tensions manifest in immigration controls when applied to domestic labour. It begins with a brief consideration of domestic labour in the UK, its multiple forms and segmentations. Deregulation and informality mean that private households are a site where people with the kinds of ambivalent immigration statuses described in Chapter 4 can find precarious work. There have also been two types of visa that have been available for domestic labour from the late 1970s onwards: the au pair visa and a visa for domestic workers who enter the UK with employers. Both visas are principally for live-in work, and both are outside the usual migrant labour channels. In this way, paid domestic labour is treated as exceptional. I will examine these visas in terms of how they help to construct the labour market for domestic services and the ways they contribute to shaping the political subjectivities of migrants.

8.1 Reproductive Labour, Domestic Work, and the Liberal Individual

Women's relation to the property in their person and therefore to their labour has always been troublesome: 'Wife and servant are the same, but only differ in the name', wrote the author and poet Lady Chudleigh in 1703. Carole Pateman has argued that the liberal selves who enter the social contract are male, and that the social contract is preceded by a 'sexual contract' granting men access to women's bodies and selves (Pateman 1988). Her analysis has been challenged on the grounds that it essentializes women's subordination and makes it inevitable and universal (Dickenson 1997; Brace 2004). Social contract theories are stories to explain and analyse relations and not actual founding events, and the case of paid domestic labour proves the importance of recognizing the historical specificity of gender relations (which are also, as discussed below, raced and classed). However, the liberal individual that structures so much of our analysis of the world is male, and it is as a (white and able-bodied) man that he can be abstracted and freed from his body. He does not menstruate, give birth, and he is a father, not a mother. This is not to say that women are any more essentially connected to bodies or to children than are men, whether through menstruation or motherhood, but that it is socially constructed maleness that is the 'normal' gender-neutral person and femaleness that is the embodied deviation.

> Men who could live and survive independently needed to be 'disengaged' selves, struggling with the external world, appropriating and improving it. They had the potential to achieve self-mastery through their mastery of the world . . . [women] cannot escape their bodies or leave them behind to enter the world of the industrious and the rational; they are not understood as independent beings in the sense of being able to control and govern themselves. (Brace 2004: 188)

Chapter 1 illustrated how vagrancy became a male crime, even as women were tightly bound into service, and the mobility of women was controlled through family subordination and prostitution (Federici 2004). These ideas have reflected and shaped ideas about citizenship, contract, and the public and the private. In the nineteenth century, respectable women's incorporation into civil society and the state was imagined and legally constructed as being through the home and their dependence on men. The Good Citizen needed a wife, and the contribution of women, though subordinated, was crucial. 'It was women who were seen as spinning the invisible thread of property into a cable, and making it part of the fabric of ethical love and equal dignity' (Brace 2004: 198). The inheritance of nationality is part of this cable, both in terms of formal citizenship but also in terms of the creation of good citizens through their upbringing in the family home.

The home is strongly imagined as structuring affective lives as the market structures the productive, but importantly, this home is a particular type of home and the story of male domination over women must be understood as overlaid by relations of race and class. One of the earliest married women's property laws in the US was in Mississippi in 1839 and was intended to protect white married women's right of ownership of slaves they acquired through inheritance or gift (Welke 2010: 46). Tellingly, we do not know what Lady Chudleigh's servants thought of her complaint, but one cannot help but suspect that she might have divined less similarity between their experiences than did Lady Chudleigh, whose plea was for the liberation of wives rather than the liberation of servants. Mothers and wives working outside the home is not a modern phenomenon. Women have long worked in exchange for money, often in the households of the wealthy which were usually managed by women not by men, by Lady and not Lord Chudleigh. Women qua women were not totally excluded, but differentially included, and mechanisms for women's differential in/exclusion were and are shaped by race, class, sexuality, and whether they were deemed 'able' in mind and body. The arrangement of domestic labour can be a powerful indication of the divisions not only between women and men, but between women across multiple axes.

One of the distinctive characteristics of domestic labour is that it is performed principally by women, and there is some discomfort in commodifying it. Domestic work in private households is part of the broader category of reproductive labour, the accommodation of the raising of children, the distribution and preparation of food, basic cleanliness and hygiene necessary to survive individually and as a species. Reproductive labour is not confined to the maintenance of physical bodies: people are social, cultural, and ideological beings (Anderson 2000). Reproductive work—mental, physical, and emotional labour—creates not simply labour units but people. It refers to the perpetuation of modes of production and social reproduction with their associated relations including those of class, race, gender, and generation. Reproductive work is not confined to the family: education and the media are clearly socially reproductive institutions. Although necessary, domestic work, as with other forms of reproductive labour, is not only performed for survival. Caring for the elderly, for example, is not about the production of labour power, but it is about being human. How a house is ordered, what food is cooked, and how children are brought up is an expression of who 'we' are as individuals, and as people within particular sets of social, cultural, and economic relations. The work of doing this is not just about the accomplishing of tasks, but the doing of tasks in a particular way. The organization of our homes and their accoutrements demonstrates our position within wider social relations. Through the doing of domestic work we literally reproduce communities and our place within them.

As reproductive work is concerned with the social and cultural reproduction of human beings, the actual doing of the work—who does it, when, and where—is a crucial part of its meaning. More than a reflection, it is an expression and reproduction of social relations. Housework is, as the title of West and Zimmerman's well-known article states, 'doing gender' (Berk 1985; West and Zimmerman 1991). The employment of a domestic worker is not the employment of a simple substitute for a housewife because who does the work is a part of the work itself (Anderson 2000). A domestic worker, like the 'mother' and the 'wife', is performing a role within the family. Even when her tasks are ostensibly the same as those performed by 'mother' or 'wife', her role is different.

8.2 Paid Domestic Labour in the UK

Domestic and caring work in the UK as elsewhere, is not fully integrated into the labour market, and there is a delicate 'equilibrium of transgression' that means that the widespread informality and illegality in the sector is generally not considered a problem. Middle-class households may be paying a person cash in hand to clean their home and as with, for example, marijuana use by middle-class teenagers, this kind of illegality is rarely regarded as a cause for concern. There have been some changes in recent years and care work has increasingly become subject to regulation because of concerns about abuse of children and the elderly. There has been a gradual rolling-out of care worker registration, beginning with the more formalized sector of care homes. However, this move was not accompanied by any plans to regulate situations where individuals directly employ a carer and do not use state funds to do so. Cleaning work in private households is similarly unregulated and there has been a proliferation of small-scale cleaning companies, often sub-contracting work to individual workers on an hourly or daily basis. There is some evidence of serious exploitation and abuse when these arrangements are used to clean commercial premises (Anderson and Rogaly 2005), but little is known about the experiences of sub-contracted workers in the domestic setting.

Domestic workers in private households share many of the problems faced by other precarious workers who are working informally or in sub-contracting chains but they also face very particular challenges. The boundary between market and non-market work, which is central to legal definitions of employment, is drawn in part by the distinction between employment and family labour, a distinction that may be drawn differently by different people, as Mrs Wang found to her detriment. It is not the nature of the task, but the social relations that govern its performance, that determine whether work is employment. As discussed in Chapter 4, these social relations are not independent of the law. The law is not simply responsive to or regulatory of pre-existing social arrangements but is part of their construction. Like 'the Migrant', 'the employee' but also 'the family' too is in part a legal creation and the domestic worker can fall between both. In the UK, this means that domestic workers can find themselves legally exempted from even minimal labour protection. Domestic workers are not covered by the weekly forty-eight-hour restriction set out in the Working Time Regulations for the limitation of working hours, and the Health and Safety Executive (HSE) has no remit to inspect private households. They are exempt from the minimum wage if they are living-in and treated 'as part of the family' (National Minimum Wage Regulations Statutory Instrument 1999: 2(iv)). This is interestingly defined in a House of Commons Library research paper as not 'employed to live as members of the family'. The idea that a person can be *employed* to be in a fictive kin relation, that is, *employed* to be not considered 'working', indicates the way in which the distinction between employment and family work is mutually constitutive: the domestic worker is not an employee when she is treated as fictive kin, but she can also be employed to be treated as fictive kin—that is, not an employee. If domestic workers are fictive kin then they are not employees and cannot rely on the protections of employment law, but the kinship is *fictive*. 'As' a member of the family indicates that a domestic worker is *not* a family member, and what it means to be treated 'as' a member of the family and yet not 'be' a member of the family is partly defined through legal cases. If a worker is an employee and not fictive kin, then he or she must reduce to contractual terms a form of relation and type of work that can be strikingly difficult to accommodate in the language of contract (for example, is a person who is responsible for an elderly person if they wake up in the night only working if the elderly person wakes them up? Or are they working all night even if they spend it asleep?). Problems arising from this are compounded by the nature of the labour process which means that workers are likely to be isolated from each other and it can be difficult to organize collective action effectively to improve overall conditions.

There are multiple different arrangements governing the organization of domestic labour in the UK. It is still overwhelmingly performed by women as wives, although there is increased participation by men in certain tasks. Much of what had in the past been conducted under non-commodified or highly informalized arrangements has moved outside the home and its organization extends into the formal and productive economies. We can buy food cooked outside in the form of ready-made meals and takeaways, washing and ironing services can be delivered to the door, etc. Some types of caring work are also done outside the home: nurseries can provide 'wrap-around care' as much concerned with childcare as with the provision of education, some elderly people live in special facilities with professional carers. These arrangements can also be mixed, combining the unpaid labour of (female) relatives with paid work covering, for example, after school pick-ups or day breaks for those caring for elderly people. The specifics of all these arrangements depend on the needs of the cared for, ideas about what is appropriate and 'good care', and what is affordable.

Some types of domestic work, such as cleaning and certain aspects of caring for dependent family members, can only be done *in situ*, and this can be done by a (paid) non-family member either on a part-time basis, or, more rarely, by living in. The likelihood is that many household services provided in this way are provided off the books. The 2010 Labour Force Survey puts numbers in the 'domestic personnel' sector at 52,000, which is likely to be a considerable underestimate (cited in Clark and Kumarappan 2011: 6). The total number of people working as care assistants and home carers in 2008 was 730,000 but this does not include the unknown number of people working for individuals who fund the costs of their care from their own resources (Moriarty 2010). There is evidence that home-based child and elder care has been growing (Cox 2006; Cangiano et al. 2009). The increase in domestic service provision has not been confined to care. Gregson and Lowe found that over one-third of middle-class dual-career families employed some kind of domestic labour, often paid for with cash, and that since the 1990s there has been a growth in the undeclared employment of cleaners (Gregson and Lowe 1994).

One reason for this is like to be the increase in female labour-market participation with women making up 46 per cent of the total waged workforce in the UK in 2008 (Davies 2011: 9). That year, more than two-thirds of working age women with dependent children were in employment in the UK (Women's Resource Centre 2010: 21). This in a context where the nature, cost, and availability of public and market childcare outside the home for pre-schoolers is very limited. Williams and Gavanas have argued that in the UK, poor public provision, the increased use of unregulated paid domestic help in the home, and the positioning of mothers as individual consumers responsible for buying services, created the cultural and material conditions for the private employment of childcare workers in the home (Williams and Gavanas 2008). They set out a framework that facilitates an analysis of how the intersections of regimes of migration, welfare, and employment, shape both demand and discourses around care work. The particularities of this vary between states but it does seem to be generally the case that, firstly, demand for low-waged care workers is structurally embedded in many European states' organization of care provision; secondly, that very different policy regimes result in ostensibly the same outcome,[1] with significant numbers of migrants working in the elderly care sector in particular (although also childcare); and thirdly, that there is a disconnection between this empirical and policy reality and states' increasingly restrictive migration policies.

Like sex work, domestic labour reveals the fiction of labour market disembodiment, and not anybody/any body will do. Demand for labour in household services is highly gendered (Rubery et al. 1999; Cancedda 2001). While men may work in certain occupations, often those to do with maintenance, or with the outside of the house such as gardening and window cleaning, most are female-dominated. There is a strong preference for female workers often because domestic and care work (especially of young children) is simply not regarded as appropriate work for men (Anderson 2007). Domestic labour is associated with women's natural qualities and feminine characteristics, and demand is racialized as well as gendered, with some groups of women considered more naturally suited to certain types of domestic work than others (Anderson 2000). Given the importance of the work of making homes to the production of nationhood, it is interesting that domestic work is (like soldiering, also important for the production of nationhood) nevertheless considered suitable for non-citizens. In private households in the UK it seems that the demand for a particular ethnicity of domestic worker is very closely, and often inextricably, related to nationality. It is not just 'race' but 'foreignness' that matters, and the foreignness is not generic, but highly differentiated. What matters is a perception of particular characteristics, often expressed in national rather than in straightforwardly racial terms and thereby associated with culture and ostensibly more acceptable. So employers and placement agencies claim that certain nationalities may be caring or docile or good with children or even 'natural housekeepers' (Anderson 2007).

8.3 Employment Relations, Migrants, and Domestic Work

Domestic work is rarely imagined straightforwardly as employment. The home is governed by relations of status rather than contract (Olsen 1983), and the introduction of relations of contract into the private sphere can be

---

[1] There is of course nevertheless considerable heterogeneity masked by this, depending on labour market segment, state of origin, employment relations, and migration status, etc.

confusing and difficult to manage: should a nanny give professional or affectionate care? What does the employment of a professional say about the care of the mother? Domestic employment can suggest mercenariness on the part of the female employee, and the female employer who would rather 'go out to work' than look after her children (Brace 2004). Domestic workers and their employers are caught between work and not work, between the language of helping and the language of contract and rights, between mercenariness and unfreedom. The relationship is difficult to contractualize, and managing this, ensuring that it does not fatally undermine gender roles and domesticity, is part of household work for both (female) employer and worker. Employers are rarely only looking for the cheapest labour, and often they are looking for a particular type of worker and social/employment relation—a cleaner or a housekeeper, an au pair or a nanny, the tasks can be the same, but the title signifies a different type of relationship. Moreover, domestic work is a sector where labour may be constructed as 'low-skilled', but the workers most definitely are not fungible. Personal relationships and trust are particularly important to employers when it comes to introducing workers into their private homes and the private sphere is an area where people are particularly likely to want 'high-quality workers for low-waged work'—even the public spirited 'Good Citizen' is likely to baulk at taking the first person in the unemployment queue.

Employment relations between migrants and those householders who directly employ them are shaped by their being foreign, but importantly they are also, as discussed in Chapter 2, by their being 'poor'. For employers and host families, 'foreignness', that is, coming from outside the UK or in practice, outside the EU 15, can indicate poverty, living a difficult life, having limited opportunities (Anderson et al. 2006). Employers can describe with real pity the miserable situation that their domestic worker or au pair has left behind, and be enthusiastic about the difference that being in the UK makes both to the Migrant and to their families:

> I really feel strongly that it's a positive thing you can do for somebody . . . I think it's liberating for a girl from the Philippines to . . . leave the rice paddyfields and the village and to be able to send back huge amounts of money and to be able to get a job in England. (Employer interviewee, 'Markets for Migrant Sex and.Domestic Workers', quoted in Anderson 2007: 254)

While some employers and host families may indeed be relating to their workers as 'windows to exotica' (Rollins 1985), it also seems that references to poverty are not simply voyeuristic but a way in which being 'foreign' as well as being 'racially' different can help employers in the managing of their relation with domestic workers (Anderson et al. 2006). Foreignness can help employers and host families manage their deep discomfort around the introduction of market relations into the home. Migrant domestic workers are imagined as coming from impoverished lands, and this goes along with the idea that there is little one can do to remedy the injustices of the world, but employing a desperate migrant is a small contribution (Anderson and O'Connell Davidson 2003). Working as a domestic worker or as an au pair in a private household can be transformed from a dead-end job to a golden opportunity when it is undertaken by a hard-pressed migrant with limited opportunities. This trick is far more difficult with British workers, where differences are directly mediated by class rather than 'poverty'. It is poverty and foreignness that allows power to be clothed in the language of obligation, support, and responsibility, rather than power and exploitation. The relationship between employer and domestic worker is one of mutual dependence: the domestic worker is impoverished and needs money and work, the employer/host family needs a 'flexible' worker, and both fulfil the other's needs. The relationship draws on notions of protection and responsibility, with the master/mistress having a duty of care towards the servant or helper, who is subject to them and bound to the family through a set of hierarchical relations but with some degree of reciprocated responsibility. By entering into such a relation, the employer/host family not only demonstrates social status, but also kindness, for which the Migrant can be grateful, a gratitude that is expressed in pleasure in service (Anderson and O'Connell Davidson 2003).

These kinds of considerations are not captured under the formalistic requirements of the immigration regime, where employment is imagined as straightforwardly contractual. The combination of deregulation and personal relations means that it is a sector where those migrants who do not fit the standard categories of employment can easily fit. This includes people whose visas permit them to work, but only temporarily or part time, or people whose visas do not permit employment, and who are looking for informal but regular work, or over-stayers and others who are illegally resident. Most 'migrant domestic workers' are not therefore on visas that are specific to this occupation. For many years there were only two visa types available for domestic work, an au pair visa and a visa for domestic workers accompanying their employers. Both were for live-in work, but for au pairs this was constructed as 'living as part of the family', while for domestic workers, this was 'employment'. The visas signalled an acknowledgement that live-in domestic work does happen in the UK, but it is imagined as exceptional; either a temporary requirement or a 'foreign' relationship. Thus the two visas have been devised to deal with quite specific situations. Nevertheless, they have been routinely reformulated and these shifting categories are highly dynamic, suggesting both the difficulty of incorporating domestic labour into the standard model of immigration controls and the difficulty of accommodating the idea of work within the ideal of the family.

8.4 Au Pair Visas: Household Employment as Servitude

As a practice, the idea of young people moving to work in households as a transition to setting up their own family has a long European history. In the early modern period in north-western Europe, late marriage meant a long gap between puberty and marriage, and an estimated three-fifths of English young people in the sixteenth to the eighteenth centuries were sent to work in other households under a system of life-cycle service, a period of protected transition from the family home to adulthood. For the majority of life-cycle servants this was a transient phase, and while elites did not send out as many young people as they hired, much movement was lateral or nearly lateral across classes, and relations were familiar. Young people moved into the homes of others of the same, or perhaps slightly better, social status and relations were familiar but they were regarded as 'junior members', subordinate but integral (Cooper 2004: 281). They performed a range of tasks including hauling water, washing laundry, gathering wood, and looking after children. These tasks were gendered, with childcare being predominantly the job of female life-cycle servants.

This bears a strong similarity to the way that the au pair regime is imagined: that it is the movement of young people, in modern times, mainly females who are child carers, it is transient and imagined as middle class. The notion of au pairing as 'cultural exchange' echoes these types of historical practices and is related to life stage in immigration practice and in the imaginations of the au pair and the host family. This is an arrangement whereby one person's stage in the life cycle, as young, without dependants, inexperienced, flexible, fits another household's life stage—overstretched, in need of 'help' with demanding young children. It draws on an idea of home as a particular safe space for girls before they settle down, offering them the opportunity for social progress without exposing them to the dangers of the market. The 1969 Strasbourg Convention formalized this process, by marking an agreement between certain European countries to facilitate cultural exchange for young people at the same time as providing help to families with young children. The Strasbourg Convention emphasized in the preamble that au pairs do not belong to the 'worker category', and described the movement of au pairs as 'an important social problem with legal, moral, cultural and economic implications' requiring special moral protections (Council of Europe 1969). The mobility of au pairs is definitely not considered economic migration. The relation between au pair and host family in the UK as in other European countries was explicitly one of fictive kin, not one of work, and they were expected to live as 'part of the family'.

In the UK (which is not in fact a signatory to the Strasbourg Convention), the immigration status of au pair was limited to people coming from named European states aged between seventeen and twenty-seven years old. Applicants also had to be single, with no dependants, and coming for the purpose of cultural exchange. The relation between au pair and host family was explicitly one of fictive kin, and au pairs were expected to live as part of the family. Host families provided accommodation and board, and in return the young person could be expected to 'help out' for a maximum of twenty-five hours and babysit twice per week, in exchange for pocket money (that is, not a wage). Au pair visas could not be renewed and were valid for a maximum of two years (with a possible six month extension).[2] The only possible switch was to a spouse visa. Immigration rules both reflected and constructed notions of what an au pair is and in the UK this meant young, European, often then coded as white and Christian (cf. Newcombe 2004; Cox 2006), and, until 1993 when the rules changed, female.

Immigration regulations also made requirements of the families that are suitable for cultural exchange: they had to be English-speaking, have a spare room, and not need too much help. If they had a pre-school age child, then there had to be another carer available. While the immigration rules described the contours of the au pair and host families, these were filled out by agencies, whose literature illustrated the wholesome au pairs and happy families they were to be welcomed into (Cox 2006). It was nevertheless the au pair that was monitored and regulated, not the host family, and this is true for both immigration controls and au pair placement agencies. In practice, there seems to have been considerable abuse of the au pair system by host families. Research conducted in 2004/5 found that many hard-pressed families were very different from the au pair ideal, and using au pairs as the only affordable form of live-in childcare for shift-working single parents for instance (Anderson et al. 2006). Moreover, au pair agencies reported considerable difficulties in managing the assumptions of whiteness of both host families and au pairs. The latter caused particular problems as generally, unlike au pairs', host families' photographs were not required for agency registration (Anderson 2007).

Immigration rules not only regulated the type of people who could be subject to the au pair arrangement, but they also described the kind of relationship that would pertain. The au pair visa institutionalized three ideas around the role of young non-citizens in British family homes: firstly, that that they were equal; secondly, that au pairing was not work; and, thirdly, that

---

[2] Across Europe these regulations vary widely: in Norway, Netherlands, Sweden, and Denmark, for instance, the movement of young people for cultural exchange more obviously includes people that in the UK would tend to be designated as 'domestic workers' from Thailand and the Philippines.

they were temporary. While, 'au pair', quite literally, designates 'equal' in French, the question of who, in practice, the au pair is equal to, can be unclear. In the context of a history of life-cycle service a certain equality of familial status might be referred to—that is, the arrangement is between equal family types, effectively families could swap their young people. However, internally, families are not equal institutions but intensely hierarchical. Are au pairs equal to big brothers, sisters, aunts, mothers, or fathers? If s/he was a helping pair of hands in the same way as an older sister this does seem to be a rather romanticized view of what might be expected from many British teenagers. Moreover, the 'equality' only extended to within the home. Unlike other young people living in the household, the au pair was not allowed to take on any form of paid employment as to do so would breach immigration conditions. The family is imagined then not only as a space of equals, but as the private sphere, completely separated from and unaffected by the market.

Au pairs were not 'migrant workers'. The tasks performed by au pairs were not work because they were performed as part of the family. Au pair agencies were extremely active in lobbying the Labour Government in the processes up to the introduction of the 1998 National Minimum Wage Act. They successfully secured an exemption for people who were being paid but living as part of the family (the 'family worker exemption'). The work done by au pairs in private households was not regarded as employment, and employment in households was equated with servitude rather than the home-making of the au pair and family members. Equality signified not getting paid; after all, wives and daughters do not get paid, but only servants, who are, implicitly, not equal. Thus the invisibility of the economic basis of the household was maintained, even as non-family members were accommodated. The Immigration Directorate's Instructions on au pairs at the time when numbers of au pair visas issued were at an all-time high suggest that the amount of money allocated to an au pair was an important indicator of the nature of this relationship. 'Reasonable allowance' was defined as up to £55 a week as 'any sum significantly in excess of this might suggest that the person is filling the position of domestic servant' (Home Office 2004: para. 4). As well as equality and not working, immigration controls imposed temporariness as a condition of the au pair visa. Temporariness is in keeping with the practices of life-cycle service, and it also facilitated the delicate imaginative and emotional balancing of maintaining the relations of fictive kin (Anderson 2007).

The enforced temporariness of the au pair visa was typically not regarded as a problem by those subject to their conditions. Rather the opposite: temporariness was part of what made au pairing tolerable. Being an au pair was not regarded as a job that the visa holder wanted to remain in for a prolonged period; rather, it represented a chance to come to the UK and to live a different kind of life for a while, improving language skills and making contacts. Au pairs were often young women at a certain life-stage with no clear migratory project, keen to emphasize their education, their aspirations, their youth, and possibilities (Anderson et al. 2006; Búriková 2006). Those who had been au pairs for a while were equally concerned to locate this role within their experience as a young person. It is not that au pairs did not recognize the demanding nature of the physical (and emotional) work of being an au pair, but that they were clear that they were seeking to move on from this work. It was not an indicator of the type of employment the au pair imagined in the future. They had little incentive to invest in achieving recognition of their work as labour, and tended to see it as drudgery rather than 'honourable labour' (Brace 2007). Their position, as footloose, young, and free could be contrasted with host mothers, often perceived as frazzled, limited by domestic responsibilities, and sometimes jealous of their au pairs' freedom. They were mobile, not just across borders, but also (unlike host mothers) within families. When there were problems with host families, most of them felt able to move on relatively quickly.

The idea of the au pair depended for many years on the architecture of immigration controls. This began to change with the free movement of European citizens, but the scheme expanded in the early 2000s to include citizens of Eastern European states who still required a visa to come to the UK. On the eve of EU Enlargement in 2004, most au pair visa holders came from the new accession states, particularly the Czech Republic. However, following EU Enlargement, nationals from the new accession states were free to work in the UK without immigration restrictions, which caused considerable anxiety for many host families (Anderson et al. 2006). In early 2004, au pair agencies reported host families as specifying that they wanted Romanian, Bulgarian, or Turkish au pairs because they could not legally leave their families to work for another one (Anderson 2007), and post-EU Enlargement there was a significant growth in these nationals working as au pairs in the UK (Torre 2008). Romanians and Bulgarians working as au pairs are required to hold an accession worker card. For these nationalities au pairing is now considered a category of employment, and they are subject to the same restrictions as other workers: they can work only for the employer named on their accession worker card and are not free to change employer. Unlike other categories of employee, they continue to be exempt from the minimum wage.

The au pair visa, with the exception of the accession workers' card (which is not a visa per se) was abolished in November 2008. The scheme was incorporated into the Temporary Youth Mobility Scheme outlined in Chapter 3 which is applicable to only seven states and is aimed at those who 'wish to experience life in the UK'. Those who enter under this scheme may both work and undertake au pair placements, but what precisely is meant by 'au pair placement' is, unlike previously, not defined. There is no need to distinguish au pairing from working in private households, because this group is allowed to work.

The discursive idea of the au pair has a strong hold, and the disappearance of the visa has not meant a disappearance of the practice and type of arrangement. There are still large numbers of au pair agencies, and it continues to signify a type of arrangement that is not straightforwardly an employment relation, often relying on fictive kin, to distinguish itself from a service relation. The current dominance of European states that are outside the EU 15 states suggests a shift in the equality of familial status aspects of au pairing: British nationals registered with au pair agencies tend to be looking for families in Austria, Spain, and Holland, or further afield in Canada, the USA, or Australia. There are very few who are looking for places in Czech Republic or Poland. The history of the au pair visa demonstrates the shifting but mutually dependent nature of citizenship, family, work, and gender, and the attempts to accommodate this within liberal discourses of equality. While the au pair visa has, for the moment, largely disappeared from the UK (it is still an important yet under-researched component of immigration controls in other European states such as Sweden and Denmark), the contradictions and tensions that gave rise to the immigration status continue to underpin domestic arrangements in unknown numbers of British households.

8.5 Domestic Worker Visa Holders: Household Employment as 'Not Slavery'

While the au pair visa was issued for non-citizens living with British families, the domestic worker visa was designed for non-citizens living and working with *non-citizen* families. It began as an immigration concession outside the rules in 1977. This followed a general tightening in immigration controls which meant that 'low-skilled' workers were not being given visas to work in the UK. It was an exception granted in the interests of wealthy employers enabling them to be accompanied by their domestic workers, not an exception granted in the interests of domestic workers. The concession gave rise to a wide range of visas: some workers would be given a visitor's visa with an 'employment prohibited' stamp, others had permission to enter to work for their employer, with the name of the employer written on their visa, others were given permission to enter as family members. The particular visa given was in practice subject to the discretion of the individual visa issuing officer, but there were discernible patterns depending on the point of origin of the family and worker. What these visas had in common was that the domestic worker did not have permission to work, and if she left the employer that she had entered with, she lost her immigration status and became an illegal resident.

The majority of those entering on domestic worker visas came from further afield than most au pairs, from places where travel is more expensive, often from Asia (the Philippines, India, and Indonesia currently account for nearly two-thirds of entries) (Lalani 2011). They were usually women with children or other dependants. Most were remitting a large portion of their wages and had migrated from developing countries often in order to support their families financially. They had a far greater age range than au pairs, with some of them in their late sixties. This is not the model of life-cycle service, but is closer to that of the nineteenth-century English domestic servant, where those who were resident were physically and psychologically more distanced from the families they lived with, and class rather than life stage was the determining factor of one's role in the family.

The employers of these domestic workers were generally wealthy foreign nationals, although they did also include returning British expatriates. The visa controls on the workers meant that they could be abused with impunity and studies found widespread evidence of exploitation and physical abuse. The immigration concession was described as the imposition of 'slavery' in modern times (Anderson 1993). Domestic workers in this situation organized around a call to be recognized as *workers*. While for au pairs in British homes, 'work' signified servitude and inequality, for domestic workers in non-citizen families 'work' signified free labour and not-slavery.

The campaign and self-organizing of domestic workers, facilitated by the trades unions, meant that in 1998 the newly elected Labour government agreed to incorporate domestic workers accompanying their employers into the immigration rules. Most of those whose stay had become illegal were given permission to stay, although the discretionary nature of the original visa which was then relied on for proof of entry meant that some found it easier to regularize than others (Anderson 1991). For new entrants, a visa was introduced that did not make them dependent for their immigration status on their employer, and gave them the right to work on their own account as long as they were restricted to private households. In terms of entry provisions, they were still dependent on their employers, and the visa continued to be for the benefit of employers. Once they had entered, the worker could in theory, gain access to employment tribunals, and join trades unions. They would also be subject to employment protections including the minimum wage. But a crucial requirement of this was that they were *not* 'family workers'—that is, they could be given a domestic worker visa and be treated as a member of the family. This would not invalidate their visa, but it would mean that the employer would not have to pay the minimum wage. This led to several high-profile cases examining what 'living as part of the family' actually means, but this still continues to be very unclear.

What was experienced by domestic workers as the most crucial change introduced in 1998, and what they and the campaign group, Kalayaan, had long campaigned for, was the right to change employers without thereby losing their right to reside. This had been possible for au pairs—until the arrangement was reconstituted as work, requiring a permit—but not for domestic workers accompanying their employers, even in cases of serious abuse. For domestic workers, the right to change employer signalled that they were not to be treated as part of the family, in a status relation, but as an independent worker. However, those subject to immigration controls who enter under worker schemes do not usually have the right to change employer, and domestic workers were therefore not asking to be accommodated within general provisions covering *migrant* labour. As discussed in Chapters 4 and 7, in general migrant workers' dependence on their employers extends beyond the employment relation and illuminates contradictions in the way that 'free labour' is imagined now for citizens and for non-citizens. On the one hand, the campaign had demanded that domestic labour be treated as a job like any other, subject to the protection of employment law. Yet if it were treated in the same way as any other job *done by a non-citizen*, this would mean withholding the right to change employer, a right that was central to their demands. So their claim for fundamental rights as workers was a claim for rights as *British* workers since workers subject to immigration controls were tied to their employers through work permit, and later, sponsorship, arrangements. This goes to the heart therefore of the confusion surrounding the distinction between slavery and indenture. While using the terminology of slavery with its implication of racialized domination the objection was rather to a system that, while sharing racialized domination with slavery, was, *as a system*, more akin to indenture. This elision was possible because neither slavery nor indenture is considered free labour, and what was seen as important was that this labour was not free.

In order to make this claim for exceptional rights as migrants, that is, to be incorporated into the immigration rules, but not incorporated into mainstream immigration for employment regulation, the campaign highlighted the specificities of domestic work and of migrant domestic workers as being their vulnerability to physical abuse and exploitation. This was tactically extremely successful. Had domestic workers initiated a joint campaign with fellow migrants calling for an end to visa sponsorship and the rights of all migrants to change employers, the likelihood is they would still be campaigning. Public sympathy seized on images of abusive male employers, and this also generated considerable parliamentary support. However, it brought with it several problems. Because most (but not all) of the families bringing in domestic workers under this visa arrangement were not British nationals, this meant that media attention focused on barbaric foreign employers, often from the Middle East. These foreign families, in stark contrast to the British host families of au pairs, were not imagined as safe spaces for women, but as cruel and exploitative places where the threat of physical and sexual abuse was ever-present. British families, comparing themselves favourably to these barbarians, began to offer 'golden opportunities' to live and work in their home for board and lodging and no pay.

The more long-term consequence to the emphasis on abuse was that it was built in to the government's response. Migrant domestic workers were given the right to change employers in the case of abuse. Employment rights were granted, not because it was a job like any other (for a British academic to be given the right to change employer if they are abused by the vice chancellor sounds absurd) but precisely because it was *not* and it was possible to ring fence domestic labour and constitute it as an exceptional case without impacting on migrant employment relations more generally.

The hard-won right to be treated as workers came under pressure only ten years later in 2008 with the difficulty of accommodating domestic workers within the PBS. Given that the UK was no longer supposed to be granting visas to 'low skilled' non-EU migrants, the domestic worker visa represented an anomaly. The Labour Government attempted to withdraw the visa, but came under pressure from domestic workers, campaigners, and trades unions, and drew back, initiating a two-year consultation period. The new coalition government reopened the debate in its pursuit of reduced net migration. It reinvigorated some of Labour's original proposals, and announced that from April 2012 domestic workers accompanying their employers would only be eligible for a six-month non-renewable visa. They would not be able to change employer, and would have to leave the UK with their employer. They would be given visas as workers, but, like Romanian and Bulgarian accession card holders, this did not mean that they would be paid the minimum wage, as the UK Border Agency claimed, 'it is not for us to say who is entitled to the National Minimum Wage'.[3] It was acknowledged by government ministers that employment in private households could be abusive, but the association of this with the foreignness of households was made explicit. Home Secretary Teresa May, for example, stated, 'We recognise that the ODW [overseas domestic worker] routes can at times result in the import of abusive employer/employee relationships to the UK' (Home Office 2012c: 2). Whereas previously vulnerability to abuse had been used to demand labour rights, these two have now been separated, and protection rather than rights invoked as the appropriate response: 'We do not necessarily believe that a right to

---

[3] Personal communication, Jenny Moss, community advocate at the migrant domestic workers' support organization Kalayaan.

change employer whatever the reason is the only way to provide protection' (Currell 2012: 12). The principle protection for migrant domestic workers was now to be refusal of entry. 'The biggest protection for these workers will be delivered by limiting access to the UK through these routes' (Home Office 2012a). Refugees may, theoretically at least, be protected by flight, but migrant workers as potential victims of trafficking are it seems protected by not being able to move in the first place.

8.6 Conclusion

Migrant domestic workers are between a rock and a hard place. Like non-migrant domestic workers they are caught between being not quite a family member and not quite an employee, but they are also, like Mrs Wang, caught between the excesses of immigration regulation on the one hand and employment deregulation on the other. Domestic work vividly illustrates many of the themes of this book: the relation between race, poverty, and immigration, the gendered consequences of our limited conceptualizations of 'skill' and the nature of the labour relation, and the problems of trafficking. It is also a reminder of the heterogeneity of migrants. Many of the employers of domestic workers are themselves 'migrants', but given that they are wealthy, their experience of immigration controls is very different.

The history of the domestic worker visa illustrates the contingency of the inclusion of domestic workers as work, both in terms of immigration and employment. It suggests that this category cannot be ignored—the businessmen and entrepreneurs and wealthy tourists 'need' their domestic worker—but this is very difficult to accommodate within the structures afforded by immigration. Immigration controls highlight the ambivalence of domestic work in employment, an ambivalence that generally goes unnoticed as hundreds of thousands of families make their own private arrangements. While viewed as exceptional because it often does not fit the conventional models of employment and contract that underpin the way waged labour is organized, care work in the most general sense has always been done, and in this respect it is not exceptional at all. Arguably, in fact what is surprising is that we tolerate an analysis that has such difficulty in accommodating care relations. Domestic and care work are not some leftover arrangements, but *precede* 'normal' employment. As wage labour has become normalized and regulated, and the wage earner constituted as the normalized subject, we have forgotten just how human the relations of care are, and how limiting our ideas of 'the job'. It is not only the domestic worker who is marginalized, but unpaid female labour, the unemployed, the informal worker, and other figures who are spectres outside the domain of political economy (Denning 2010).

9

Conclusion

Making the Difference

In the fairy story of the Introduction, the wealth of the kingdom and the poverty of the woodcutter were not related. If the woodcutter had become impoverished because the kingdom had chopped the forest down to satisfy its requirement for fuel, his gratitude at being permitted admittance might have been more muted. Chapters 1 and 2 indicated the relation between kingdom and forest, their continuing inter-relatedness, and the importance of history for understanding this. Uncovering the relation between the different ways that states both directly control the mobility of citizens (through emigration, registration, and regimes of imprisonment, for example), and help shape their mobility more indirectly, though policies like welfare benefit, transportation, and housing, can help to give new political perspectives deriving from, but not confined to, migration. As outlined in Chapters 3 and 4, the hard and soft borders that confront the non-citizen, like the 'national labour market', for example, or the minimum income requirements for family reunion, also have consequences for citizens. Chapter 5 discussed how the situation of migrants reveals the importance of analysing citizenship as a global system as well as a relation between an individual and a state and the ways in which citizenship signifies closure and exclusion at the same time as it claims universalism and inclusion. Indeed, as discussed in Chapters 6 and 7, the increase in in-country immigration enforcement affects citizens as well as migrants. In Chapter 8, the case of domestic labour was examined, and the choice offered to migrant workers made explicit: either accept being tied to employers or do not work in the UK at all. Here is an alternative fairy story: the woodcutter is a woman, and the guards gently inform her that she will not be treated well in the kingdom, and turn her away for her own good.

Us and Them has started to consider the implications of the kingdom not being a community of value populated solely by good citizens. There is conflict, exclusion, and failure inside as well as outside the kingdom. Previous chapters have examined how the 'them' that is implied by 'us' becomes explicit when it comes to immigration, and how 'us' is consonant with the nation but also with an imagined community of value. The community of value is both local and national at the same time. Defined from inside by the 'failed citizen', its borders can coincide with an imagined 'local community', and defined from the outside by the 'non-citizen', its borders are strongly associated with 'the nation'. The good citizens of the community of value are social beings shaped by national culture, national obligations, and national history, and the borders of the nation can also be called upon to exclude the Failed Citizen (who can be presented as not having national values).

Nationalism is, as Benedict Anderson notes, 'the most universally legitimate value in the political life of our time' (Anderson 1991: 3). While often associated with the political far right, its assumptions structure much of our daily lives and our politics. From the sports pages to the editorials, the national 'us' is placed in a world of homelands (Billig 1995; Sharma 2006). The nation sets the community of value within a historical trajectory, and links the individual to a community of people and to a heritage. The history of the nation is imagined as an interweaving of ancestral histories (the word 'nation' is derived from *natio* or 'that which has been born'; Zernatto and Mistretta 1944), that connects an imagined 'us' to the past through ancestry. Relating to the past through ancestry can offer anchorage through the nation when the nation is linked to a historic homeland (which may be metaphorically lost, even if currently inhabited—consider the English Defence League, for example).

Ancestral histories are not only correlated with nations. They may trace the contours of religion, class, race, ethnic, and other affiliations that are, through these historical relations, rendered authentic and claimable by particular contemporary populations. The suffering or triumph of literal but also metaphorical ancestors can be claimed as a 'heritage' by some, but not by others. This claim is often a means to assert a right to membership in the community of value. 'They' were rejected and dismissed, but 'they' were misunderstood, pioneers, before their time, overcoming overwhelming odds, made crucial contributions, etc. This ancestry also serves to delimit 'us' from 'them' from the past through to the present. Anchorage and authenticity set the boundaries of the historical 'we'. For example, the vagrancy ordinances and statutes prefigure and shape the institutions, laws, and habits of thought that contemporaneously control labour mobility and welfare benefits. However, while the homeless, the tramp, and the beggar may make a claim to the history of the unsettled poor in England, this is far more difficult for the Migrant. Given the history of transportation, press gangs, clearances, and compulsory service, those who today theoretically could trace their ancestry back to a fourteenth-century English vagrant are as likely to live outside the UK as inside. Nevertheless it is a history that is easier to claim for those whose immediate families have been in the UK for a couple of generations than for those whose near relatives have not, and it is easier to claim for those who are 'white' than for those who are not.

Migrants must claim their history in their 'own' origins, not in the institutions, laws, and history of their country of residence. This means that migration histories, whether of individuals or of groups, often reproduce an imagined trajectory from origin to integration, from a time of original settlement and belonging, to a 'new community'. This is typically how the history of Britain's 'migrant communities' is depicted. There is a deeply sedentarist bias to this: the Migrant qua migrant has no history but rather an origin. Yet, as stated at the outset, the history of the world is a history of human mobility. Situating migration within a broader history of often unruly mobilities, and in this way unmooring people, nation, and state, offers opportunities for developing a new perspective on migration, one that does not essentialize (and thereby recreate) the figure of the Migrant. This unmooring invites a critique of investment in the imaginaries, not only of nation but also of ancestry, and asks how one can reclaim histories and acknowledge their importance without thereby falling into ideas of authenticity, autochthony, and belonging.

Historical comparison is important for the questions it raises about the limits of contemporary liberalism. Previous chapters have noted the dislike of the terminology of 'deportation' because of its resonance with the deportations of the Second World War, and the political application of the language of 'slavery', with its associations of racial domination, violence, and systemic exploitation to contemporary migrants. Foreshadowing, parallels, institutions, influences can help nuance ideas of heritage and 'identity' without neutralizing them and open ways of relating to the past that are not driven solely by ancestral thinking and national imaginaries. Thinking historically about migration reveals the contingency of contemporary institutions and systems, and crucially the relation of privilege, power, and poverty to questions of mobility and state development. The wealth of the kingdom is not independent of the poverty of the woodcutter. The guards' 'protection' of the woman who seeks to enter must be understood in the context of economically, socially, and historically shaped inequalities.

The response to this, 'Let me in, I can make my own choices', could be cast as the migrant dilemma. Migrants are caught between life and work in liberal democracies as imagined and rhetorically portrayed—free labour, justly rewarded—and the harsh realities of low-waged labour in those same liberal democracies—the only realistic option. 'There is no easy answer to the question and answer often heard in emigration areas, "What is worse than being 'exploited' abroad? Not being 'exploited' abroad"' (Martin 2003: 30). That despite such limited rights, so many migrants still attempt to enter, legally and illegally, in order to live and work in wealthy countries, suggests not only that those migrants who are admitted are better off than those who are not, but also that they are prepared to tolerate limitations on their rights as part of a 'trade-off' that facilitates their entry (Ruhs and Martin 2008). Migrants are doing the global equivalent of getting on their bike, taking their skills and their labour to where it brings most profit. If they choose to be exploited from a universe of admittedly constrained options, then this choice should be theirs to make. The argument goes that those who are more economically privileged should be careful about claiming to protect those in more constrained circumstances from risks by further limiting their options.

There is a sleight of hand here, however. For the original observation by economist Joan Robinson in 1962 is 'the misery of being exploited by capitalists is nothing compared to the misery of not being exploited at all' (Robinson 2006: 45). The 'choice' to be exploited and its associated misery is not confined to migrants. Many citizens, particularly those in low-waged work, do not work in marvellous jobs, free from exploitation, expressing themselves and achieving their potential through their labour, gaining a sense of contribution to a greater good. Similarly, while migrants struggle to have their family relations, including heterosexual marriage, recognized and respected, the relational possibilities for all of us, migrants and citizens, are heavily constrained through ideals of heteronormativity, monogamy, and exclusion. This is not to deny that to be able to work in a job, to be acknowledged as a monogamous partner, to vote or stand in an election, are precious rights for those who are denied them, and their recognition can change lives. However, they are also limited. Recognizing simultaneously the artificiality and the consequences of the categorizing of people into migrants and citizens reveals that the politics of migration are far broader than immigration policy.

The migration fairy story is just that; a fairy story. The kingdom is not a place of harmony and justice, its wealth is not independent of the poverty of the forest and the inhabitants of the kingdom do not live happily ever after. Moreover, the guards find it singularly difficult to keep out the woodcutter, and her friends and family. No set of border controls has ever worked to contain fully people's desire and need to move. In this sense, national borders are a dystopian/utopian project. No state, however powerful and well resourced, will manage to control migration and ensure that only those with the right motivation, values, and plans cross the border in the right direction. The logic of job, family, and citizenship, assumes a certain community of value. Moving beyond the choice between exclusion or exploitation through beginning, not with a job, but with the need for subsistence, not with a spouse, but with the need for mutual care and support, and not with the right to exclude, but with the assumption of people's full inclusion, has the potential to open up politics and analysis. It invites an open, complex, and multifaceted contemporary 'us' that has the possibility of being shaped by shared imagined futures as well as shared imagined pasts.

Bibliography

Act for the Better Releife of the Poore of this Kingdom 1662. *13 + 14 Charles II c.12*. London.

Act for the Punishment of Sturdy Vagabonds and Beggars 1536. *27 Henry VIII c.25*. London.

ADAMS, J., GRIEG, M. & MCQUAID, R. W. 2002. Mismatch in Local Labour Markets in Central Scotland: The neglected role of demand. *Urban Studies*, 39, 1399–416.

AGUSTÍN, L. 2007. *Sex at the Margins*, London, Zed Books.

AHMAD, A. 2008. Dead Men Working: Time and space in London's (illegal) migrant economy. *Work, Employment and Society*, 22, 301–18.

ALDIN, V., JAMES, D. & WADSWORTH, J. 2010. The Changing Shares of Migrant Labour in Different Occupations and Sectors of the UK: An overview. *In:* RUHS, M. & ANDERSON, B. (eds.) *A Need for Migrant Labour? Labour shortages, immigration and public policy*, Oxford, Oxford University Press.

Aliens Act 1905. *5 Edward VII c.13*. London.

ALLEN, E. 2010. Vanished. *Oxford Mail*, November 22.

ANDERSON, B. 1991. *The devil is in the Detail: Some lessons to be drawn from the UK, government's recent regularisation of migrant domestic workers*. Available at <http://www.childtrafficking.com/Docs/anderson_1999_devil_detail_0108.pdf> (accessed 14 March 2012).

ANDERSON, B. 1993. *Britain's Secret Slaves: Migrant domestic workers in the UK*, London, Kalayaan and Anti-Slavery International.

ANDERSON, B. 2000. *Doing the Dirty Work? The global politics of domestic labour*, London, Zed Books.

ANDERSON, B. 2007. A Very Private Business: Exploring the demand for migrant domestic workers. *European Journal of Women's Studies*, 14, 247–64.

ANDERSON, B. 2009. What's in a Name? Immigration controls and subjectivities: The case of au pairs and domestic worker visa holders in the UK. *Subjectivity*, 29, 407–24.

ANDERSON, B. 2010a. Migration, Immigration Controls and the Fashioning of Precarious Labour. *Work, Employment and Society*, 24, 300–17.

ANDERSON, B. 2010b. Mobilising Migrants Making Citizens: Migrant domestic workers as political agents. *Ethnic and Racial Studies*, 33, 60–74.

ANDERSON, B. & ANDRIJASEVIC, R. 2008. Sex, Slaves and Citizens: The politics of anti-trafficking. *Soundings*, 40, 135–45.

ANDERSON, B. & BLINDER, S. 2011. *Who Counts as a Migrant? Definitions and their consequences* Oxford, The Migration Observatory, COMPAS.

ANDERSON, B., GIBNEY, M. & PAOLETTI, E. 2011. Citizenship, Deportation and the Boundaries of Belonging. *Citizenship Studies*, 15, 547–63.

ANDERSON, B. & HANCILOVA, B. 2011. Migrant Labour in Kazakhstan: A cause for concern? *Journal of Ethnic and Migration Studies*, 37, 467–83.

ANDERSON, B. & O'CONNELL DAVIDSON, J. 2003. *Is Trafficking in Human Beings Demand Driven? A multi-country pilot study*, Geneva, International Organization for Migration.

ANDERSON, B. & ROGALY, B. 2005. *Forced Labour and Migration to the UK*. London, Trades Union Congress.

ANDERSON, B. & RUHS, M. 2010. Migrant Workers: Who needs them? A framework for the analysis of shortages, immigration, and public policy. *In:* RUHS, M. & ANDERSON, B. (eds.) *Who Needs Migrant Workers? Labour shortages, immigration, and public policy*, Oxford, Oxford University Press.

ANDERSON, B., RUHS, M., ROGALY, B. & SPENCER, S. 2006. *Fair Enough? Central and East European migrants in low-wage employment in the UK*, London, Joseph Rowntree Foundation.

ANDRIJASEVIC, R. 2007. Beautiful Dead Bodies: Gender, migration and representation in anti-trafficking campaigns. *Feminist Review*, 86, 24–44.

Anti-Trafficking Monitoring Group 2010. Wrong Kind of Victim? One year on: an analysis of UK measures to protect trafficked persons. London, ATMG.

ATFIELD, G., GREEN, A. E., PURCELL, K., STANIEWICZ, T. & OWEN, D. 2011. The Impact of Student and Migrant Employment on Opportunities for Low Skilled People. *Evidence Report*. London, UK Commission for Employment and Skills.

BACH, S. 2008. Staff Shortages and Immigration in the Health Sector: A report prepared for the Migration Advisory Committee, London, Migrant Advisory Committee.

BACK, L., KEITH, M., KHAN, A., SHUKRA, K. & SOLOMOS, J. 2002. The Return of Assimilationism: Race, multiculturalism and New Labour. *Sociological Research Online*, 7, 2.

BALE, T. 2011. The Right Side of the Argument? The centre-left's response to migration and multiculturalism. *Exploring the Cultural Challenges to Social Democracy*, London, The Policy Network.

BALES, K. 2000. *Disposable People: New slavery in the global economy*, Berkeley, University of California Press.

BALES, K. 2005. *Understanding Global Slavery*, Berkeley, University of California Press.

BALIBAR, E. 1991. Racism and Nationalism. *In:* BALIBAR, E. & WALLERSTEIN, I. (eds.) *Race, Nation, Class: Ambiguous identities*, London, Verso.

BALIBAR, E. 2004. *We, the People of Europe? Reflections on transnational citizenship*, Princeton, Princeton University Press.

BANKS, J. 2008. The Criminalisation of Asylum Seekers and Asylum Policy. *Prison Service Journal*, 175, 43–9.

BARBIER, J.-C., BRYGOO, A. & VIGUIER, F. 2002. Defining and Assessing Precarious Employment in Europe: A review of main studies and surveys, a tentative approach to precarious employment in France, Paris, Centre d'Etude de l'Emploi.

BARDSLEY, F. 2008. Aunt Ordered Out of UK. *Oxford Mail,* 10 December.

BARRETT, D. 2011. Killer of Gurkha's Son Wins Right to Stay in Britain. *Daily Telegraph*, *16 January*.

BARROW, B. 2006. East Europe Migrants Help Take Jobless to Six-year High. *Daily Mail*, 17 August.

BARTELS, E. 2006. Too Many Blackamoors: Deportation, discrimination and Elizabeth. *SEL Studies in English Literature 1500–1900*, 46, 305–22.

BAUDER, H. 2006. *Labor Movement: How migration regulates labor markets*, Oxford, Oxford University Press.

BECK, U. 1992. *Risk Society: Towards a new modernity*, New Delhi, Sage.

BEIER, A. L. 1978. Social Problems in Elizabethan London. *The Journal of Interdisciplinary History*, 9, 203–21.

BEIER, A. L. 1985. *Masterless Men: The vagrancy problem in England 1560–1640*, London, Methuen.

BELT, V. & RICHARDSON, R. 2005. Social Labour, Employability and Social Exclusion: Pre-employment training for call centre work. *Urban Studies*, 42, 257–70.

BENNETT, J. 2010. Compulsory Service in Late Medieval England. *Past and Present*, 209, 7–51.

BENTHAM, J. 1796. *Management of the poor or, a plan, containing the principle and construction of an establishment, in which persons of any description are to be kept under inspection*, Dublin, James Moore.

BERK, S. 1985. *The Gender Factory: The appointment of work in American households*, London, Plenum.

BERLIN, I. 1969. Two Concepts of Liberty. *In*: BERLIN, I. *Four Essays on Liberty*, Oxford, Oxford University Press.

BERR 2008. Agency Working in the UK: A review of the evidence. *Employment Relations Research Series 87* London, Department for Business Enterprise & Regulatory Reform.

BILLIG, M. 1995. *Banal Nationalism*, London, Sage.

BINDÉ, J. 2000. Toward an Ethics of the Future. *Public Culture* 12, 51–72.

BLEICHMAR, J. 1999. Deportation as Punishment: A historical analysis of the British practice of banishment and its impact on modern constitutional law. *Georgetown Immigration Law Journal*, 14, 115–64.

BLINDER, S. 2011a. Deportations, Removals and Voluntary Departures from the UK. *Migration Observatory Briefing*, Oxford, Centre on Migration, Policy and Society (COMPAS).

BLINDER, S. 2011b. UK Public Opinion Towards Immigration: Overall attitudes and level of concern. *Migration Observatory Briefing*. Oxford, Centre on Migration, Policy and Society (COMPAS).

BLINDER, S. 2011c. UK Public Opinion Towards Migration: Determinants of attitudes. *Migration Observatory Briefing*, Oxford, Centre on Migration, Policy and Society (COMPAS).

BLINDER, S. 2012. Briefing: Settlement in the UK. *Migration Observatory Briefing*, Oxford, Centre on Migration, Policy and Society (COMPAS).

BOSNIAK, L. 2006. *The Citizen and the Alien: Dilemmas of contemporary membership*, Princeton, Princeton University Press.

BOSWELL, C. 2007. Theorizing Migration Policy: Is there a Third Way? *International Migration Review*, 41, 75–100.

BOSWORTH, M. 2008. Border Control and the Limits of the Sovereign State. *Social and Legal Studies*, 17, 199–215.

BOSWORTH, M. 2011a. Ambivalence and Detention. A Chrysalis for Every Kind of Criminal? Mobility, crime and citizenship, Seminar, 20 October, Oxford, COMPAS.

BOSWORTH, M. 2011b. Deportation, Detention and Foreign National Prisoners in England and Wales. *Citizenship Studies*, 15, 583–95.

BOSWORTH, M. & GUILD, M. 2008. Governing Through Migration Control: Security and citizenship in Britain. *The British Journal of Criminology*, 48, 703–19.

BOYD, R. 2011. Letter to Editor. *Oxford Magazine*. Oxford.

BRACE, L. 2004. *The Politics of Property: Labour, freedom and belonging*, Edinburgh, Edinburgh University Press.

BRACE, L. 2010. The Opposites of Slavery? Contract, freedom and labour. Human Rights, Victimhood and Consent Workshop, Bergen, Rokkan University Centre.

BRADDICK, M. J. 2000. *State Formation in Early Modern England c.1550–1700*, Cambridge, Cambridge University Press.

BRETTELL, C. & HOLLIFIELD, J. (eds.) 2000. *Migration Theory: Talking across disciplines*, London, Routledge.

BREWER, R. & HEITZEG, N. 2008. The Racialization of Crime and Punishment: Criminal justice, color-blind racism, and the political economy of the prison industrial complex. *American Behavioral Scientist*, 51, 625–44.

British Nationality and Status of Aliens Act 1914. *4 + 5 George V c.17*. London.

BROWN, W. 2006. *Regulating Aversion: Tolerance in the age of identity and empire*, Princeton, Princeton University Press.

BUERKLE, T. 2000. Chinese Gang is Suspected in Smuggling into Dover: A deadly traffic in humans. *International Herald Tribune*, 21 June.

BÚRIKOVÁ, Z. 2006. The Embarrassment of Co-presence: Au pairs and their rooms. *Home Cultures*, 3, 99–122.

BURRIDGE, A. 2009. Differential Criminalization under Operation Streamline: Challenges to freedom of movement and humanitarian aid provision in the Mexico-US borderlands. *Refuge*, 26, 78–91.

CAMERON, D. 2011. *Immigration, Not Mass Immigration*. <http://www.conservatives.com/News/Speeches/2011/04/David_Cameron_Good_immigration_not_mass_immigration.aspx> (accessed 1 February 2012).

CANCEDDA, A. 2001. Employment in Household Services, Dublin, European Foundation for the Improvement of Living and Working Conditions.

CANGIANO, A., SHUTES, I., SPENCER, S. & LEESON, G. 2009. *Migrant Care Workers in Ageing Societies: Research Findings in the United Kingdom*, Oxford, COMPAS.

CANTLE, T. 2001. *Community Cohesion: A report of the Independent Review Team*, Chaired by Ted Cantle, London, HMSO.

CARENS, J. 2002. Citizenship and Civil Society: What rights for residents? *In:* HANSEN, R. & WEIL, P. (eds.) *Dual Nationality, Social Rights and Federal Citizenship in the US and Europe: The reinvention of citizenship*, New York, Berghahn Books.

CARENS, J. 2008. Live-In Domestics, Seasonal Workers, Foreign Students and Others Hard to Locate on the Map of Democracy. *Journal of Political Philosophy*, 16 (4), 419–45.

CARLYLE, T. 1849. Original Discourse on the Negro Question. *Fraser's Magazine for Town and Country*, XL.

CHAMBLISS, W. 1964. A Sociological Analysis of the Law of Vagrancy. *In:* CARSON, W. G. & WILES, P. (eds.) *The Sociology of Crime and Delinquency in Britain,* London, Martin Robertson.

CHAN, P., CLARKE, L. & DAINTY, A. 2010. The Dynamics of Migrant Employment in Construction: Can supply of skilled labour ever match demand? *In:* RUHS, M. & ANDERSON, B. (eds.) *Who Needs Migrant Workers? Labour shortages, immigration and public policy*, Oxford, Oxford University Press.

CHANTLER, K., GANGOLI, G. & HESTER, M. 2009. Forced Marriage in the UK: Religious, cultural, economic or state violence? *Critical Social Policy*, 29, 587–612.

CHATTERJEE, P. 1993. *The Nation and its Fragments*, Princeton, Princeton University Press.

CHENG, S. 2010. *On the Move for Love: Migrant entertainers and the U.S. military in South Korea*, Philadelphia, University of Pennsylvania Press.

CHERNILO, D. 2006. Social Theory's Methodological Nationalism: Myth and reality. *European Journal of Social Theory*, 9, 5–22.

CHOWERS, E. 2002. Gushing Time: Modernity and the multiplicity of temporal homes. *Time & Society*, 11, 233–49.

CHUANG, J. 2010. Rescuing Trafficking from Ideological Capture: Prostitution reform and Anti-Trafficking law and policy. *University of Pennsylvania Law Review*, 158, 1655–728.

CLARK, N. & KUMARAPPAN, L. 2011. *Turning a Blind Eye: The British state and migrant domestic workers' employment rights,* London, London Metropolitan University.

COHEN, R. 1994. *Frontiers of Identity: The British and the others*, London, Addison Wesley.

COHEN, R. 1997. *The New Helots: Migrants in the international division of labour*, Oxford, Oxford Publishing Services.

COHEN, S. 1972. *Folk Devils and Moral Panics: The creation of the Mods and Rockers*, London, MacGibbon and Kee Ltd.

COHEN, S. 2005. *That's Funny You Don't Look Anti-Semitic: An anti-racist analysis of left anti-semitism.* <http://www.engageonline.org.uk/ressources/funny/thats_funny.pdf> (accessed 2 September 2011).

COLE, P. 2000. *Philosophies of Exclusion: Liberal political theory and immigration*, Edinburgh, Edinburgh University Press.

COLE, P. 2010. Introduction: 'Border Crossings'—The dimensions of membership. *In:* CALDER, G., COLE, P. & SEGLOW, J. (eds.) *Citizenship Acquistion and National Belonging: Migration, membership and the liberal democratic state*, Basingstoke, Palgrave Macmillan.

COLEMAN, D. 2010. When Britain Becomes 'Majority Minority'. *Prospect*, 17 November, 177. <http:/www.prospectmagazine.co.uk/magazine/when-britain-becomes-majority-minority> (accessed 1 February 2012).

COMAROFF, J. 1997. Reflections on the Colonial State, in South Africa and Elsewhere: Fractions, fragments, facts and fictions. *Bulletin of the Institute of Ethnology, Academia Sinica*, 83, 1–50.

Commissioner for Human Rights 2010. Criminalisation of Migration in Europe: Human rights implications. CommDH/Issue Paper (2010) 1.

Communities and Local Government 2010. 2008–09 Citizen Survey: Community cohesion topic report. *Citizen Survey*, London, Department for Communities and Local Government.

COOPER, S. M. 2004. From Family Member to Employee: Aspects of continuity and discontinuity in English domestic service 1600–2000. *In:* FAUVE-CHAMOUX, A. (ed.) *Domestic Service and the Formation of European Identity: Understanding the globalization of domestic work, 16th–21st centuries*, Bern, Peter Lang.

COUNCIL OF EUROPE 1969. European Agreement on 'Au Pair' Placement. Strasbourg: 24.XI.

COUSSEY, M. 2004. *Annual Report of the Independent Race Monitor 2003/4*, London, Immigration and Nationality Department.

COX, R. 2006. *The Servant Problem: Domestic employment in a global economy*, London, I. B. Tauris.

CPS 2011. *Violence Against Women and Girls Crime Report 2010–2011*, London, Equality and Diversity Unit.

CURRELL, J. 2012. *Response to the OSCE Report on Human Trafficking*, London, Organised and Financial Crime Unit, HMSO.

CURRIE, S. 2008. *Migration, Work and Citizenship in the Enlarged European Union*, Farnham, Ashgate.

CURTIS, S. & LUCAS, R. 2001. A Coincidence of Needs? Employers and full-time students. *Employee Relations*, 23, 38–54.

CWERNER, S. 2001. The Times of Migration. *Journal of Ethnic and Migration Studies*, 27, 7–36.

Daily Mail 2011. Fraudsters Who Work While on the Dole Cost the Taxpayer More Than £100m in ONE Year. *Daily Mail*, 22 April 2011.

DAVIDOFF, L. 1979. Class and Gender in Victorian England: The diaries of Arthur J. Munby and Hannah Cullwick. *Feminist Studies*, 5, 86–141.

DAVIES, J. 2010. *Temporary Labour Migration to the UK: Does it all have to end in 'tiers'?*, Dhaka, Bangladeshi Trade Support Programme.

DAVIES, L. 2011. *Women on Boards*, London: BIS.

DAVIES, N. 2009. Inquiry Fails to Find Single Trafficker Who Forced Anybody Into Prostitution. *The Guardian*, 20 October.

DEAN, M. 1991. *The Constitution of Poverty: Toward a genealogy of liberal governance*, London, Routledge.

DE GENOVA, N. 2002. Migrant 'Illegality' and Deportability in Everyday Life. *Annual Review of Anthropology*, 31, 419–47.

DE GENOVA, N. & PEUTZ, N. (eds.) 2010. *The Deportation Regime: Sovereignty, space and the freedom of movement*, New York, Duke University Press.

DENCH, S., HURSTFIELD, J., HILL, D. & AKROYD, K. 2006. Employers' use of Migrant Labour. Home Office Online Report.

DENNING, M. 2010. Wageless Life. *New Left Review*, 66, 79–97.

Department of Trade and Industry 2006. Success At Work: Protecting vulnerable workers, supporting good employers, London.

Detention Services Order. 2008. <http://www.ukba.homeoffice.gov.uk/sitecontent/documents/policyandlaw/detention-services-orders/paid-work.pdf?view=Binary>.

DEVINS, D. & HOGARTH, T. 2005. Employing the Unemployed: Some case study evidence on the role and practice of employers. *Urban Studies*, 42, 245–56.

DICKENSON, D. 1997. *Property, Women and Politics*, Cambridge, Polity Press.

DOEZEMA, J. 2000. Loose Women or Lost women? The re-emergence of the myth of white slavery in contemporary discourses of trafficking in women. *Gender Issues*, 24, 23–50.

DOEZMA, J. 2010. *Sex Slaves and Discourse Masters: The construction of trafficking*, London, Zed Books.

DORRE, K., KRAEMER, K. & SPEIDEL, F. 2006. The Increasing Precariousness of the Employment Society—Driving force for a new right-wing populism? 15th Conference of Europeanists. Chicago.<http://natlex.ilo.ch/wcmsp5/groups/public/—ed_dialogue/—actrav/documents/meetingdocument/wcms_161354.pdf>.

DOYLE, J. & SLACK, J. 2011. Shipped back to Britain: Australians say career thug is a risk to the public—so they've sent him home to the UK . . . as a free man. *Daily Mail*, 19 April.

DRINKWATER, S. 2007. Written Evidence. House of Lords Select Committee on Economic Affairs.

DUBOURG, R., FAROUK, S., MILLER, L. & PRICHARD, S. 2007. People Trafficking for Sexual Exploitation. *In:* DUBOURG, R. & PRICHARD, S. (eds.) *Organised Crime: revenues, economic and social costs, and criminal assets available for seizure*, London, Home Office.

DUMMETT, A. 2001. *Ministerial Statements: The immigration exception in the Race Relations (Amendment) Act 2000*, London, ILPA.

DUMMETT, A. & NICOL, A. 1990. *Subjects, Citizens, Aliens and Others: Nationality and immigration Law*, London, Weidenfeld and Nicolson.

DUNCAN SMITH, I. 2011. Marriage Week Speech, 8 February. Available: <http://www.dwp.gov.uk/newsroom/ministers-speeches/2011/08-02-11.shtml> (accessed 20 February 2012).

DWORKIN, R. 2011. *Justice for Hedgehogs*, Cambridge, MA, Harvard University Press.

DYER, C. 2008. Briton Sues Over Deportation as Failed Asylum Seeker. *The Guardian*, 7 June.

Economist 2012. Sons and Lovers: Bit by bit, Britain is closing its borders to immigrants. *The Economist,* 16 June.

EHRKAMP, P. 2010. The Limits of Multicultural Tolerance? Liberal democracy and media portrayals of muslim migrant women in Germany. *Space and Polity*, 14, 13–32.

ELLERMANN, A. 2006. Street-level Democracy? How immigration bureaucrats manage public opposition. *West European Politics*, 29, 287–303.

EMIRBAYER, M. & MISCHE, A. 1998. What is Agency? *American Journal of Sociology*, 103, 962–1023.

Employment Markets Analysis and Research (EMAR) 2008. Agency Working in the UK: A review of the evidence. *Employment Relations Research Series.* London: Department for Business, Enterprise and Regulatory Reform.

Encyclopedia Britannica 1911. <http://www.1911encyclopedia.org/Main_Page> (accessed 17 March 2012).

European Court of Human Rights 2010. *Case of A. W. Khan v. The United Kingdom.* Strasbourg, ECHR.

FAIFE, C. 2010. Modern Times: Osman Rasul In memory. *Ceasefire*, 3 August. <http://ceasefiremagazine.co.uk/modern-times-osman-rasul-in-memory>.

FAMILY IMMIGRATION ALLIANCE. 2011. *Our Story.* <http://familyimmigrationalliance.wordpress.com/2011/12/> (accessed 17 July 2012).

FANTONE, L. 2007. Precarious Changes: Gender and generational politics in contemporary Italy. *Feminist Review*, 87, 5–20.

FARLEY, M. 2003. Prostitution and the invisibility of harm Invisibility of Harm. *Women and Therapy*, 26, 247–80.

FEDERICI, S. 2004. *Caliban and the Witch: Women, the body and primitive accumulation*, New York, Autonomedia.

FEINGOLD, D. 2010. Trafficking in Numbers: The social construction of human trafficking data. *In:* ANDREAS, P. & GREENHILL, K. (eds.) *Sex, Drugs and Body Counts: The politics of numbers in global crime and conflict*, New York, Cornell University Press.

FELDMAN, D. 2003. Migrants, Immigrants and Welfare From the Old Poor Law to the Welfare State. *Transactions of the Royal Historical Society*, 13, 79–104.

FELDMAN, D. 2011. Why the English like Turbans: Multicultural politics in British history. *In:* FELDMAN, D. & LAWRENCE, J. (eds.) *Structures and Transformations in Modern British History,* Cambridge: Cambridge University Press.

FELDMAN, D. 2012. Settlement and the Law in the Seventeenth Century. (unpublished).

FEVRE, R. 2007. Employment Insecurity and Social Theory: The power of nightmares. *Work, Employment and Society*, 21, 517–35.

FIRTH, C. H. (ed.) 1901. *The Clarke Papers: Selections from the papers of William Clarke, Secretary to the Council of the Army, 1647–1649, and to General Monck and the Commanders of the Army in Scotland, 1651–1660*, London, The Camden Society.

FLYNN, D. 2003. Tough as Old Boots? Asylum, immigration and the paradox of New Labour policy. Immigration Rights Project discussion series, London, Joint Council for the Welfare of Immigrants.

FOOTE, C. 1956. Vagrancy Type Law and Its Administration. *University of Pennsylvania Law Review*, 104.

FOUCAULT, M. 2003. *Society Must be Defended: Lectures at the College de France, 1975–1976*, New York, Picador.

FRANCESCO, M. 2008. The Concept of 'Persecution' in Refugee Law: Indeterminacy, context-sensitivity, and the quest for a principled approach. On Persecution EUI, Florence, 17 October 2008. <http:dossiersgrihl.revues.org/3896> (accessed 3 March 2012).

FRANKENBERG, R. 2001. The Mirage of an Unmarked Whiteness. *In:* RASUMUSSEN, B. B., KLINENBERG, E., NEXICA, I. & WRAY, M. (eds.) *The Making and Unmaking of Whiteness,* Durham, Duke University Press.

FREEDMAN, J. 2011. The Réseau Éducation Sans Frontières: Reframing the campaign against the deportation of migrants. *Citizenship Studies,* 15, 613–26.

FREEMAN, G. P. 1994. Can Liberal States Control Unwanted Migration. *Annals of the American Academy of Political and Social Science,* 534, 17–30.

FROISSART, J. *c*.1563. *Here begynnith the firste volum of Syr Iohn Froissart: of the cronycles of Englande, Fraunce, Spayne, Portyngale, Scotlande, Bretaine, Flaunders and other places adioynynge,* London. <http://searchworls.stanford.edu/view/5162516> (accessed 17 July 2012).

FRYER, P. 1984. *Staying Power: The history of black people in Britain since 1504,* London, Pluto Press.

FUDGE, J. 2011. The Precarious Migrant Status and Precarious Employment: The paradox of international rights for migrant workers, Metropolis British Columbia: Centre of Excellence for Research on Immigration and Diversity Working Paper No. 11–15.

FUMERTON, P. 2006. *Unsettled: The culture of mobility and the working poor in early modern England,* Chicago, University of Chicago Press.

GALLAGHER, A. 2001. Human Rights and the New UN Protocols on Trafficking and Migrant Smuggling: A preliminary analysis. *Human Rights Quarterly,* 23, 975–1004.

GARNER, S. 2010. *The Entitled Nation: How people make themselves white in contemporary Britain.* <http://www.sens-public.org/spip.php?article729&lang=fr> (accessed 3 March 2012).

GHALI, K. 2008. No Slavery Except as a Punishment for Crime: The punishment clause and sexual slavery. *UCLA Law Review,* 55, 607–42.

GIBNEY, M. 2001. The State of Asylum: Democratization, judicialization and evolution of refugee policy in Europe. *New Issues in Refugee Research: UNHCR Working Paper No.50.* Oxford, Refugee Studies Centre.

GIBNEY, M. 2008. Asylum and the Expansion of Deportation in the United Kingdom. *Government and Opposition,* 43, 146–67.

GIBNEY, M. 2011. Should Citizenship be Conditional? *Refugee Studies Working Paper Series.* Oxford, Refugee Studies Centre.

GIBNEY, M. & HANSEN, R. 2003a. Deportation and the Liberal State: The involuntary return of asylum seekers and unlawful migrants in Canada, the UK and Germany. *New Issues in Refugee Research: UNHCR Working Paper* Geneva, UNHCR.

GIBNEY, M. & HANSEN, R. 2003b. Asylum Policy in the West: Past trends, future possibilities. Discussion Paper, 2003/68. <http://archive.unu.edu/hq/library/Collection/PDF_files/WIDER/WIDERdp2003.68.pdf> (accessed 2nd September 2011).

GILROY, P. 2004. *After Empire: Melancholia or convivial culture?* London, Routledge.

GILROY, P. & HALL, S. 2007. *Black Britain: A photographic history,* London, Saqi Books.

GOLDBERG, D. T. 1993. *Racist Culture: philosophy and the politics of meaning,* Oxford, Blackwell Publishers Ltd.

GOLDBERG, D. T. 2002. *The Racial State,* Oxford, Blackwell.

GOOS, M. & MANNING, A. 2007. Lousy and Lovely Jobs: The rising polarisation of work in Britain. *Review of Economics and Statistics,* 89, 118–33.

GORDON, I., SCANLON, K., TRAVERS, T. & WHITEHEAD, C. 2009. Economic impact on London and the UK of an earned regularisation of irregular migrants in the UK, Interim Report, London, London School of Economics.

GORDON, J. & LENHARDT, R. A. 2008. Rethinking Work and Citizenship. *UCLA Law Review*, 55, 1161–238.

GRAYLING, C. & GREEN, D. 2012. Labour Didn't Care Who Landed in Britain: The last government had lax immigration and a chaotic way of controlling foreign benefit claimants. *Daily Telegraph*, 20 January 2012.

GREEN, D. 2010. The Real Immigration Question: Speech at the Royal Commonwealth Society, 7 Sept. <http://www.homeoffice.gov.uk/media-centre/speeches/Damian-Green-real-immigration> (accessed 24 February 2012).

GREEN, D. 2011. *Equality (Transit Visa, Entry Clearance, Leave to Enter, Examination of Passengers and Removal Directions) Authorisation 2011*, London, HMSO.

GREGSON, N. & LOWE, M. 1994. *Servicing the Middle Classes: Class, gender and waged domestic labour in contemporary Britain*, London, Routledge.

GRIFFITHS, M., ROGERS, A. & ANDERSON, B. 2012. Migration, Time and Temporalities: Review and prospect, Oxford, COMPAS.

Guardian 2010. Iraqi Asylum-seeker Who Killed Girl in Hit and Run Allowed to Stay in UK. *The Guardian*, 16 December.

GWYNN, R. 2001. *Huguenot Heritage: The history and contribution of the Huguenot's in Britain*, Brighton, Sussex Academic Press.

HAGE, G. 2000. *White Nation: Fantasies of white supremacy in a multicultural society*, London, Routledge.

Halifax Courier 2011. How to Spot a Bogus Wedding. *Halifax Courier*, 30 August.

Hansard 2006. HC Deb. 2 October 2006 vol.449, col. 2618W.

Hansard 2007. HC Deb 26 November 2007 vol. 468, cols 7–10.

Hansard 2010. HL Deb 14 October 2010 vol. 721, cols 594–621.

Hansard 2011. HC Deb. 10 October 2011 vol. 533 col. 81W.

HANSEN, R. 2000. *Citizenship and Immigration in Post-war Britain*, Oxford, Oxford University Press.

HARVEY, D. 2005. *A Brief History of Neoliberalism*, Oxford, Oxford University Press.

HARVEY, M. 2001. *Undermining Construction: The corrosive effects of false self-employment*, London, The Institute of Employment Rights.

HAYCRAFT, T. W. 1897. Alien Legislation and the Prerogative of the Crown. *Law Quarterly Review*, 13, 165–86.

HEAL, F. 1990. *Hospitality in Early Modern England*, Oxford, Clarendon Press.

HERZENBERG, S. A., ALIC, J. A. & WIAL, H. 2000. *New Rules for a New Economy: Employment and opportunity in Postindustrial America*, Ithaca and London, Cornell University Press.

HEYMAN, J. 1999. State Escalation of Force: A Vietnam/US-Mexico border analogy. *In:* HEYMAN, J. (ed.) *States and Illegal Practices*. Oxford, Berg.

HILL, C. 1972. *The World Turned Upside Down*. London, Penguin.

HINDESS, B. 2000. Citizenship in the International Management of Population. *The American Behavioral Scientist*, 43, 1486–97.

HINDLE, S. 1998. Power, Poor Relief and Social Relations in Holland Fen, *c.* 1600–1800. *The Historical Journal*, 41, 67–96.

HOERDER, D. 2002. *Cultures in Contact: World migrations in the second millennium*, Durham, Duke University Press.

HOLDEN-SMITH, B. 1996. Lynching, Federalism, and the Intersection of Race and Gender in the Progressive Era. *Yale Journal of law and Feminism*, 8, 1–31.

HOLEHOUSE, M. 2012. Damian Green: Britain has become addicted to immigration. *Daily Telegraph*, 6 March.

Home Office 2002a. Control of Immigration Statistics United Kingdom 2001. *Command Paper*, London, HMSO.

Home Office 2002b. *Secure Borders, Safe Haven: Integration with diversity in modern Britain*, London, HMSO.

Home Office 2003. The New and the Old: The report of the 'Life in the United Kingdom' advisory group, London, HMSO.

Home Office 2004. 'Au Pair' Placements.: Immigration Directorates' Instructions: Chp 4, Section 1, Annex A.

Home Office 2005. *The Economic and Social Costs of Crime Against Individuals and Households 2003/04*, London, HMSO.

Home Office 2006a. *Life in the United Kingdom: A journey to citizenship*, London, HMSO.

Home Office 2006b. A Points-Based System: Making migration work for Britain, London, HMSO.

Home Office 2006c. *Tackling Human Trafficking—Consultation on proposals for a UK action plan*, London, HMSO.

Home Office 2007a. Control of Immigration Statistics United Kingdom 2006. *Command Paper*, London, HMSO.

Home Office 2007b. Enforcing the Rules: A strategy to ensure and enforce compliance with our immigration laws, London, HMSO.

Home Office 2007c. UK Action Plan on Tackling Human Trafficking, London, HMSO.

Home Office 2008. Enforcing the Deal: Our plans for enforcing the immigration laws in the United Kingdom's communities, London, HMSO.

Home Office 2009. Control of Immigration Statistics United Kingdom 2008. *Statistical Bulletins*, London, HMSO.

Home Office 2010a. *Booklet AN: Naturalisation Booklet—The requirements*, London, HMSO.

Home Office 2010b. *Guide AN: Naturalisation as a British citizen—A guide for applicants*, London, HMSO.

Home Office. 2010c. RE: Letter, 29 September. To Andrew Smith MP.

Home Office 2010d. Prevention of Illegal Working: Immigration, Asylum and Nationality Act 2006, London, HMSO.

Home Office 2010e. *Protecting our Border, Protecting the Public*, London, HMSO.

Home Office 2011a. *Employment-related Settlement, Tier 5 and Overseas Domestic Workers: A consultation*, London: UKBA, HMSO.

Home Office 2011b. *Family Migration: A consultation*, London, HMSO.

Home Office 2011c. *Family Migration: Evidence and analysis*, 2nd edn, London, HMSO.

Home Office 2011d. *Human Trafficking: The government's strategy*, London, HMSO.

Home Office 2011e. *Immigration Statistics—April to June 2011, British citizenship*, London, HMSO.

Home Office 2012a. Immigration (Employment-related settlement, Overseas Domestic Workers, Tier 5 of the Points Based System and Visitors). statement of Intent: 29 February 2012, London, HMSO.

Home Office 2012b. *Removals and Voluntary Departures Data Tables Immigration Statistics October–December 2011*, London, HMSO.

Home Office 2012c. Immigration (Employment-related Settlement, Overseas Domestic Workers, Tier 5 of the Points Based System and Visitors). Available: <http://www.parliament.uk/documents/commons-vote-office/February_2012/29-02-12/6.Home-Immigration.pdf> (accessed 29 February 2012).

Homeless Link 2008. *Survey of Needs and Provision Report*, London, Homeless Link.

HONIG, B. 2003. *Democracy and the Foreigner*, Princeton, Princeton University Press.

House of Lords 2008. The Economic Impact of Immigration, 1st Report of Session 2007–08. Select Committee on Economic Affairs, London, HMSO.

HUSAK, D. 2008. *Overcriminalization: The limites of the criminal law*, Oxford, Oxford University Press.

HYNES, H. P. & RAYMOND, J. 2002. Put in Harm's Way: The neglected health consequences of sex trafficking in the United States. *In:* BHATTACHARJEE, A. & SILLIMAN, J. (eds.) *Policing the National Body: Sex, race and criminalization.* Cambridge, South End Press.

Immigration Directorate 2006. Instructions, Chp. 8 Unmarried & Same-sex Relationships, Section 9, Annex Z. <http://www.ukba.homeoffice.gov.uk/sitecontent/documents/policyandlaw/IDIs/idischapter8/section9/annexz.pdf?view=Binary> (accessed 20 February 2012).

Immigration Directorate 2011. Instructions, Chp. 8 Family Members, Section 6 Dependent Relatives, Annex 5. <http://www.ukba.homeoffice.gov.uk/sitecontent/documents/policyandlaw/IDIs/idischapter8/08section6/section6.pdf?view=Binary> (accessed 20 February 2012).

Independent 2010. Gang Treated Migrant Workers 'Like Slaves'. *The Independent*, 7 December.

International Labour Office 1930. Convention 29—Forced Labour Convention, Geneva, ILO. <http://www.ilo.org/dyn/normlex/en/f?p+1000:12100:0::NO::P12100_INSTRUMENT_ID:31274>.

International Labour Office 2008. *Fighting Human Trafficking: The forced labour dimensions (Background Paper)*, Geneva, ILO.

Investigating Prison Labour 2009. The Documents. Available: <http://www.prisonlabour.org.uk/documents.htm> (accessed 25 February 2012).

JAYAWEERA, H. & ANDERSON, B. 2008. *Migrant Workers and Vulnerable Employment: A review of existing data*, London, Trades Union Congress.

Joint Committee on Human Rights 2006. *Twenty-Sixth Report*, London, House of Commons & House of Lords.

JONES, A. 2010. Immigration and the UK Labour Market in Financial Services: A case of conflicting policy challenges? *In:* RUHS, M. & ANDERSON, B. (eds.) *A Need for Migrant Labour? Labour shortages, immgiration and public policy*, Oxford, Oxford University Press.

JONES, S. 1974. Working-class Culture and Working-class Politics in London, 1870–1900: Notes on the remaking of a working class. *Journal of Social History*, 7, 460–508.

JONES, S. 2009. Rate Pushes UK Population to Greatest Increase in Almost 50 Years. *The Guardian*, 27 August.

JOPPKE, C. 1999. Immigration Challenges to the Nation-state. *In:* JOPPKE, C. (ed.) *Challenge to the Nation-State: Immigration in western Europe and the United States*, Oxford, Oxford University Press.

JOPPKE, C. 2004. The Retreat of Multiculturalism in the Liberal State: Theory and practice. *The British Journal of Sociology*, 55, 237–57.

Justice for Domestic Workers 2011. Rally Leaflet, 4 September. J4DW.

KANSTROOM, D. 2010. *Deportation Nation: Outsiders in American History*, Harvard, Harvard University Press.

KAY, D. & MILES, R. 1988. Refugees or Migrant Workers? The Case of the European Volunteer Workers in Britain (1946–1951). *Journal of Refugee Studies*, 1, 214–36.

KILLINGRAY, D. (ed.) 1994. *Africans in Britain*, London, Frank Cass & Co. Ltd.

KING, R. 2002. Towards a New Map of European Migration. *International Journal of Population Geography*, 8, 89–106.

KRAUSE, M. 2008. Undocumented Migrants: An Arendtian Perspective. *European Journal of Political Theory* 7, 331–48.

LALANI, M. 2011. *Ending the Abuse: Policies that work to protect migrant domestic workers*, London, Kalayaan.

LANDAU, N. 1990. The Regulation of Immigration, Economic Structures and Definitions of the Poor in Eighteenth-Century England. *Historical Journal*, 33, 541–71.

LAPE, S. 2010. *Race and Citizen Identity in the Classical Athenian Democracy*, Cambridge, Cambridge University Press.

LAYTON-HENRY, Z. (ed.) 1980. *Conservative Party Politics*, London, Macmillan.

Learning and Skills Council 2007. *National Employers Skills Survey 2007: Main report*, Coventry, LSC.

LECADET, C. 2013 forthcoming. From Migrant Destitution to Self-organisation into Transitory National Communities: The revival of citizenship in post-deportation experience in Northern Mali, in B. ANDERSON, M. GIBNEY & E. PAOLETTI (eds.) *Deportation and the Constitution and Contestation of Citizenship*, New York, Springer.

LEVY, A. 2010a. British Grandmother Returns Home after 23 Years in Spain . . . and is Branded an Asylum Seeker. *Daily Mail,* 24 April.

LEVY, A. 2010b. Swans Killed and Fish Vanish as 'Migrants Pillage River for Food'. *Daily Mail* 24 March.

LILLIE, N. & GREER, I. 2007. Industrial Relations, Migration and Neo-liberal Politics: The case of the European construction sector. *Politics & Society*, 35, 551–81.

LINDSAY, C. & MCQUAID, R. W. 2004. Avoiding the 'McJobs': Unemployed job seekers and attitudes to service work. *Work, Employment and Society*, 18, 297–394.

LINEBAUGH, P. 2008. *The Magna Carta Manifesto: Liberties and commons for all*, Berkeley, University of California Press.

LLOYD, C. & PAYNE, J. 2009. 'Full of Sound and Fury, Signifying Nothing': Interrogatingthe new skill concepts in service work—The view from two call centres. *Work, Employment and Society*, 24, 617–34.

LOCKE, J. [1689] 1993. *Second Treatise of Government*, London, Penguin Classics.

LUCAS, R. & MANSFIELD, S. 2008. *Staff Shortages and Immigration in the Hospitality Sector. A report prepared for the Migration Advisory Committee*, London, Migrant Advisory Committee. <http://www.ukba.homeoffice.gov.uk/sitecontent/documents/aboutus/workingwithus/mac/239769/lucasandmansfield2008>.

LUCASSEN, J. & LUCASSEN, L. 2009. The Mobility Transition Revisited, 1500–1900: What the case of Europe can offer to global history. *Journal of Global History*, 4, 347–77.

LUIBHÉID, E. 2002. *Entry Denied: Controlling sexuality at the border*, Minneapolis, University of Minnesota Press.

MACKAY, L. 1997. The Mendicity Society and its Clients: A cautionary tale. *Left History* 5, 39–64.

MACKENZIE, R. & FORDE, C. 2009. The Rhetoric of the 'Good Worker' Versus the Realities of Employers' Use and the Experiences of Migrant Workers. *Work, Employment and Society*, 23, 142–59.

MAJOR, J. 1993. Speech to the Conservative Group for Europe, 22 April 1993. <http://www.johnmajor.co.uk/page1086.html> (accessed 9 March 2012).

MALKKI, L. 1996. Speechless Emissaries: Refugees, humanitarianism and dehistoricization. *Cultural Anthropology*, 11, 377–404.

MAMDANI, M. 2011. The Invention of the Indigène. *London Review of Books*, 33, 2.

MANNING, P. 2005. *Migration in World History*, New York, Routledge.

MARKON, J. 2007. Human Trafficking Evokes Outrage, Little Evidence. *Washington Post*, 23 September.

MARTIN, P. 2003. *Managaing Labor Migration: Temporary worker programs for the 21st century*, Geneva, ILO.

MASSEY, D. S. 1990. Social structure, household strategies, and the cumulative causation of migration. *Population Index*, 56, 3–26.

MAY, J., WILLS, J., DATTA, K., EVANS, Y., HERBERT, J. & MACILWAINE, C. 2006. *The British State and London's Migrant Division of Labour*, London, Queen Mary College, University of London.

MAY, T. 2010. The Home Secretary's Immigration Speech, 5 November, London. <http://www.homeoffice.gov.uk/media-centre/speeches/immigration-speech> (accessed 1 March 2012).

MAYO, M. & ROOKE, A. 2006. *Active Learning for Active Citizenship*, London, DCLG.

MCCLINTOCK, A. 1995. *Imperial Leather: Race, Gender and Sexuality in the Colonial Conest*, New York, Routledge.

MCDOWELL, L. 2005. *Hard Labour: The forgotten voices of Latvian migrant 'volunteer; workers*, London, UCL Press.

MCKEOWN, A. 2004. Global Migration 1846–1940. *Journal of World History*, 15, 155–89.

MCPHEE, P. 2006. *Daily Life in the French Revolution*. <http://www.hfrance.net/rude/rude%20volume%20ii/McPhee%20Final%20Version.pdf> (accessed 18 July 2012).

Migrants Rights Network 2008. 'Papers Please': The Impact of the Civil Penalty Regime on the Employment Rights of Migrants in the UK. *In:* FLYNN, D. & GROVE-WHITE, R. (eds.) *MRN Migration Perspectives Series*, London, Migrants Rights Network.

Migration Advisory Committee 2008. *Skilled, Shortage, Sensible: The recommended shortage occupation lists for the UK and Scotland*, London, Migration Advisory Committee.

Migration Advisory Committee 2010a. *Analysis of the Points Based System: London weighting*, London.

Migration Advisory Committee 2010b. *Skilled, Shortage, Sensible: Third review of the recommended shortage occupation lists for the UK and Scotland: Spring 2010*, London, Migrant Advisory Committee.

Migration Advisory Committee 2011. *Review of the Minimum Income Requirement for Sponsorship Under the Family Migration Route*, Migrant Advisory Committee.

Migration Advisory Committee 2012. *Analysis of the Impacts of Migration*, London, Migrant Advisory Committee.

Migration Observatory 2011. Thinking Behind the Numbers: Understanding public opinion on immigration in Britain, Oxford, Migration Observatory and COMPAS.

MILES, R. 1987. *Capitalism and Unfree Labour: Anomaly or necessity?*, London, Tavistock Publications Ltd.

MILL, J. S. 1948. *On Liberty*, London, J. M. Dent and Sons.

MILLINGTON, G. 2010. Racism, Class Ethos and Place: The value of context in narratives about asylum-seekers. *The Sociological Review*, 58, 361–80.

MILLS, C. 1997. *The Racial Contract*, New York, Cornell University Press.

MILLS, C. 1998. *Blackness Visible: Essays on philosophy and race*, New York, Cornell University Press.

MILLS, M., BLOSSFELD, H. & KLIJZING, E. 2005. Becoming an Adult in Uncertain Times: A 14 country comparison of the losers of globalization. *In:* BLOSSFELD, H., KLIJZING, E., MILLS, M. & KURZ, K. (eds.) *Globalization, Uncertainty and Youth in Society*, Abingdon, Routledge.

MITCHELL, T. 2002. *Rule of Experts: Egypt, technopolitics, modernity*, Berkeley, University of California Press.

MORE, T. 1992 (1516). *Utopia*, London, David Campbell.

MORGAN, K. 1985. The Organization of the Convict Trade to Maryland: Stevenson, Randolph and Cheston, 1768–1775. *The William and Mary Quarterly*, 42, 201–27.

MORIARTY, J. 2010. Competing with Myths: Migrants and social care. *In:* RUHS, M. & ANDERSON, B. (eds.) *A Need for Migrant Labour? Labour shortages, immigration and public policy*, Oxford, Oxford University Press.

MORTON, A. L. 1965. *A People's History of England*, London, Lawrence & Wishart.

MURDOCH, J. L. 1991. Encouraging Citizenship: Report of the Commission on Citizenship. *The Modern Law Review*, 54, 439–41.

MURPHY, A., MUELLBAUER, J. & CAMERON, G. 2006. Housing Market Dynamics and Regional Migration in Britain. CEPR Discussion Paper.

MURRAY, A. 2011. *Britain's Points Based Migration System*, London, CentreForum.

National Audit Office 2005. Returning Failed Asylum Applicants HC 76 Session 2005–2006, Appendix 2:44, London: National Audit Office.

National Centre for Social Research 2003. *British Social Attitudes Survey 2003.* <http://nesstar.esds.ac.uk/webview/index.jsp?v=2&mode=documentation&sub mode=abstract&study=http%3A%2F%2Fnesstar.esds.ac.uk%3A80%2Fobj%2Ff Study%2F5235&top=yes> (accessed 1 March 2012).

National Statistics 2007. *Marriage, Divorce and Adoption Statistics: Review of the Registrar General on marriages and divorces in 2004, and adoptions in 2005, in England and Wales. FM2*, London, ONS. <http://www.ons.gov.uk/ons/rel/vsob1/marriage–divorce-and-adoption-statistics–england-and-wales–series-fm2-/no–35–2007/marriage–divorce-and-adoption-statistics–england-and-wales–series-fm2-.pdf> (accessed 1 March 2012).

Naturalisation Act 1870. *33 + 34 Victoria c.14*. London.

NEWCOMBE, E. 2004. Temporary Migration to the UK as an Au Pair: Cultural Exchange or Reproductive Labour? Sussex Migration Working Paper No. 21. University of Sussex.

NEWLAND, K. 1995. The Impact of U.S. Refugee Policies on U.S. Foreign Policy: A case of the tail wagging the dog. In: TEITELBAUM, M. (ed.) *Threatened Peoples,Threatened Borders: World migration and U.S. policy*, New York, W. W. Norton.

NZONGOLA-NTALAJA, G. 2002. *The Congo from Leopold to Kabila: A people's history*, London, Zed Books.

OCOBOCK, P. 2008. Introduction: Vagrancy and homelessness in global and historical perspective. In: BEIER, A. L. & OCOBOCK, P. (eds.) *Cast Out: Vagrancy and homelessness in global and historical perspective*, Ohio, Ohio University Press.

O'CONNELL DAVIDSON, J. 2005. *Children in the Global Sex Trade*, Cambridge, Polity.

O'CONNELL DAVIDSON, J. 2006. Will the Real Sex Slave Please Stand Up? *Feminist Review*, 83, 4–22.

O'CONNELL DAVIDSON, J. 2008. Trafficking, Modern Slavery and the Human Security Agenda: Guest editorial *Human Security Journal*, 6, 8–15.

O'CONNELL DAVIDSON, J. 2009. 'Sex Workers, More or Less', BBC Radio 4 programme, 9 January.

O'CONNELL DAVIDSON, J. 2010. New Slavery, Old Binaries: Human trafficking and the borders of 'freedom'. *Global Networks*, 10, 244–61.

O'CONNELL DAVIDSON, J. 2011. Outside Liberal Fictions of Disembodiment: Dilemmas of intimate labour. Rethinking Intimate Labor through Inter-Asian Migrations Workshop, Bellagio, 6–10 June.

OLSEN, F. 1983. The Family and the Market: A study of ideology and legal reform. *Harvard Law Review*, 96, 1497–578.

Ordinance of Labourers 1349. *23 Edward III*. London.

PAI, H.-H. 2008. *Chinese Whispers: The true story behind Britain's Hidden Army of labour*, London, Penguin.

PANDYA, A. 2012. 200,000 Children to Go Without a Place in School: Where on earth are the controls on immigration? *Daily Mail*, 24 January.

PAPADOPOULOS, D., STEPHENSON, N. & TSIANOS, V. 2008. *Escape Routes: Control and subversion in the 21st century*, London, Pluto Press.

Parliamentary Ombudsman 2010. Fast and Fair: A report by the Parliamentary Ombudsman on the UK Border Agency. <http://www.ombudsman.org.uk/__data/assets/pdf_file/0016/673/UKBA-2010-02-09.pdf>.

PATEMAN, C. 1988. *The Sexual Contract*, Cambridge, Polity Press.

PATTERSON, O. 1982. *Slavery and Social Death: A comparative study*, Cambridge MA, Harvard University Press.

PATTIE, C., SEYD, R. & WHITLEY, P. 2004. *Citizenship in Britain: Values, participation and democracy*, Cambridge, Cambridge University Press.

PETTIT, P. 1997. *Republicanism: A theory of freedom and government*, Oxford, Oxford University Press.

PHELPS, J. 2009. *Detained Lives: The real cost of indefinite immigration detention*, London, London Detainee Support Group.

PHELPS, J. 2010. *No Return, No Release, No Reason: Challenging indefinite detention*, London, London Detainee Support Group.

PHELPS, J. 2011. Who is the Figure of the Foreign National Prisoner Who Must Be Detained but Not Punished? A chrysalis for every kind of criminal? Mobility, Crime and Citizenship Seminar, 1 December, COMPAS, University of Oxford.

PHILLIPS, T. 2011. The Three I's: Immigration, integration and Islam. *In:* MCTERNAN, M. (ed.) *Exploring the Cultural Challenges to Social Democracy: Anti-migration populism, identity and community in an age of insecurity*, London, Policy Network.

PIORE, M. J. 1979. *Birds of Passage: Migrant labour and industrial societies*, Cambridge, Cambridge University Press.

POLLARD, N., LATORRE, M. & SRISKANDARAJAH, D. 2008. *Floodgates or Turnstiles? Post-EU enlargement migration flows to (and from) the UK*, London, IPPR.

Poor Law Amendment Act 1834. *4 + 5 William IV c.76.*

POWELL, E. 2007. 'Rivers of Blood' speech. *Daily Telegraph*, 6 November.

POYNTER, J. R. 1969. *Society and Pauperism: English ideas on poor relief, 1795–1834*, London, Routledge & Kegan Paul.

PREIBISCH, K. & BINFORD, L. 2007. Interrogating Racialized Global Labour Supply: An exploration of the racial/national replacement of foreign agricultural Workers. *The Canadian Review of Sociology and Anthropology/La revue canadienne de sociologie et d'anthropologie* 44, 5–36.

RANCIÈRE, J. 2004. Who Is the Subject of the Rights of Man? *South Atlantic Quarterly*, 103, 297–310.

RATTANSI, A. 2002. Who's British? Prospect and the new assimilationism. *Cohesion, Community and Citizenship: Proceedings of a Runnymede Conference*, London, LSE.

RAYMOND, J. 1999. The Health Effects of Prostitution. *In:* HUGHES, D. M. & ROCHE, C. (eds.) *Making the Harm Visible: Global sexual exploitation of women and girls*, Kingston, Rhode Island, Coalition Against Trafficking in Women.

ROBINSON, J. 2006. *Economic Philosophy*, Chicago, Aldine.

ROCHE, B. 2000. UK Migration in a Global Economy. <http://www.ippr.org/events/54/5875/uk-migration-in-a-global-economy?siteid=ipprnorth> (accessed 20 February, 2012).

RODGERS, G. & RODGERS, J. 1989. *Precarious Jobs in Labour Market Regulation: The growth of atypical employment in Western Europe*, Brussels, International Labour Organisation.

ROGALY, B. & TAYLOR, B. 2010. 'They Called Them Communists Then...What d'you call 'em now?...Insurgents?' Narratives of British military expatriates in the context of the new imperialism. *Journal of Ethnic and Migration Studies*, 36, 1335–51.

ROGALY, B. & TAYLOR, B. 2011. What Does Migration Mean for the 'White Working Class' in the UK? *COMPAS Break East Briefings,* Oxford, COMPAS.

ROLLINS, J. 1985. *Between Women: Domestic workers and their employers,* Philadelphia, Temple University Press.

ROSENHEK, Z. 2003. The Political Dynamics of a Segmented Labour Market: Palestinian citizens, Palestinians from the occupied territories and migrant workers in Israel. *Acta Sociologica,* 46, 231–49.

RUBERY, J., SMITH, M. & FAGAN, C. 1999. *Women's Employment in Europe: Trends and prospects,* London, Routledge.

RUHS, M. & ANDERSON, B. (eds.) 2010a. *A Need for Migrant Labour? Labour shortages, immigration and public policy,* Oxford, Oxford University Press.

RUHS, M. & ANDERSON, B. 2010b. Semi-Compliance and Illegality in Migrant Labour Markets: An analysis of migrants, employers and the state in the UK. *Population, Space and Place,* 16, 195–212.

RUHS, M. & MARTIN, P. 2008. Numbers vs Rights: Trade-offs and guest worker programmes. *International Migration Review,* 42, 249–65.

RUTTER, J., LATORRE, M. & SRISKANDARAJAH, D. 2008. *Beyond Naturalisation: Citizenship policy in an age of super mobility,* London, Institute for Public Policy Research.

RYAN, B. 2010. Integration Rules in Immigration and Nationality Law: The case of the United Kingdom, Nijmengen, European Integration Fund.

SALTER, M. 2007. Governmentalities and an Airport: Heterotopia and confession. *International Political Sociology,* 1, 49–66.

SAWYER, C. 2006. Not Every Child Matters: The UK's expulsion of British citizens. *The International Journal of Children's rights,* 14, 157–85.

SAWYER, C. 2010. *EUDO Citizenship Observatory Country Report: United Kingdom,* Florence, Robert Schuman Centre for Advanced Studies, European University Institute.

SCHUSTER, L. 2005. Sledgehammer to Crack a Nut: Deportation, detention and dispersal in Europe. *Social Policy and Administration,* 39, 606–21.

SCIORTINO, G. 2004. Between Phantoms and Necessary Evils: Some critical points in the study of irregular migration to Western Europe. *IMIS-Beitrage,* 24, 17–24.

SEAMARK, M. & COHEN, T. 2011. Asylum Seeker Who Claimed to have been Gang-raped and Witnessed Family's Murder in Somalia Exposed as £250k Benefit Fraudster. *Daily Mail,* 11 January.

SENNETT, R. 1998. *The Corrosion of Character: The personal consequences of work in the new capitalism,* New York, W. W. Norton & Company.

SHACHAR, A. 2009. *The Birthright Lottery: Citizenship and global inequality,* London, Harvard University Press.

SHARMA, N. 2006. *Home Economics: Nationalism and the making of 'migrant workers' in Canada,* Toronto, University of Toronto Press.

SHARMA, N. & WRIGHT, C. 2008. Decolonizing Resistance, Challenging Colonial States. *Social Justice,* 35, 93–111.

Bibliography

SHELLEY, T. 2007. *Exploited: Migrant labour in the new global economy*, London, Zed.

SIGONA, N. & HUGHES, V. 2010. Being Children and Undocumented in the UK: A background paper. COMPAS Working Paper, No. 78.

SIMMEL, G. 1976. The Stranger. *In:* WOLFF, K. (ed.) *The Sociology of Georg Simmel*, New York, Free Press.

SIMMONS, T. 2008. Sexuality and Immigration: UK family reunion policy and the regulation of sexual citizens in the European Union. *Political Geography*, 27, 213–30.

SINGHA, R. 2000. Settle, Mobilize, Verify: Identification practices in Colonial India. *Studies in History*, 16, 151–98.

SLACK, J. 2007. Government Finally Admits: Immigration IS placing huge strain on Britain. *Daily Mail*, 17 October.

SOLOMOS, J. 1993. *Race and Racism in Contemporary Britain*, London, MacMillan.

SPENCER, S. 2011. *The Migration Debate*, Bristol, The Policy Press.

Statute of Cambridge 1388. *12 Richard II c.7*. London.

Statute of Labourers 1351. *25 Edward III stat.2*. London.

Statutory Instrument 1999. National Minimum Wage Regulations. *SI 1999/584.* SI 1999/584. UK.

STEINFATT, T., Baker, S. & Beesey, A. 2003. Measuring the Number of Trafficked Women and Children in Cambodia: A direct observation field study. Accepted for presentation at the Human Rights Challenge of Globalization in Asia-Pacific-US: The trafficking in persons, especially women and children. Sponsored by the Office to Combat and Monitor Trafficking, U.S. State Department. Globalization Research Center—University of Hawaii-Manoa, Honolulu, Hawaii, USA, 13–15 November. <http://slate.msn.com/Features/pdf/Trfcamf3.pdf> (accessed 11 October 2011).

STEINFELD, R. J. 1991. *The Invention of Free Labor: The employment relation in English and American law and culture, 1350–1870*, Chapel Hill, University of North Carolina Press.

STEINFELD, R. J. 2001. *Coercion, Contract and Free Labor in the Nineteenth Century*, Cambridge, Cambridge University Press.

STEINFELD, R. J. 2008. Coercion/Consent in Labour. COMPAS Annual Conference: Theorizing Key Migration Debates, St Anne's College, University of Oxford.

STEPNITZ, A. 2012. A Lie More Disastrous than the Truth: Asylum and the identification of trafficked women in the UK. *Anti-Trafficking Review Issue*, 1, 104–19.

STEVENS, D. 1998. The Case of UK Asylum Law and Policy: Lessons from history? *In:* NICHOLSON, F. & TWOMEY, P. (eds.) *Current Issues of UK Asylum Law and Policy*, Aldershot, Ashgate.

STEVENS, D. 2004. *UK Asylum Law and Policy: Historical and Contemporary Perspectives*, London, Sweet & Maxwell.

STEVENS, J. 2011. U.S. Government Unlawfully Detaining and Deporting U.S. Citizens as Aliens. *Virginia Journal of Social Policy and the Law*, 18, 606–720.

STOLER, L. A. 1995. *Race and the Education of Desire*, Durham, Duke University Press.

STONE, L. 1966. Social Mobility in England, 1500–1700. *Past & Present*, 33, 16–55.

STORY, B. 2005. Politics as Usual: The criminalization of asylum seekers in the United States. RSC Working Paper, 26.

Sunday Express 2006. Halt the Tide of EU Migrants. *Sunday Express*, 20 August.

TALAVERA, V., NÚÑEZ-MCHIRI, G. & HEYMAN, J. 2010. Deportation in the U.S.-Mexico Borderlands: Anticipation, experience, and memory. *In:* DE GENOVA, N. & PEUTZ, N. (eds.) *The Deportation Regime: Sovereignty, space and the Freedom of Movement*, Durham, Duke University Press.

TALWAR, J. P. 2002. *Fast Food, Fast Track: Immigrants, big business and the American Dream big business and the American Dream*, Boulder, CA, Westview.

TIEDEMAN, C. 1886. *A Treaty of the Limits on the Police Power in the United States Considered from Both a Civil and Criminal Standpoint*, St. Louis, F. H. Thomas Law Book Co.

TORPEY, J. 2000. *The Invention of the Passport: Surveillance, citizenship and the state*, Cambridge, Cambridge University Press.

TORRE, A. 2008. *Living Transnationally: Romanian migrants in London*, Runnymede Trust.

TRAVIS, A. 2009. War Protest Migrants May Face Passport Penalties. *The Guardian*, 3 August.

TRAVIS, A. 2011. Workers Face Curb on Bringing Foreign-born Spouses to UK. *The Guardian*, 16 November.

TRAVIS, A. 2012. Heathrow to Get Fast-track Passport Lanes for 'Low-risk' Countries: Citizens of Australia, Canada, New Zealand, Japan and the US will benefit from post-Olympic launch. *The Guardian*, 10 July.

TUC & NUS 2006. All Work and Low Pay: The growth in UK student employment, London TUC, NUS.

TUC Commission on Vulnerable Employment 2008. Hard Work, Hidden Lives: The full report of the Commission on Vulnerable Employment. London, Trades Union Congress.

UK Border Agency 2009a. UK Border Agency Business Plan, April 2009–March 2012, London, HMSO.

UK Border Agency. 2009b. *Accession Monitoring Report, May 2004–March 2009*, London, HMSO. <http://www.bia.homeoffice.gov.uk/sitecontent/documents/aboutus/reports/accession_monitoring_report/> (accessed 13 November, 2009).

UK Border Agency 2011. *UK Border Agency Business Plan April 2011–March 2015: Securing our border, controlling migration*, London, HMSO.

UK Border Agency. 2012. *SET05—Unmarried and Same-sex Partners*. <http://www.ukba.homeoffice.gov.uk/policyandlaw/guidance/ecg/set/set5/> (accessed 24 February, 2012).

UNHCR 2001. *Asylum Applications in Industrialized Countries 1980–1999: Trends in asylum applications lodged in 27, mostly industrialized countries*, Geneva, UNHCR.

United Kingdom Human Trafficking Centre 2009. *United Kingdom Pentameter 2 Statistics of Victims Recovered and Suspects Arrested During the Operational Phase*, London, UKHTC.

United Nations 1949. Convention for the Suppression of the Traffic in Persons and of the Exploitation of the Prostitution of Others. <http://www2.ohchr.org/english/law/trafficpersons.htm>.

United Nations 2000. *Protocol to Prevent, Suppress and Punish Trafficking in Persons, Especially Women and Children, Supplementing the United Nations convention Against Transnational Organized Crime*, Vienna, United Nations Office on Drugs and Crime.

United States' Government Accountability Office 2006. *Human Trafficking: Better data, strategy and reporting needed to enhance U.S. anti-trafficking efforts abroad*, Washington, DC, US GAO.

VARELA, A. 2009. Residency Documents for All! Notes to understand the movement of migrants in Barcelona. *Refuge*, 26, 121–32.

VINE, J. 2011. A *Thematic Inspection of How the UK Border Agency Manages Foreign National Prisoners, February–May 2011*, London, Independent Chief Inspector of the UK Border Agency.

VOSKO, L. F., ZUKEWICH, N. & CRANFORD, C. 2003. Precarious Jobs: A new typology of employment. *Perspectives on Labour and Income*, 4, 10, 16–26.

WACQUANT, L. 2007. *Urban Outcasts: A comparative sociology of advanced marginality*, Cambridge, Polity Press.

WAITE, L. 2007. Migrant Labourers: The new 'precariat'. Annual meeting of the Association of American Geographers, San Francisco.

WALDINGER, R. D. & LICHTER, M. 2003. *How the Other Half Works: Immigration and the social organization of labor*, Berkeley, University of California Press.

WALTERS, S. 2006. Secret Report Warns of Migration Meltdown in Britain. *Daily Mail*, 30 July.

WALTERS, S. 2012. Cameron to Axe Housing Benefits for Feckless Under 25s as He Declares War on Welfare Culture. *Daily Mail*, 23 June.

WALTERS, W. 2010. Deportation, Expulsion and the International Police of Aliens. *In:* DE GENOVA, N. & PEUTZ, N. (eds.) *The Deportation Regime: Sovereignty, Space and the Freedom of Movement*. Durham, Duke University Press.

WALTERS, W. 2011. Foucault and Frontiers: Notes on the Birth of the humanitarian border. *In:* ULRICH BRÖCKLING, SUSANNE KRASMANN & THOMAS LEMKE, R. (eds.) *Governmentality: Current issues and future challenges*, New York, Routledge.

WARREN, T. 2003. Class and Gender-based Working Time? Time poverty and the division of domestic labour. *Sociology*, 37, 733–52.

WATT, N. & WINTOUR, P. 2010. Parents Must Prepare for Work or Face Sanctions—Iain Duncan Smith. *The Guardian*, 11 November.

WEBBER, F. 2008. *Border Wars and Asylum Crimes*, London, Statewatch.

WEBER, L. & BOWLING, B. 2008. Valiant Beggars and Global Vagabonds: Select, eject, immobilize. *Theoretical Criminology*, 12, 355–75.

WEBSTER, C. 2008. Marginalized White Ethnicity, Race and Crime. *Theoretical Criminology*, 12, 293–312.

WEITZER, R. 2010. The Mythology of Prostitution: Advocacy research and public policy. *Sexuality Research Social Policy*, 7, 15–29.

WELKE, B. 2010. *Law and the Borders of Belonging in the Long Nineteenth Century United States*, New York, Cambridge University Press.

WEST, C. & ZIMMERMAN, D. 1991. Doing Gender. *In:* LORBER, J. & FARRELL, S. (eds.) *The Social Construction of Gender*, London, Sage.

WICKHAM, J. & BRUFF, I. 2008. Skills Shortages Are Not Always What They Seem: Migration and the Irish software industry. *New Technology, Work and Employment*, 23, 30–43.

WILLIAMS, F. & GAVANAS, A. 2008. The Intersection of Childcare Regimes and Migration Regimes: A three-country study. *In:* LUTZ, H. (ed.) *Migration and Domestic Work: A European perspective on a global theme*. Aldershot, Ashgate.

WILSHER, D. 2012. *Immigration Detention: Law, History, Politics*, Cambridge, Cambridge University Press.

WILSON, G. 2009. Foreigners Grab 200,000 Brit Jobs. *The Sun*, 12 February.

WINNETT, R. 2012. 370,000 Migrants on the Dole. *Daily Telegraph*, 19 January.

WIRED-GOV. 2008. Large Scale Expansion of Britain's Detention Estate, Home Office Press Release, 19 May 2008. <http://www.wired-gov.net/wg/wg-news-1.nsf/0/8436C7FCA243D94A8025744E0036573A?OpenDocument> (accessed 1 March, 2012).

WISTRICH, H., ARNOLD, F. & GINN, E. 2008. *Outsourcing Abuse: The use and misuse of state-sanctioned force during the detention and removal of asylum seekers*, London: Birnberg Peirce and Partners, Medical Justice, National Coalition of Anti-Deportation Campaigns.

WITTENBURG, V. 2008. *The New Bonded Labour? The impact of proposed changes to the UK immigration system on migrant domestic workers*, London, Kalayaan and Oxfam.

Women's Resource Centre 2010. *Briefing: Statistics about women in the UK*, London, Women' Resource Centre.

WOODFIELD, K., SPENCER, L., PURDON, S., PASCALE, J., LEGARD, R., ANIE, A., NDOFOR-TAH, C., MOUDEN, J. & BRENNAN, F. 2007. Exploring the Decision Making of Immigration Officers: A research study examining non-EEA passenger stops and refusals at UK ports. *Home Office Online Report*, London, HMSO.

WOODWARD, D. 1980. The Background to the Statute of Artificers: genesis of Labour policy, 1558–63. *The Economic History Review*, 33, 1.

WRIGHT, T. & MCKAY, S. 2007. *United Kingdom Country Report: Undocumented worker transitions*, London, Working Lives Research Institute.

YouTube. 2011. David Starkey Tries to Talk About the English Riots on Newsnight. <http://www.youtube.com/watch?v=bAGTE_RGN4c> (accessed 15 March 2012).

ZATZ, N. 2009. Prison Labor and the Paradox of Paid Nonmarket Work. *In:* BANDELJ, N. (ed.) *Economic Sociology of Work*, Bingley, Emerald Press.

ZEDNER, L. 2010. Security, the State and the Citizen: The changing architecture of crime control. *New Criminal Law Review*, 13, 379–403.

ZERNATTO, G. & MISTRETTA, A. 1944. Nation: The history of a word. *The Review of Politics*, 6, 351–66.

Index